Prentice Hall LITERATURE

PENGUIN EDITION

Unit One
Resources

Grade Ten

PEARSON

Upper Saddle River, New Jersey
Boston, Massachusetts
Chandler, Arizona
Glenview, Illinois

BQ Tunes Credits
Keith London, Defined Mind, Inc., Executive Producer
Mike Pandolfo, Wonderful, Producer
All songs mixed and mastered by Mike Pandolfo, Wonderful
Vlad Gutkovich, Wonderful, Assistant Engineer
Recorded November 2007 – February 2008 in SoHo, New York City, at
Wonderful, 594 Broadway

PEARSON

ISBN-13: 978-0-13-366458-4
ISBN-10:   0-13-366458-9

6 7 8 9 10 V011 13
CC

CONTENTS
UNIT 1

"Marian Anderson: Famous Concert Singer" by Langston Hughes

"Tepeyac" by Sandra Cisneros

Writing Workshop: Narration—Autobiographical Narrative

Writing Workshop: Using Possessive Nouns Correctly

Benchmark Test 1

Skills Concept Map 2

"Contents of the Dead Man's Pocket" by Jack Finney

"Games at Twilight" by Anita Desai

"Like the Sun" by R. K. Narayan

"The Open Window" by Saki

About the Unit Resources

The *Prentice Hall Literature Unit Resources* provide manageable, comprehensive, and easy-to-use teaching materials to support each Student Edition unit. You can use these resources to address your students' different ability levels and learning styles, customize instruction to suit your teaching needs, and diagnose and assess student progress. All of these materials are also available at *PHLitOnline*, a rich, online source of personalized instruction and activities.

Here is a brief description of each element of the *Unit Resources*:

UNIT-LEVEL FEATURES

Big Questions (grades 6–10)

Support for the Big Questions includes complete lyrics to BQ Tunes (engaging songs that incorporate Big Question Vocabulary; available on CD); unit-opener worksheets that practice Big Question Vocabulary, an Applying the Big Question chart, re-rendered from the Student Edition.

Essential Questions (The American Experience; The British Tradition)

Support for the Essential Questions includes unit-opener worksheets that focus on each Essential Question individually and a worksheet to support the end-of-unit Essential Question Workshop.

Skills Concept Maps

Each map presents a graphic look at the relationship between the literature and the skills taught in the unit, with space provided for students' notes.

Vocabulary Workshop, Writing Workshop, and Communications Workshop support

End-of-unit worksheets provide opportunities for students to practice vocabulary, and gather and organize information for their Student Edition assignments.

SELECTION-LEVEL SUPPORT

Vocabulary and Reading Warmups

These exercises and easy reading passages provide selection vocabulary practice for students reading at one or two levels below grade level

Writing About the Big Question (grades 6–10)

These worksheets tie the Big Question to individual selections, while giving students additional practice using the Big Question Vocabulary.

Literary Analysis, Reading, and Vocabulary Builder

A series of worksheets that provide extra practice on each of the main skill strands in the Student Edition. You can find more support for the Literary Analysis and Reading strands in the separate Graphic Organizers Transparencies component.

Integrated Language Skills

The Student Edition Integrated Language Skills features are supported by grammar worksheets and additional pages containing graphic organizers and questions to help students gather and organize information to complete their Student Edition Writing and Listening and Speaking or Research and Technology assignments.

Enrichment

These activities give opportunities for advanced students to focus more closely on topics related to the content or theme of the literature selection.

ASSESSMENT

Diagnostic Tests

The beginning of each Unit 1 Resources book features a Diagnostic Test. Thereafter, each even-numbered Benchmark Test ends with a 20-question diagnostic component called Vocabulary in Context. Teachers desiring a larger sample for measuring students' reading ability can find an additional 20 questions at *PHLitOnline*.

Benchmark Tests

Twelve Benchmark Tests, spaced evenly throughout the year, assess students' mastery of literary, reading, vocabulary, grammar, and writing skills. A diagnostic Vocabulary in Context, described above, ends each even-numbered Benchmark Test.

Open-Book Tests

For every selection or grouping of selections, there is an Open-Book Test featuring short-answer and extended-response questions and opportunities for oral response. Most Open-Book-Tests also contain a question requiring students to represent information in a graphic organizer. These tests are available as a computer test bank on CD-ROM and at *PHLitOnline*.

Selection Tests

For every selection or grouping of selections, there are two closed-book Selection Tests (A and B) featuring multiple-choice and essay questions. Both tests assess essentially the same material; however Test A is designed for lower-level students, and Test B is designed for students average and above.

ADDITIONAL SUPPORT IN *UNIT ONE RESOURCES*

Pronunciation Guide

A two-page student guide to understanding diacritical marks given in standard dictionary pronunciations; includes practice

Form for Analyzing Primary Source Documents

In support of Primary Sources features in *The American Experience* and *The British Tradition*, a form for analyzing various types of primary sources.

Teaching Guides

To support fluency monitoring, Guide for Assessing Fluency; to support vocabulary instruction through music, a Guide for Teaching with BQ Tunes.

Name _____ Date _____

Guide for Assessing Fluency

The students' *All-in-One Workbooks* feature a series of twelve expository and narrative reading passages to be used to assess reading fluency. The passages have lexiles of increasing difficulty within the grade level range. They are designed to test students' reading accuracy and pace. An optional question is provided to assess comprehension.

The following oral reading rates are recommended goals:

ORAL READING RATES	
Grade	Words per Minute
6	115–145 with 90% accuracy
7	147–167 with 90% accuracy
8	156–171 with 90% accuracy
9–10	180–200 with 90% accuracy

Instructional Routine

- Hold reading practice sessions. Choose an appropriate practice passage of about 250 words from the literature students are studying or from another source. You will find a lexile score for each literature selection in your *Teacher's Edition* Time and Resource Managers. You may also use as practice passages the Warm-ups in the *Unit Resources* books and, for grade 6–8, articles in the *Discoveries* series and *Real-Life Readings*.

- Students should read the passage once silently, noting any unfamiliar words. Have them define or explain those words before reading the passage aloud. (Students may add these words to a *Word Wall* later.)

- Then, have students work in pairs to rehearse their oral fluency. (Alternatively, you may lead the class in a choral reading of a single passage.)

- After students have read the passage(s) with understanding, they may time themselves or each other for practice before the formal timed readings are conducted.

Formal Fluency Assessment

- From the students' All-in-One workbook, select a passage at the appropriate lexile level.

- Using an audio recorder, instruct the student to read the passage aloud at a normal pace. Alternatively, you may ask the student to read as you follow along, marking the text. Time the student for one minute.

- Note these types of errors: mispronunciations, omissions, reversals, substitutions, and words with which you have to help the student, after waiting two or three seconds.

- Mark the point in the passage that the student reaches after one minute.

- Use the formula below for determining accuracy and rate.

- Determine the rate by calculating the total number of WCPM (word correct per minute) and comparing the student's results against the goals indicate in the chart above.

- Analyze the results and create a plan for continued student improvement.

Name _____ Date _____

Guide for Assessing Fluency

Calculating Fluency

Use this formula to calculate reading fluency:

Total words read correctly (both correctly read and self-corrected) in one minute *divided by* total words read (words read correctly + errors) × 100 = % accuracy

---

$$\frac{\text{number of words read correctly}}{\text{number of words read}} \times 100 = \text{WCPM}$$

Example: $\frac{137}{145} \times 100 = 94\%$

Post-reading Comprehension Activity

A short test item allows you quickly to assess student's comprehension. The items include these formats:

- matching
- fill-in-the-blank
- true/false
- short answer

If the student demonstrates difficulty in understanding the passage, you may remediate using selected leveled resources in the *Prentice Hall Literature* program. These components include the Vocabulary and Reading Warm-ups in the *Unit Resources;* the *Reading Kit* Practice and Assess pages, which are aligned with specific skills; and the scaffolded support for comprehension and other ELA skills in the *Reader's Notebooks: Adapted* and *English Learner's Versions.*

Name _____ Date _____

Pronunciation Key Practice—1

Throughout your textbook, you will find vocabulary features that include pronunciation for each new word. In order to pronounce the words correctly, you need to understand the symbols used to indicate different sounds.

Short Vowel Sounds

These sounds are shown with no markings at all:

a   as in <u>a</u>t, c<u>a</u>p   e   as in <u>e</u>nd, f<u>ea</u>ther, v<u>e</u>ry
i   as in <u>i</u>t, g<u>y</u>m, <u>ea</u>r   u   as in m<u>u</u>d, t<u>o</u>n, tr<u>ou</u>ble

Long Vowel Sounds

These sounds are shown with a line over the vowel:

ā   as in <u>a</u>te, r<u>ai</u>n, br<u>ea</u>k   ē   as in s<u>ee</u>, st<u>ea</u>m, p<u>ie</u>ce
ī   as in n<u>i</u>ce, l<u>ie</u>, sk<u>y</u>   ō   as in n<u>o</u>, <u>oa</u>t, l<u>ow</u>

A. DIRECTIONS: *Read aloud the sounds indicated by the symbols in each item. Then write the word the symbols stand for.*

1. kap _____   6. ker _____
2. kāp _____   7. wird _____
3. tīp _____   8. swet _____
4. klōz _____   9. swet _____
5. tuf _____   10. nīt _____

Other Vowel Sounds

Notice the special markings used to show the following vowel sounds:

ä   as in father, far, heart   ô   as in all, law, taught
ഠo   as in look, would, pull   o͞o   as in boot, drew, tune
yo͞o as in cute, few, use   oi   as in oil, toy, royal
ou   as in out, now   ʉ   as in her, sir, word

B. DIRECTIONS: *Read aloud the sounds indicated by the symbols in each item. Then write the word the symbols stand for.*

1. boi _____   6. wʉrk _____
2. kär _____   7. lʉr _____
3. koͦod _____   8. kôt _____
4. lo͞oz _____   9. myo͞o _____
5. kroun _____   10. rä _____

Pronunciation Key Practice—2

Some Special Consonant Sounds

These consonant sounds are shown by special two-letter combinations:

hw	as in which, white
sh	as in shell, mission, fiction
ŋ	as in ring, anger, pink
ch	as in chew, nature

zh	as in vision, treasure
th	as in threw, nothing
th	as in then, mother

Syllables and Accent Marks

Your textbook will show you how to break a word into syllables, or parts, so that you can pronounce each part correctly. An accent mark (´) shows you which syllable to stress when you pronounce a word. Notice the differences in the way you say the following words:

bā´ bē   ō bā´   den´ im   dē ni´

Sounds in Unaccented Syllables

You will often see the following special symbols used in unaccented syllables. The most common is the schwa (ə), which shows an unaccented "uh" sound:

ə   as in ago, conceited, category, invisible
'l   as in cattle, paddle
'n   as in sudden, hidden

Light and Heavy Accents

Some long words have two stressed syllables: a heavy stress on one syllable and a second, lighter stress on another syllable. The lighter stress is shown by an accent mark in lighter type, like this: (´)

C. DIRECTIONS: *With a partner, read aloud the sounds indicated by the symbols in each item. Say the words that the symbols stand for.*

1. kôr´əs
2. kən pash´ən
3. brē *th*iŋ
4. ig nôrd´

5. mezh´ ər
6. des´ pər ā´ shən
7. im´ ə choor´
8. plunj´ iŋ

9. fər bid´ 'n
10. hwim´ pər
11. fun´ də ment´ 'l
12. rek´ əg nīz´

D. DIRECTIONS: *With a partner, read aloud the sounds indicated by the symbols in the following lines. Each group of lines represent the words of a small poem.*

1. ī ēt mī pēz wi*th* hun´ ē.
    īv dun it ôl mī līf.
    it māks *th*ə pēz tāst fun´ ē.
    but it kēps *th*em än *th*ə nīf.

2. dōnt wʉr´ ē if yoor jäb iz smôl
    and yoor ri wôrdz´ är fyoo.
    ri mem´ bər *th*at *th*ə mīt´ ē ōk
    wuz wuns ə nut līk yoo.

Name _____   Date _____

BQ Tunes Activities

Use **BQ Tunes** to engage students in learning each unit's Big Question vocabulary and introduce the issue that the Big Question raises. You can access **BQ Tunes** recordings and lyrics at *PHLitOnline* or in *Hear It*, the Prentice Hall Audio Program. The lyrics are also provided in your **Unit Resources** books and in the students' **All-in-One Workbooks**. Below are suggested activities for using the songs with your class. Each activity takes 20–25 minutes. Students should have copies of the lyrics available.

Listening Exercise

OBJECTIVE: *To familiarize students with the song vocabulary and initiate discussion of definitions*

1. Instruct students to listen to the selected song, listing any words they do not know.
2. Play the selected song.
3. Afterward, ask students to raise their hands if they know the definitions of words they listed, and call on individuals to share their definitions. Write the words on the board as they are called out.
4. Then, ask students to share words for which they did *not* know the definitions, and call on them individually. Write the words on the board as they are called out.
5. Direct students to turn to the selected lyrics, and instruct students to infer definitions for the remaining words in the lyrics. If they experience difficulty, encourage them to work in pairs or direct them to a dictionary.
6. Play song again, and instruct students to read the lyrics to reinforce the exercise.

Vocabulary Game Exercise

OBJECTIVE: *To reinforce students' knowledge of Big Question vocabulary in the songs, and to initiate class discussion of definitions*

1. Divide the students into two teams, each on one side of the room.
2. Play the selected song to the class. Then, play it again as students follow along reading the lyrics.
3. Afterward, read the song's lyrics aloud and, alternating sides, ask each team to define key words as they come upon them. Award a point for each correct definition.
4. Write the words on the board as they are defined, and keep score as the teams win points.
5. Declare the team with the most points the winners.
6. Review vocabulary missed by both teams, and field any questions the students may have.

BQ Tunes Activities

Writing Exercise, Stage 1

OBJECTIVE: *To build students' writing skills, leveraging newly acquired vocabulary*

1. Instruct students to write three contextual sentences, each using a single vocabulary word present in the selected song. The sentences *do not* have to be related to one another.
2. Allow 5 to 7 minutes for students to complete the task.
3. Afterward, ask random students to read what they have composed.
4. Then, ask the class if the sentences satisfied the "contextual" criteria, and discuss the responses.
5. Repeat with as many students as time permits.
6. Field any questions the students may have.

Writing Exercise, Stage 2

OBJECTIVE: *To build students' composition skills, leveraging newly acquired vocabulary*

1. Instruct students to write three contextual sentences, each using a single vocabulary word present in the selected song. The sentences *must* be related to one another, as in a paragraph.
2. Allow 5 to 7 minutes for students to complete the task.
3. Afterward, ask random students to read what they've composed.
4. Then, ask the class if the sentences satisfied the "contextual" criteria and the "relationship" criteria, and discuss the responses.
5. Repeat with as many students as time permits.
6. Field any questions the students may have.

BQ Tunes

The Difference, performed by Fake Gimms

Uncertainty. I can't be sure of what you say until I've checked it out.
Evaluate. Look through the facts just to **confirm**,
Prove what really went down.

As I weigh the situation
The **context** becomes clear.
And my **perception** strengthens as I understand
The difference between reality and truth.

Attempt to **discern**, to recognize and clearly see,
Verify and prove the truth.
Look past the lies to what is solid and **concrete**,
The **evidence** and the proof.
As I weigh the situation
The context becomes clear.
And my perception strengthens as I **comprehend**
The difference between reality and . . .

What's the **objective**?
What is your plan?
Don't be so **subjective**.
It can't only be about how you feel.
It's highly unlikely, **improbable** at best,
To **differentiate**.
To know the difference,
The difference between **reality** and truth

Song Title: **The Difference**
Artist / Performed by Fake Gimms
Vocals & Guitar: Joe Pfeiffer
Guitar: Greg Kuter
Bass Guitar: Jared Duncan
Drums: Tom Morra
Lyrics by the Fake Gimms
Produced by the Fake Gimms
Studio Production: Mike Pandolfo, Wonderful
Executive Producer: Keith London, Defined Mind

Unit 1: Fiction and Nonfiction
Big Question Vocabulary—1

The Big Question: Is there a difference between reality and truth?

In your textbook, you learned words that are useful for talking about reality and truth. In literature as well as in our everyday lives, we sometimes struggle to identify what is real or true, as opposed to what is fictional or false.

DIRECTIONS: *Review the following definitions of words you can use when talking about reality and truth.*

comprehend: to understand the nature or meaning of something

concrete: able to be seen and touched

confirm: to verify the truth, accuracy, or genuineness of something

context: the set of circumstances that surround a particular event or situation

differentiate: to perceive the difference in or between two or more things

A. *Now, for each Big Question vocabulary word, write a synonym, an antonym, and a sentence in which you use the word correctly.*

Word	Synonym	Antonym	Example Sentence
1. comprehend			
2. concrete			
3. confirm			
4. context			
5. differentiate			

B. *Write two to three sentences in which you use three or more of the vocabulary words on this page to write a generalization about reality and truth.*

_____

_____

_____

_____

Unit 1: Fiction and Nonfiction
Big Question Vocabulary—2

The Big Question: Is there a difference between reality and truth?

DIRECTIONS: *Review the following definitions of words you can use when talking about reality and truth.*

discern: to recognize something as distinct or different

evaluate: to judge or determine the significance, worth, or quality of

evidence: that which tends to prove or disprove something

improbable: not likely

objective: unbiased

Now, decide whether each statement below is true or false, based on the meanings of the underlined vocabulary words. Circle T or F, and then explain any true answers. If a statement is false, rewrite it so that it is true. Do not change the underlined vocabulary words.

1. One can <u>discern</u> the truth of a situation by stating a falsehood.
   T / F _____
   _____

2. To determine whether or not a person's opinion is valid, you should <u>evaluate</u> the facts the person used to reach such a conclusion.
   T / F _____
   _____

3. In a debate, the winning side is usually the one that provides the best <u>evidence</u> to support its arguments.
   T / F _____
   _____

4. The sun rising each morning is completely <u>improbable</u>.
   T / F _____
   _____

5. An <u>objective</u> opinion is one that is based entirely on one's emotions and internal reactions to a situation.
   T / F _____
   _____

Unit 1: Fiction and Nonfiction
Big Question Vocabulary—3

The Big Question: Is there a difference between reality and truth?

DIRECTIONS: *Review the following definitions of words you can use when talking about reality and truth.*

perception: one's understanding of something, especially as seen through the filter of that person's emotions, experiences, and biases

reality: the state or quality of being real and provable

subjective: existing in the mind and influenced by moods, attitudes, opinions

uncertainty: the state of being in doubt or hesitant

verify: to confirm or prove the truth of something

Now, use the word or words given in parentheses to answer each question.

1. What is truth? **(verify)**

   _____

   _____

2. How can one person see something as a truth while another person does not? **(perception)**

   _____

   _____

3. How might a person's emotions influence his or her opinions on an issue? **(perception, subjective)**

   _____

   _____

4. If you are not sure about what is supposed to be real in a novel you are reading, how might you determine it? **(reality, uncertainty)**

   _____

   _____

5. Why is it important to understand the difference between reality and truth? **(reality, perception, subjective)**

   _____

   _____

Unit 1: Fiction and Nonfiction
Applying the Big Question

The Big Question: Is there a difference between reality and truth?

DIRECTIONS: *Complete the chart below to apply what you have learned about the difference between reality and truth. One row has been completed for you.*

Example	Reality	Truth	Difference Between Reality and Truth	What I Learned
From Literature	The game of hide-and-seek in "Games at Twilight" is just a game and does not really matter.	Winning the game carries a deep life lesson for Ravi about how insignificant he really is.	In reality the game is just a game, but the truth to Ravi is that the game is proof of his place in the world.	A person's perception of reality is often subjective.
From Literature				
From Science				
From Social Studies				
From Real Life				

Diagnostic Test

Identify the answer choice that best completes the statement.

1. Each week, Mom gives us each ten dollars for our_____.
   - A. treasury
   - B. luxury
   - C. allowances
   - D. cashed

2. I could buy the black shoes or the brown shoes, but I think I will choose the_____.
   - A. midst
   - B. genuine
   - C. latter
   - D. extreme

3. Once the ingredients for the bread are in the bowl, I will show you how to_____the dough.
   - A. knead
   - B. pursue
   - C. waver
   - D. barbecue

4. I was so thirsty that I was feeling_____.
   - A. awaiting
   - B. parched
   - C. subdued
   - D. revealed

5. If you do not take care of your teeth, you will likely have_____.
   - A. brittle
   - B. mottled
   - C. agitated
   - D. cavities

6. When the firefighters arrived on the scene, the warehouse was already_____.
   - A. brazier
   - B. astray
   - C. sabotage
   - D. ablaze

7. I decided to use a ladder to clean the leaves out of the_____ around the house.
   - A. abode
   - B. drainpipes
   - C. casements
   - D. parapets

8. These spices will give your dish a very special, _____ taste.
   A. pungent
   B. bland
   C. dank
   D. extraordinarily

9. The school policy states that for every six students, there must be at least one_____ on field trips.
   A. governess
   B. reveler
   C. chaperone
   D. reinforcement

10. Thousands of years ago, monks lived, worked, and prayed in this old_____.
    A. sloop
    B. elementary
    C. abbey
    D. stucco

11. After teaching for several years, he was hired to be the_____ of the boarding school.
    A. scribe
    B. associate
    C. headmaster
    D. colleague

12. After the concert in the park, the crowd_____.
    A. separation
    B. unseated
    C. overrun
    D. dispersed

13. When the jury members did not reach a verdict by the end of the day, they were_____ overnight.
    A. coded
    B. sequestered
    C. termination
    D. clinched

14. I try to exercise and read some uplifting_____ quietly every day.
    A. sayings
    B. assumptions
    C. pacts
    D. meditations

15. Those movies about exploring outer space started his _____ with spaceships.
    A. passionate
    B. characterization
    C. scenario
    D. preoccupation

16. He did not do his job, and he _____ his duties.
    A. ejected
    B. analyze
    C. persecuted
    D. shirked

17. I shouldn't take the vacation time now _____ I do need a break.
    A. logical
    B. consequence
    C. albeit
    D. doubtless

18. When we arrived in the city, we were amazed at the traffic and the _____.
    A. monumental
    B. skyscrapers
    C. hillocks
    D. gothic

19. While serious areas of disagreement remain, our views are now more _____.
    A. assailed
    B. recurred
    C. spectral
    D. convergent

20. At our graduation ceremony, we walked onto the stage and were handed our _____.
    A. diplomas
    B. proverbs
    C. rubles
    D. postscripts

21. This beautiful jewelry looks very old, and I would not be surprised if it was an _____.
    A. creation
    B. antique
    C. recent
    D. structured

22. Does this CD player come with a written _____ ?
   A. guidance
   B. guarantee
   C. effective
   D. qualification

23. The block tower was certain to fall because it looked so crooked and _____ .
   A. lopsided
   B. fantastic
   C. collapse
   D. uncertainty

24. The heat was turned up high in this room, and it had become _____ .
   A. lofty
   B. scalded
   C. vivid
   D. stifling

25. The butterfly flitted among the flowers before it came to _____ on the red rose.
   A. alight
   B. whitewashed
   C. shrouded
   D. ominous

26. She thought she was better than all of us, which led to her very _____ attitude.
   A. respectably
   B. imperious
   C. virtuous
   D. enthusiastic

27. She was in a happy mood and skipped _____ down the street.
   A. ghastly
   B. apprehensively
   C. jauntily
   D. merciful

28. The farmer took a break from his work only after the entire field was _____ .
   A. fulfilled
   B. straddled
   C. pealed
   D. sowed

29. Words used in a harsh way and meant to hurt are_____ to me.
    A. impassive
    B. offensive
    C. nonchalant
    D. burdening

30. This steak was so easily cut that it was the_____ piece of meat I ever ate.
    A. animated
    B. wholesale
    C. tenderest
    D. exceptional

31. That expensive beaded evening gown is the most_____ dress I have ever seen.
    A. luxurious
    B. leisurely
    C. vainly
    D. humble

32. Just as you asked, everything has been taken care of in_____ with your wishes.
    A. strategic
    B. proposition
    C. censorship
    D. accordance

33. I think that I will sew a new shirt from this_____ fabric.
    A. calico
    B. girdle
    C. sandpaper
    D. overcoat

34. Some day soon, you will see houses where you now see just_____ land.
    A. rectangular
    B. undeveloped
    C. amongst
    D. tier

35. When talking about the contract, the lawyer answered our questions_____ .
    A. distinguished
    B. emphatic
    C. decisively
    D. tranquilly

36. The lecture was not very interesting, and I thought I would doze off out of _____ .
    A. boredom
    B. withstanding
    C. persecution
    D. consolation

37. When she could not find her car keys, she ran around the house searching for them in a near _____ .
    A. surveillance
    B. intercept
    C. frenzy
    D. infuriated

38. The fever was so high that he became _____ .
    A. delirious
    B. writhed
    C. lighthearted
    D. vibrant

39. May I ask you a simple question about an unimportant and _____ matter?
    A. consequence
    B. trifling
    C. intricate
    D. extraordinary

40. After the bitter defeat, he shut himself off in _____ .
    A. sedate
    B. monotonous
    C. intrigue
    D. seclusion

Unit 1: Fiction and Nonfiction Skills Concept Map—1

Is there a difference between reality and truth?

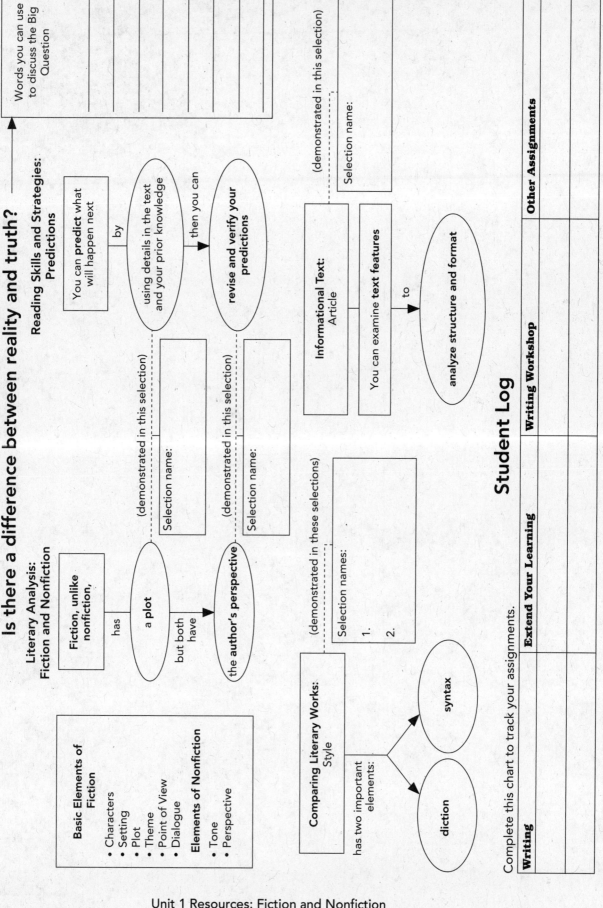

Literary Analysis:
Fiction and Nonfiction

Fiction, unlike nonfiction, — has — a plot

but both have — the **author's perspective**

(demonstrated in this selection)

Selection name: _____

(demonstrated in this selection)

Selection name: _____

Basic Elements of Fiction

- Characters
- Setting
- Plot
- Theme
- Point of View
- Dialogue

Elements of Nonfiction

- Tone
- Perspective

Reading Skills and Strategies:
Predictions

You can **predict** what will happen next — by — using details in the text and your prior knowledge — then you can — **revise and verify your predictions**

Words you can use to discuss the Big Question

Informational Text:
Article

You can examine **text features** — to — analyze structure and format

(demonstrated in this selection)

Selection name: _____

Comparing Literary Works:
Style

has two important elements: — syntax / diction

(demonstrated in these selections)

Selection names:

1. _____
2. _____

Student Log

Complete this chart to track your assignments.

Writing	Extend Your Learning	Writing Workshop	Other Assignments

Vocabulary Warm-up Word Lists

Study these words. Then, complete the activities that follow.

Word List A

auctioned [AWK shuhnd] *v.* sold in a public sale to the highest bidder
   My mother plans to bid on the table that will be <u>auctioned</u> tomorrow.

chronology [kruh NAH luh jee] *n.* the order of events
   A timeline can help you understand the <u>chronology</u> of historic events.

defiance [di FY uhns] *n.* resistance to authority; refusal to conform
   The runner showed her <u>defiance</u> by refusing to follow the coach's orders.

entailed [en TAYLD] *v.* involved; required
   Becoming a lawyer <u>entailed</u> many years of long and difficult study.

eroded [i ROH did] *v.* wore away; caused to decrease
   My cousin <u>eroded</u> my trust in him when he told me a lie.

locales [loh KAHLZ] *n.* locations, especially places connected with events
   The story is set in two <u>locales</u>: a shopping mall and a graveyard.

whim [HWIM] *n.* a sudden fancy or impulse
   We passed the museum and on a <u>whim</u> we decided to go inside.

yield [YEELD] *v.* to produce
   Studying carefully for a test is likely to <u>yield</u> a passing grade.

Word List B

artful [ART fuhl] *adj.* skillful; clever
   She was such an <u>artful</u> writer that even her notes were fun to read.

evocative [i VAH kuh tiv] *adj.* causing strong memories or images
   The band played a tune that was <u>evocative</u> of dance clubs in the 1970s.

excessive [ek SES iv] *adj.* too much; overdone
   His blue shoes, socks, and shirt showed his <u>excessive</u> fondness for blue.

ferociously [fuh ROH shuhs lee] *adv.* fiercely; greatly; intensely
   The team worked <u>ferociously</u> to complete the science project.

lute [LOOT] *n.* an early stringed instrument with a pear-shaped body and a long neck
   The musician played a <u>lute</u> to bring a medieval sound to the song.

meticulous [muh TIK yoo luhs] *adj.* extremely careful
   I am <u>meticulous</u> about my clothes, so they are always neat and clean.

muslin [MUZ lin] *n.* a strong cotton cloth
   The monk's robes were made of heavy brown <u>muslin</u>.

trivia [TRI vee uh] *n.* insignificant, unimportant matters
   Grandma tells me to focus on the important things in life, not on <u>trivia</u>.

"Magdalena Looking" and "Artful Research" by Susan Vreeland
Vocabulary Warm-up Exercises

Exercise A *Fill in each blank in the paragraph below with an appropriate word from Word List A. Use each word only once.*

I forget some of the details, but I still recall the basic [1] _____

of events. One Sunday last year, my grandfather and I were bored. On a

sudden [2] _____, we decided to clean out the attic. The job

[3] _____ sorting through a lot of junk. Then, I saw a trunk covered with

stickers from interesting [4] _____ from around the world. "I bet there's a

treasure in this thing," he said. My confidence in him was [5] _____ when

we opened the trunk and it was empty. "It's only a big box," I said, stamping my foot to

show my [6] _____ of his optimism. Of course, grandfather was right. The

antique trunk will be [7] _____ to the highest bidder next week. The

dealer expects the sale will [8] _____ more than five hundred dollars!

Exercise B *Answer the questions with complete explanations.*

Example: How can you tell if the emotions of the actors in a movie are <u>excessive</u>?
If the emotions are too great for the situation, they are <u>excessive</u>.

1. What is one good job for someone who is very <u>meticulous</u>?

_____

2. Who among your friends would probably win a <u>trivia</u> contest? Why?

_____

3. Would you like to have a winter scarf made of <u>muslin</u>? Why or why not?

_____

4. Do you think a <u>lute</u> sounds more like a guitar or a piano? Why?

_____

5. How can you tell if someone is <u>ferociously</u> devoted to a hobby or sport?

_____

6. Is an <u>artful</u> solution always the best solution?

_____

7. What kind of music do you think is <u>evocative</u> of outer space?

_____

"Magdalena Looking" and "Artful Research" by Susan Vreeland
Reading Warm-up A

Read the following passage. Pay special attention to the underlined words. Then, read it again, and complete the activities. Use a separate sheet of paper for your written answers.

The life of Dutch painter Johannes Vermeer remains a mystery. Historians identify only basic dates in the chronology of his life, including his birth in 1632, his marriage in 1653, and his death in 1675. Vermeer is remembered as the painter of about 35 paintings. Time has eroded the details of Vermeer's life, but his reputation has been built up by this small collection of wonderful masterpieces.

Vermeer's father became an art dealer the year before Vermeer was born. Paintings are sometimes auctioned to the highest bidder; other times they are sold by a dealer at a set price. Because his father bought and sold art, it is probable that Vermeer's youth entailed plenty of chances to observe and study paintings.

Most of Vermeer's works show everyday people in common situations. In several paintings, a woman reads or writes a letter. The locales are mostly interiors, often with a window nearby. Vermeer creates a delicate sense of light that many viewers find magical. Vermeer is also well known for his masterful placement of objects. Nothing is left to whim or chance. Every detail, from a single earring to a milk jug, is carefully selected and positioned.

Close inspection of Vermeer's paintings can yield plenty of information about the way he used paint to create his rich illusions. In some paintings, he applied the paint thickly to build up a heavy surface. In others, he used many layers of paints and transparent glazes. These layers help create depth and light.

Some artists become famous for their defiance of accepted traditions. They boldly toss aside the normal ways of painting and follow their own goals. Instead, Vermeer brought the accepted style to a new height with his careful, shimmering works.

1. Circle three events in the chronology of Vermeer's life. Then, explain what a *chronology* is.

2. Underline the words that tell what time eroded. Then, describe what happens when a rock is *eroded* by wind or water.

3. Circle the word that names something that can be auctioned. Then, name two other items that might be *auctioned* today.

4. Underline the words that tell what Vermeer's youth entailed. Then, tell what *entailed* means.

5. Circle the word that names the locales of most of Vermeer's paintings. Then, describe two *locales* in a movie you have seen recently.

6. Underline the words that describe something that is the opposite of a whim. Then, tell about a decision you once made on a *whim*.

7. Underline the words that tell what close inspection of Vermeer's paintings can yield. Then, tell what *yield* means.

8. Underline the sentence that describes how an artist might show defiance. Then, tell what *defiance* is.

"Magdalena Looking" and "Artful Research" by Susan Vreeland
Reading Warm-up B

Read the following passage. Pay special attention to the underlined words. Then, read it again, and complete the activities. Use a separate sheet of paper for your written answers.

Vermeer lived in Holland during the seventeenth century, a period known as the golden age of Dutch art. During this time, artists produced between five million and ten million works. This fact is not mere trivia, but an important reflection of the enormous artistic activity during this time. Almost every Dutch household had at least one work of art, whether it was a simple print or an original painting. Most of these were the careful works of meticulous artists who wanted to get each detail just right.

Today, these Dutch landscapes and scenes from daily life are richly evocative, giving modern viewers insight into a world hundreds of years in the past. When you look at one of these paintings, you enter a clear picture of another time. Many historical facts are presented in nearly photographic detail. In one family scene, an artist might clearly show the difference between the rich velvet and satin worn by a wealthy merchant and the simple cotton muslin worn by the servants. We can draw conclusions about the importance of music when we view a portrait of a singer plucking the strings of a lute or another musician playing a tune on a piano.

In seventeenth-century Holland, young men who wanted to become painters had to work as apprentices to a member of St. Luke's Guild. They had to pay for this chance to work with a master painter for four to six years. Girls were seldom allowed to become apprentices. First, apprentices learned to make exact copies of drawings and paintings. Then, they learned how to make artful drawings of the human body, working from plaster models. The artists who taught apprentices were often ferociously critical, forcing apprentices to redo work again and again. Some apprentices quit, finding the hours excessive and the conditions unreasonable. However, apprentices who finished the training were well prepared to carry on in the footsteps of their teachers.

1. Circle the words that mean the opposite of trivia. Tell one *trivia* fact you know.

2. Underline the words that describe what a meticulous artist wants. Describe a friend who is *meticulous*.

3. Underline the words that tell why Dutch landscapes can be evocative. Then, tell what *evocative* means.

4. Circle fabrics that are not like muslin. Name what you might make out of *muslin*.

5. Underline the words that tell how someone plays a lute. Describe two other instruments in the *lute* family.

6. Underline what apprentices learned before they made artful drawing. Tell something that you can do in an *artful* way.

7. Underline the words that describe what ferociously critical teachers did. Then, tell what *ferociously* means.

8. Circle a synonym for excessive. Describe what you think is an *excessive* amount of exercise.

Susan Vreeland
Listening and Viewing

Segment 1: Meet Susan Vreeland
- How did an ancient glass pitcher inspire Susan Vreeland to write about visual arts? What type of art would you like to write about?

_____

_____

_____

Segment 2: Fiction and Nonfiction
- How did Susan Vreeland's nonfiction writing lead her to writing fiction about art? Why is writing descriptively important in fiction?

_____

_____

_____

_____

Segment 3: The Writing Process
- What does Susan Vreeland look to edit when revising a draft? In what ways do you agree or disagree with Susan Vreeland that revising is the most important part of the writing process?

_____

_____

_____

_____

Segment 4: The Rewards of Writing
- What does Susan Vreeland hope readers can "get out of" reading her stories? What do you think you can learn by reading books about art?

_____

_____

_____

_____

Learning About Fiction and Nonfiction

Literature may be either **fiction** or **nonfiction.** The following chart compares and contrasts these two types of literature.

Characteristics	Fiction	Nonfiction
Overall Features	Fiction is prose that tells a story from the author's imagination. The individuals who take part in the story are **characters.** They experience a series of related events called the **plot.** The plot begins with a **conflict,** or problem; rises to a **climax,** or point of great intensity; and ends with a **resolution,** or conclusion.	Nonfiction is prose that presents information about real people, events, or ideas. The author of a nonfiction work may include opinions or impressions along with facts.
Sample Forms	short stories, novellas, novels	speeches, articles, news reports, essays, biographies
Author's Purpose	to entertain	to persuade, inform, or entertain

DIRECTIONS: *Read each item. Decide whether it is a work of fiction or nonfiction, and then write fiction or nonfiction on the line provided.*

_____ 1. a piece of literature that tells how a real-life mystery was solved

_____ 2. a piece of literature that tries to persuade readers to plant trees

_____ 3. a piece of literature about a group of people who travel to another galaxy

_____ 4. a piece of literature that compares American pizza to Italian pizza

_____ 5. a piece of literature about highways in outer space

_____ 6. a piece of literature about an imaginary girl who lived in Spain in the 1600s

_____ 7. a piece of literature that summarizes and reviews a new work of fiction

_____ 8. a piece of literature that states the author's opinions about country music

_____ 9. a piece of literature that tells about two boys who time-travel to the year 3007

_____ 10. a piece of literature that explains how to start your own pet care business

"Magdalena Looking" by Susan Vreeland
Model Selection: Fiction

Fiction is prose that tells about individuals and events from the author's imagination. The individuals who take part in the story are **characters.** They experience a series of related events called the **plot.** The plot begins with a **conflict,** or problem; rises to a **climax,** or point of intensity; and ends with a **resolution,** or conclusion. The action takes place at a certain time and location, called the **setting.**

In fiction, the perspective from which a story is told is called **point of view. First-person point of view** is the perspective of a character who participates in the story. **Third-person point of view** is the perspective of a narrator outside the story. A third-person narrator might be **omniscient,** or all-knowing. The narrator might also be **limited,** reporting the perspective of only one character.

The underlying message or insight a story conveys is its **theme.** If a theme applies to all people in all cultures, it is a **universal theme.**

DIRECTIONS: *Read this passage from "Magdalena Looking," and answer the questions that follow.*

In 1696, just after their only living child, Magritte, damp with fever, stopped breathing in her arms, Magdalena read in the *Amsterdamsche Courant* of a public auction of one hundred thirty-four paintings by various artists. "Several outstandingly artful paintings," the notice said, "including twenty-one works most powerfully and splendidly painted by the late J. Vermeer of Delft, will be auctioned May 16, 1:00, at the Oude Heeren Logement." Only a week away. She thought of Hendrick [the baker]. Of course he couldn't be expected to keep those paintings forever. Hers might be there. The possibility kept her awake nights.

1. What is the setting of this passage? _____

2. What event advances the plot in this passage? _____
_____

3. A. Which characters are involved in this passage? _____
_____

   B. How does each character relate to the events that are occurring? _____
_____
_____

4. A. Is this passage told from the first-person, third-person omniscient, or third-person limited point of view? Explain. _____
_____

   B. Why do you think the author uses this point of view? _____
_____

"Artful Research" by Susan Vreeland
Model Selection: Nonfiction

Nonfiction is prose in which an author presents information about real people, events, or ideas. Unlike fiction, which contains invented characters and events, nonfiction can *only* present facts and discuss real-world ideas.

Nonfiction is presented directly by the author, whose **perspective,** or viewpoint, colors the work. Through his or her word choices and details, the author expresses a particular attitude toward the subject and the readers. This attitude is known as **tone.**

Authors of nonfiction works have a definite **purpose for writing.** Some include the following purposes:

- to explain ("How To Juggle")
- to entertain ("Life *IS* Stranger than Fiction")
- to share thoughts and experiences ("Skiing: My Downfall as an Athlete")
- to persuade ("Adopt a Pet!")
- to inform ("Why Glow Worms Glow")

DIRECTIONS: *Answer the following questions about "Artful Research."*

1. Which real people does the author mention? _____
_____

2. From whose perspective is it told? _____

3. Summarize a real-life experience that the author shares with her readers. _____
_____
_____

4. List two facts that the author presents. _____
_____
_____

5. List two opinions that the author presents. _____
_____
_____

6. What is the author's attitude toward her subject? How do you explain this attitude? ____
_____

"Magdalena Looking" and "Artful Research" by Susan Vreeland
Open-Book Test

Short Answer *Write your responses to the questions in this section on the lines provided.*

1. How can you tell that "Magdalena Looking" is a work of fiction, even though Johannes Vermeer was a real person? Remember that a piece of writing is fiction if it includes anything imaginary.

   _____

   _____

2. What makes "Magdalena Looking" a short story rather than a novella or a novel? Think about its size and scope. In your explanation, show your understanding of all three terms.

   _____

   _____

   _____

   _____

3. What is the general setting of "Magdalena Looking"? In what specific settings do the opening and closing incidents of the story take place? Fill in your answers on the chart below. Then, on the line below, explain why Vreeland keeps the setting simple and focused.

General Setting	
Time:	Place:
Opening Setting	
Time:	Place:
Closing Setting	
Time:	Place:

   _____

4. From what point of view is "Magdalena Looking" told? Briefly explain your answer.

   _____

   _____

   _____

5. Why does the young Magdalena leave her house and go up to the sentry post at the beginning of the story? Provide at least two details to support your answer.

_____

_____

_____

_____

6. What is it about Magdalena's father that most pains her? What does she most admire about him?

_____

_____

_____

7. Magdalena hates mending so much that she screams out loud in *defiance*. What would be another example of an act of *defiance* in Magdalena's situation?

_____

_____

8. Consider the ideas about art that "Magdalena Looking" conveys. What main theme is stressed by Magdalena's thoughts in the final paragraph?

_____

_____

9. Judging from the tone of "Artful Research," what seems to be Vreeland's attitude toward research?

_____

_____

10. The three main purposes of nonfiction are to persuade, to inform, and to entertain. What is Vreeland's main purpose in "Artful Research"? What sorts of people does she seem to envision as her main audience?

_____

_____

_____

Essay

Write an extended response to the question of your choice or to the question or questions your teacher assigns you.

11. Near the end of "Magdalena Looking," Magdalena is described as "a woman overcome with wishes." In an essay, identify Magdalena's most powerful wish. Then, state whether or not it comes true, and explain why.

12. In nonfiction works, authors use facts for several different purposes. In an essay, analyze Vreeland's use of facts in "Artful Research." What kinds of facts does she include? Does she simply want to inform the reader of facts, or do the facts help her accomplish another purpose, such as persuading the reader or illustrating her points? Cite examples of Vreeland's facts as you answer these questions in your essay.

13. In "Artful Research," Vreeland claims that research "gives direction, depth, and authority" to her writing. Having read "Magdalena Looking," do you agree with Vreeland's claim? What details or aspects of the story reflect the author's research? In your opinion, do these details enrich the story or detract from its appeal? Why? Write an essay in which you examine Vreeland's use of research in "Magdalena Looking" and its effects on the reader.

14. **Thinking About the Big Question: What is the difference between reality and truth?** The social reality in seventeenth-century Europe made it difficult for females to become artists. In truth, however, many girls and women had the talent to be fine artists. In a brief essay, explain how this contrast between reality and truth is a key idea in "Magdalena Looking." Explore the social conflict Magdalena faces, as well as the talents and interests she seems to have. Support your answer with examples from the story.

Oral Response

15. Go back to short answer question 2, 5, 7, or 8 or to the question your teacher assigns you. Take a few minutes to expand your answer and prepare an oral response. Find additional details in "Magdalena Looking" that support your points. If necessary, make notes to guide your response.

"Magdalena Looking" and **"Artful Research"** by Susan Vreeland
Selection Test A

Critical Thinking *Identify the letter of the choice that best answers the question.*

_____ 1. Which statement is true about **nonfiction?**
    A. It is told by an omniscient narrator.
    B. It contains only provable facts.
    C. It contains a series of imaginary events.
    D. It is presented directly by the author.

_____ 2. Which term names the part of a **plot** that concludes a work of fiction?
    A. climax
    B. resolution
    C. setting
    D. conflict

_____ 3. Read these sentences from the beginning of a short story.

    I guess I should have known not to adopt a hedgehog. At the time, though, it
    seemed like such a good idea.

    From what **point of view** is this story told?
    A. first person
    B. third person limited
    C. third person omniscient
    D. the reader's point of view

_____ 4. Which of the following is an example of **fiction?**
    A. a political speech
    B. a newspaper article
    C. a short story
    D. a biography

_____ 5. In a nonfiction work, what is **tone?**
    A. how the main character feels and thinks
    B. the author's purpose for creating a mood
    C. how the setting relates to the subject matter
    D. the author's attitude toward the subject

Critical Reading

___ 6. Who narrates "Magdalena Looking"?
A. Magdalena
B. a famous painter
C. an outside narrator
D. Hendrick the baker

___ 7. In "Magdalena Looking," what is Magdalena's greatest wish in life?
A. to paint what she sees
B. to leave her hometown
C. to be a beautiful woman
D. to collect works of art

___ 8. In "Magdalena Looking," what is Magdalena's main feeling toward her father?
A. distrust
B. awe
C. hatred
D. affection

___ 9. Why does Magdalena go to the art auction in "Magdalena Looking"?
A. to look for her father
B. to look for a painting
C. to find an old friend
D. to sell a painting

___ 10. Which event is the climax of "Magdalena Looking"?
A. Magdalena's father decides to paint Magdalena.
B. Magdalena sells the painting of herself to Hendrick.
C. Magdalena marries a saddlemaker named Nicolaes.
D. Magdalena attempts to buy the painting of herself.

___ 11. What message about art does the story "Magdalena Looking" convey?
A. Art can connect people to one another.
B. Art will lead only to disappointment.
C. Art is best left to experts and geniuses.
D. Art is a good hobby for a young girl.

___ 12. How can you tell that "Artful Research" is a work of nonfiction?

    A. It includes made-up events and characters.

    B. It refers to distant times and places.

    C. The author describes her own experiences.

    D. The narrator has an outsider's viewpoint.

___ 13. Who is Vreeland's main audience in "Artful Research"?

    A. writers

    B. librarians

    C. artists

    D. teachers

___ 14. How does Vreeland feel about research?

    A. She sees it as a chore.

    B. She prefers it to writing.

    C. She believes it has no value.

    D. She sees it as an adventure.

Essay

15. In the scene in the auction gallery in "Magdalena Looking," Magdalena is "struck again by that keenest of childhood wishes" and regrets that she did not pursue this wish. In an essay, explain Magdalena's wish. If Magdalena had followed her wish, do you think she would have succeeded? Provide at least two examples from the story to support your ideas.

16. In "Artful Research," Susan Vreeland explains that she uses factual material in her works of fiction. In an essay, define the concept of *fiction*. Then, explain how Vreeland uses factual information in "Magdalena Looking." According to Vreeland, how can facts add to a fictional work?

17. **Thinking About the Big Question: Is there a difference between reality and truth?** In seventeenth-century Europe, it was difficult for females to become artists. They were not thought to be talented enough. In truth, however, many girls and women had the talent to be fine artists. In a brief essay, explain how Magdalena faces this conflict. First, describe Magdalena's talents and interests in art. Then explain how other people, such as Magdalena's father, expect her to do something different with her life. Support your answer with examples from the story.

"Magdalena Looking" and **"Artful Research"** by Susan Vreeland
Selection Test B

Critical Thinking *Identify the letter of the choice that best completes the statement or answers the question.*

____ 1. Which statement is true about **nonfiction?**
   A. It can contain imaginary characters.
   B. It presents facts *and* made-up details.
   C. It presents only ideas and opinions.
   D. It presents only facts and ideas.

____ 2. Which statement is true about **fiction?**
   A. It can contain only real people.
   B. It can contain imaginary people.
   C. It cannot contain any facts.
   D. It cannot contain any details.

____ 3. Which of the following is NOT a part of the **plot** in a work of fiction?
   A. climax
   B. resolution
   C. introduction
   D. conflict

____ 4. Which statement is true about a third-person omniscient narrator?
   A. The narrator is a character and plays a role in the story's development.
   B. The narrator knows the thoughts and feelings of all the characters.
   C. The narrator knows only what a single character is thinking and feeling.
   D. The narrator shares only his or her own thoughts and experiences.

____ 5. Which of the following groups contains one example of **fiction?**
   A. autobiography, novel, letter
   B. essay, diary, editorial
   C. biography, letter, speech
   D. speech, autobiography, article

____ 6. Which of the following is NOT an example of **nonfiction?**
   A. a textbook chapter about rainy climates
   B. an essay that urges readers to collect rainwater
   C. an article that describes fun rainy-day activities
   D. a short story about a raindrop's journey

Critical Reading

____ 7. Which statement is true about "Magdalena Looking"?
   A. Its narrator is Magdalena.
   B. Its narrator is Johannes Vermeer.
   C. Its narrator is an art dealer.
   D. Its narrator is not a character.

___ 8. In "Magdalena Looking," why does Magdalena go up to the sentry post?
   A. to practice painting
   B. to avoid her work
   C. to look and dream
   D. to meet people

___ 9. In "Magdalena Looking," which statement describes Magdalena's main conflict?
   A. She wants to learn how to paint.
   B. She hopes to end her family's debt.
   C. She does not enjoy mending.
   D. She resents caring for her siblings.

___ 10. What about her father most pains Magdalena in "Magdalena Looking"?
   A. He shows little interest in her as a person.
   B. He prefers to paint her sister and her mother.
   C. He does not take her out on the boat often.
   D. He does not earn enough to support the family.

___ 11. "Magdalena Looking" is set in Europe over 300 years ago. How does this setting relate to the story's events?
   A. It helps explain why Magdalena's family was not wealthy.
   B. It helps explain why Magdalena's father was a painter.
   C. It helps explain why Magdalena liked going to the sentry post.
   D. It helps explain why Magdalena was not encouraged to paint.

___ 12. In "Magdalena Looking," Magdalena encounters a painting of herself after twenty years. What does she see?
   A. She sees a young, foolish girl with impossible dreams.
   B. She sees a young girl filled with innocence and longing.
   C. She sees a girl already worn down by life's difficulties.
   D. She sees a girl preoccupied with the task of mending.

___ 13. Which is a theme of "Magdalena Looking"?
   A. Most hopes and dreams lead only to disappointment.
   B. Artistic endeavors are best left to artistic experts.
   C. Art can connect us to ourselves and to other people.
   D. It is through love—not art—that we can find meaning.

___ 14. What is a likely reason that Susan Vreeland chose the title "Artful Research" for her essay?
   A. Her essay demonstrates how research can enrich a fiction writer's work.
   B. Her essay explains what she has learned about art through research.
   C. Her essay expresses the opinion that research is more important than art.
   D. Her essay argues that many painters could benefit from research.

___ 15. What makes "Artful Research" a work of nonfiction?
   A. The author uses imaginary characters to convey certain ideas.
   B. The author sets the work in a distant time and place.
   C. The author describes her own experiences.
   D. The author uses a third-person narrator to express her views.

____ 16. Who is Vreeland's main audience in "Artful Research"?
   A. artists who enjoy historical fiction
   B. readers of historical fiction
   C. writers of historical fiction
   D. fans of *Girl in Hyacinth Blue*

____ 17. From the tone of "Artful Research," what seems to be the author's attitude toward research?
   A. The author sees research as a necessary drudgery.
   B. The author sees research as a promising adventure.
   C. The author sees research as preferable to actual writing.
   D. The author sees research as a complete waste of time.

____ 18. According to "Artful Research," how did Vreeland's research on windmills help her write *Girl in Hyacinth Blue*?
   A. It helped her better understand the novel's setting.
   B. It gave her an idea for the main character's conflict.
   C. It helped her envision the entire novel as a machine.
   D. It gave her a new way of thinking about a character.

____ 19. According to "Artful Research," at what point does Vreeland think a writer should stop researching and start writing?
   A. when the story comes alive in the writer's mind
   B. when the first relevant fact has been discovered
   C. when all necessary knowledge has been gained
   D. when the "safety" of research is no longer needed

Essay

20. Near the end of "Magdalena Looking," Magdalena is described as "a woman overcome with wishes." In an essay, identify Magdalena's most powerful wish. Does her wish come true? Why or why not? Based on this outcome, what might Vreeland be urging her readers to learn or to do? Support your answers to these questions with at least two examples from the story.

21. In nonfiction works, authors use facts to serve different purposes. Sometimes, they use facts to instruct or inform their audience. Other times, they use facts to persuade their audience or to illustrate a particular idea. In an essay, analyze how Vreeland uses facts in "Artful Research." What kinds of facts does she include? Does she want the reader to remember the facts for their own sake? Or, do the facts help Vreeland accomplish another purpose? Use at least two details from the essay to support your analysis.

22. In "Artful Research," Vreeland claims that research "gives direction, depth, and authority" to her writing. Having read "Magdalena Looking," do you agree with Vreeland's claim? What details or aspects of the story point back to the author's research? In your opinion, do these details enrich the story or detract from it? Support your answers with at least two details from the story.

23. **Thinking About the Big Question: Is there a difference between reality and truth?** The social reality in seventeenth-century Europe made it difficult for females to become artists. In truth, however, many girls and women had the talent to be fine artists. In a brief essay, explain how this contrast between reality and truth is a key idea in "Magdalena Looking." Explore the social conflict Magdalena faces, as well as the talents and interests she seems to have. Support your answer with examples from the story.

Vocabulary Warm-up Word Lists

Study these words. Then, complete the activities that follow.

Word List A

dubiously [DOO bee uhs lee] *adv.* doubtfully
   The repairman looked <u>dubiously</u> at the bent skateboard.

haste [HAYST] *n.* great speed, particularly when time is limited
   His <u>haste</u> was so great he forgot to put on his shoes.

persisted [puhr SIS tid] *v.* continued steadily; refused to give up
   The dog <u>persisted</u> in barking even when scolded.

preoccupied [pree AHK yoo pyd] *adj.* completely absorbed in something else
   I was so <u>preoccupied</u> with work I did not hear the phone ring.

pursued [puhr SOOD] *v.* followed; strived for
   The artist <u>pursued</u> her goal by painting every day.

torrent [TAWR uhnt] *n.* quick, violent flood; heavy rush of liquid
   The <u>torrent</u> of rain completely soaked the lawn.

unnecessary [uhn NES uh ser ee] *adj.* not needed; not required
   The extra-credit reading is <u>unnecessary</u> but helpful.

virtues [VER chooz] *n.* good qualities; morally excellent qualities
   My grandfather's <u>virtues</u> include honesty and reliability.

Word List B

absentmindedly [ab suhnt MYN duhd lee] *adv.* unaware of surroundings or actions
   I often tap my foot <u>absentmindedly</u> while I work.

aghast [uh GAST] *adj.* horrified; struck with amazement
   My best friend was <u>aghast</u> when she saw what I had done to my hair.

apparel [uh PA ruhl] *n.* clothing
   The new clothing store will sell both men's and women's <u>apparel</u>.

coincidence [koh IN suh duhns] *n.* events occurring at the same time by accident but seeming to have a connection
   Is it a <u>coincidence</u> when you see a friend you were just thinking about?

consequences [KAHN suh kwen siz] *n.* results of an action
   The student will have to face the <u>consequences</u> of his carelessness.

impressive [im PRES iv] *adj.* striking; tending to make a favorable impression
   The movie was so <u>impressive</u> that I remember it two years later.

sinister [SIN is tuhr] *adj.* evil; dishonest; threatening harm
   The stranger's <u>sinister</u> smile made me nervous.

talisman [TAL is muhn] *n.* object believed to bring luck or supernatural powers
   I carry a smooth stone as a <u>talisman</u> to keep worries away.

Unit 1 Resources: Fiction and Nonfiction
30

"The Monkey's Paw" by W. W. Jacobs
Vocabulary Warm-up Exercises

Exercise A *Fill in each blank in the paragraph below with an appropriate word from Word List A. Use each word only once.*

Adam and I were riding our bicycles when we were caught in a sudden

[1] _____ of rain. The heavy downpour [2] _____,

and we got wetter and wetter. Adam suggested that we stop for a while, but I

became [3] _____ with getting home as quickly as possible. I sped

up as Adam [4] _____ me at a safer speed. Unfortunately, in my

[5] _____ to get home, I forgot the rules of safety. I lost control of my

bicycle and crashed. Adam arrived and looked [6] _____ at the

wrecked frame. He didn't say anything because he knew that scolding was

[7] _____. Luckily, one of Adam's [8] _____ is that

he never says "I told you so."

Exercise B *Revise each sentence so that the underlined vocabulary word is used in a logical way. Be sure to keep the vocabulary word in your revision.*

Example: She knew that she was chewing her pencil <u>absentmindedly</u>.
She had no idea that she was chewing her pencil <u>absentmindedly</u>.

1. It was a <u>coincidence</u> that Jane and I wore different shirts today.

   _____

2. The ending of the story was so predictable that I felt <u>aghast</u>.

   _____

3. My sister hopes to get <u>apparel</u> like a camera or a compact disc for her birthday.

   _____

4. Many people keep a horseshoe as an unlucky <u>talisman</u>.

   _____

5. The politician seems <u>sinister</u>, so his promises can be trusted.

   _____

6. Your story was so <u>impressive</u> that I forgot it right away.

   _____

7. He accepted the <u>consequences</u> of his crime by breaking out of prison.

   _____

"The Monkey's Paw" by W. W. Jacobs
Reading Warm-up A

Read the following passage. Pay special attention to the underlined words. Then, read it again, and complete the activities. Use a separate sheet of paper for your written answers.

"Hello, Amy, this is your old pal Jackie. Can you believe it's been twenty-three years since geometry class?"

The instant she heard Jackie's voice, Amy felt a <u>torrent</u> of emotions, as though she were being flooded by the past.

Amy and Jackie had been neighbors and best friends in high school, but they had <u>pursued</u> very different paths since then. Amy went to college, studied media and communications, and eventually became a news writer for a local radio station. Jackie moved to Mexico immediately after graduation, got married, and soon had four children.

"Can you meet for lunch?" asked Jackie. "Sorry about the last-minute call, but in my <u>haste</u> to catch the plane, I completely forgot to call you."

Jackie had many <u>virtues</u>, but planning and time management skills were not among them. "No problem," she told her friend, "advance warning isn't required between friends—it's <u>unnecessary</u>."

Yet, Amy was surprised when a tall woman looked down at her. "Jackie," Amy asked <u>dubiously</u>, questioning her own memory as well as the stranger, "is that you?"

"Of course it's me," said the woman. "I can't have changed as much as all that, can I?"

Throughout lunch, Amy's doubts about Jackie identity <u>persisted</u>. Jackie seemed to know the details of their high school years, but it was as if she had studied the facts from a book. By the end of lunch, Amy simply couldn't believe that this woman was really her long-lost friend.

Then, Jackie said that she had a big favor she needed to ask, but Amy never heard the favor. She was completely <u>preoccupied</u> with her own internal questions. Was this stranger really her old friend, or was Jackie an imposter?

1. Underline the words that describe the <u>torrent</u> that Amy feels. Then, tell what a *torrent* is.

2. Underline the words that tell what the friends <u>pursued</u>. Then, describe a goal that you have *pursued*.

3. Underline the words that say what Jackie did in her <u>haste</u>. How you can tell if you are acting in *haste*?

4. Circle the words that name <u>virtues</u> that Jackie does *not* have. Describe *virtues* you look for in a friend.

5. Circle the word that means the opposite of <u>unnecessary</u>. Then, tell what *unnecessary* means.

6. Underline the words that tell what Amy did <u>dubiously</u>. Then, write what *dubiously* means.

7. Underline the words that describe the way in which Amy's doubts <u>persisted</u>. Give a synonym for *persisted*.

8. Underline the words that tell what happened because Amy was <u>preoccupied</u>. Write a sentence about what can make someone *preoccupied*.

"The Monkey's Paw" by W. W. Jacobs
Reading Warm-up B

Read the following passage. Pay special attention to the underlined words. Then, read it again, and complete the activities. Use a separate sheet of paper for your written answers.

A talisman is an object that some people believe can attract good luck the way that a magnet attracts lead. Anything from a special stone to an unusual plant might do, depending on your point of view.

According to some traditions, items of apparel can be talismans. For example, a bride may promote a happy marriage by wearing "something old, something new, something borrowed and something blue." An athlete might wear a lucky shirt before a game.

Even a gesture might encourage a positive outcome as in "keep your fingers crossed." Many people perform these gestures absentmindedly, hardly aware of their actions. You might have seen someone knock on wood to prevent something bad from happening. Maybe you were more aware of this action than he was.

Good luck talismans vary from culture to culture. For example, in China, a cricket in the home is a sign of good fortune. Coins spread on the floor might attract wealth; rice also has many positive associations.

Just as some objects have associations with luck and good fortune, others are emotionally linked to bad luck. Some people believe that sinister omens such as black cats or the number thirteen predict unfortunate events. Others fear the serious and unfortunate consequences of breaking a mirror or spilling salt.

Observers with a strictly logical outlook might be aghast at these beliefs, viewing them as mere superstitions. Suppose that someone finds a four-leaf clover and then wins a huge prize in a contest. A nonbeliever will view the second event as an unrelated coincidence. However, to a believer, this chain of events would be impressive proof of the clover's power.

It is possible to believe in omens and talismans without relying on them. As Thomas Jefferson remarked, "I'm a great believer in luck, and I find the harder I work the more I have of it."

1. Underline the words that tell what a talisman can do. Then, explain what a *talisman* is.

2. Circle the words that describe different kinds of apparel. Then, tell what *apparel* means.

3. Underline the words that describe people who do things absentmindedly. What does *absentmindedly* mean?

4. Underline the words that tell what sinister omens can do. Then, write a sentence that describes a *sinister* plan.

5. Circle the words that describe the consequences of breaking a mirror. Then, tell what *consequences* are.

6. Write a sentence that tells something that you would be *aghast* to see.

7. Underline the example of a coincidence. Then, write your own example of a *coincidence*.

8. Underline the words that describe what impressive proof can do. Then, write a sentence about something *impressive* you have seen this year.

"The Monkey's Paw" by W. W. Jacobs

Writing About the Big Question

Is there a difference between reality and truth?

Big Question Vocabulary

comprehend	concrete	confirm	context	differentiate
discern	evaluate	evidence	improbable	objective
perception	reality	subjective	uncertainty	verify

A. *Use one or more words from the list above to complete each sentence.*

1. It seemed _____ that he could win the race with a broken foot.

2. To _____ between reality and truth, consider facts objectively.

3. Sometimes your _____ of an event can be colored by emotions.

4. His behavior confused me, and I could not _____ his actions.

B. *Follow the directions in responding to each of the items below.*

1. Identify a situation in world events in which the reality of the situation might be different from the truth about the situation.

_____

_____

2. Write two sentences explaining your response in the preceding item. Use at least two of the Big Question vocabulary words.

_____

_____

_____

_____

C. *Complete the sentence below. Then, write a short paragraph in which you connect this experience to the Big Question.*

When people face personal hardship, they often _____.

_____

_____

_____

_____

_____

_____

Unit 1 Resources: Fiction and Nonfiction

"The Monkey's Paw" by W. W. Jacobs
Literary Analysis: Plot

A **plot** is the sequence of related events that make up a story. A typical plot concerns a **conflict**—a struggle between opposing forces—and follows a pattern.

- In the **exposition,** the writer gives background information about the characters and the situation.
- During the **rising action,** events occur that intensify the conflict.
- At the **climax,** the tension reaches its highest point because the outcome of the conflict is about to be revealed.
- The tension lessens during the **falling action.**
- The **resolution** is the final outcome of the conflict. The resolution often involves a change or an insight.

Writers use various techniques to add tension to a story. One technique is **foreshadowing**—giving details that hint at coming events. For instance, when a character leaves a door unlocked in her haste, it may foreshadow a later event—a pet getting loose, for example.

In this passage, the character Morris is speaking about a monkey's paw with a spell on it.

If you keep it, don't blame me for what happens.

Here, the author uses foreshadowing to hint at a future event relating to the monkey's paw.

DIRECTIONS: *Identify each passage below as* exposition, rising action, climax, falling action, *or* resolution. *Then, tell what each passage foreshadows.*

1. "Hark at the wind," said Mr. White, who, having seen a fatal mistake after it was too late, was amiably desirous of preventing his son from seeing it.

   Part of plot: _____ Foreshadows: _____

   _____

2. He wanted to show that fate ruled people's lives, and that those who interfered with it did so to their sorrow. He put a spell on it so that three separate men could each have three wishes from it.

   Part of plot: _____ Foreshadows: _____

   _____

3. "The first man had his three wishes, yes," was the reply; "I don't know what the first two were, but the third was for death."

   Part of plot: _____ Foreshadows: _____

   _____

4. Herbert sat alone in the darkness, gazing at the dying fire, and seeing faces in it. The last face was so horrible and so simian that he gazed at it in amazement.

   Part of plot: _____ Foreshadows: _____

   _____

Name _____ Date _____

"The Monkey's Paw" by W. W. Jacobs
Reading: Use Prior Knowledge to Make Predictions

A **prediction** is an idea about what will happen in a story. To make predictions, pay attention to story details and **use your prior knowledge.**

- Your knowledge of plot structure will help you predict that a character will experience difficulties. If you know other stories with similar plots, you might predict that similar things will happen.
- You can also use your prior knowledge of human nature. Think about how people you know react to events. Your insights into their behavior can help you predict how characters will act.

Read the following passage from "The Monkey's Paw."

"I should like to see those old temples and fakirs and jugglers," said the old man. "What was that you started telling me the other day about a monkey's paw or something, Morris?"

"Nothing," said the soldier, hastily. "Leastways nothing worth hearing."

You can use your prior knowledge of the structure of short stories to predict that the monkey's paw will play an important part in this story. The fact that the story's title is "The Monkey's Paw" and the introduction of the paw into conversation are clues to its importance.

DIRECTIONS: *Read each passage from the story. Make a prediction about what will happen based on the clues and your prior knowledge. List one clue and one piece of prior knowledge that helped you make each prediction.*

1. "It had a spell put on it by an old fakir," said the sergeant major, "a very holy man. He wanted to show that fate ruled people's lives, and that those who interfered with it did so to their sorrow."

Prediction: _____

Clue: _____

Prior knowledge: _____

2. A fine crash from the piano greeted the words, interrupted by a shuddering from the old man. His wife and son ran toward him.

"It moved," he cried with a glance of disgust at the object as it lay on the floor. "As I wished it twisted in my hand like a snake."

Prediction: _____

Clue: _____

Prior knowledge: _____

3. "The paw!" she cried wildly. "The monkey's paw!"

He started up in alarm. "Where? Where is it? What's the matter?"

She came stumbling across the room toward him. "I want it," she said quietly.

Prediction: _____

Clue: _____

Prior knowledge: _____

"The Monkey's Paw" by W. W. Jacobs
Vocabulary Builder

Word List

apathy   credulity   furtively   grave   maligned   oppressive

A. DIRECTIONS: *Think about the meaning of each italicized word. Then, answer the question.*

1. If you saw someone moving *furtively* around your home, what should you do?

   _____

2. If a new movie was *maligned* by a critic, would you want to see it? Why or why not?

   _____

3. If voters had *apathy* toward a political candidate, what do you think would happen in the election?

4. If a coach had a *grave* expression at the end of a game, did the team win or lose? Explain.

   _____

5. Will your *credulity* cause you to question every claim made by a politician?

   _____

6. If an employer's work load is *oppressive*, how does that person probably feel about the job?

   _____

B. WORD STUDY: The Latin root *-cred-* means "believe." Answer the following questions using one of these words that contain the root *-cred-: credence, credo, discredit.*

1. Would you have *credence* in a report presented by someone known for giving false information?

2. If your *credo* is "Live and Let Live," are you a tolerant person?

3. Why would you be unhappy if someone tried to *discredit* your results on a test?

"The Monkey's Paw" by W. W. Jacobs
Enrichment: Problematic Wishes

In "The Monkey's Paw," as in many stories that feature wishes, the wishes that characters make have terrible results. Any wish for change can have both positive and negative consequences if it comes true. Use the following chart to list six wishes you might like to make, and include each wish's positive and possible negative consequences.

Wish	Positive Consequences	Possible Negative Consequences

Name _____ Date _____

"The Monkey's Paw" by W. W. Jacobs
Open-Book Test

Short Answer *Write your responses to the questions in this section on the lines provided.*

1. What is family life like in the White household when "The Monkey's Paw" opens? Think about what the characters are doing and saying to each other. Support your description with two details from the story.

   _____

   _____

2. In "The Monkey's Paw," how do Sergeant Major Morris's comments foreshadow the harm that the monkey's paw will cause? Identify two remarks.

   _____

   _____

   _____

3. When the Whites acquire the paw in "The Monkey's Paw," Herbert predicts that it will make them rich, famous, and happy. Based on the plots of other works you have read, heard, or seen, why might this prediction be wrong? Provide one example.

   _____

   _____

   _____

4. In the boxes below, list three chronological events that are part of the rising action in "The Monkey's Paw." Then, on the line below, explain how you know these events are part of the rising action.

   ┌─────────────────────────────────────┐
   │   │
   └─────────────────────────────────────┘
                    ↓
   ┌─────────────────────────────────────┐
   │   │
   └─────────────────────────────────────┘
                    ↓
   ┌─────────────────────────────────────┐
   │   │
   └─────────────────────────────────────┘

   _____

5. In "The Monkey's Paw," the firm of Maw and Meggins is prepared to pay the Whites to avoid legal responsibility for Herbert's death. What earlier details help the reader predict that the payment will amount to two hundred pounds? Provide two details.

_____

_____

6. According to the narrator of "The Monkey's Paw," the Whites accept Herbert's death with resignation that should not be confused with *apathy*. Explain why their feelings should not be confused with *apathy*.

_____

_____

7. What event would you consider the climax of "The Monkey's Paw"? Briefly explain why this event qualifies as the climax.

_____

_____

_____

8. In "The Monkey's Paw," Mrs. White makes her husband wish that their son Herbert will come back to life. What does this wish show about Mrs. White's feelings about Herbert and his death?

_____

9. The narrator never directly tells us Mr. White's third wish in "The Monkey's Paw," but the story's events suggest the answer. What is Mr. White's third wish? How did you come to that conclusion?

_____

_____

_____

_____

10. In "The Monkey's Paw," why is Mr. White afraid that his second wish will be granted?

_____

_____

_____

Essay

Write an extended response to the question of your choice or to the question or questions your teacher assigns you.

11. Many details foreshadow future events in "The Monkey's Paw." Write a paragraph in which you identify two examples of foreshadowing and explain the specific events they foreshadow. For example, reread the sergeant major's comments about fate. What later events can be tied to these comments?

12. According to the sergeant major in "The Monkey's Paw," the fakir "wanted to show that fate ruled people's lives, and that those who interfered with it did so to their sorrow." In an essay, explain how the events of the plot teach this lesson. Also indicate which character learns (or does not learn) this lesson.

13. In "The Monkey's Paw," Mr. White makes several decisions that influence events in the plot. In a brief essay, describe and evaluate two of Mr. White's decisions. Explain what these decisions show about the kind of person he is.

14. **Thinking About the Big Question: What is the difference between reality and truth?** In "The Monkey's Paw," both Mr. and Mrs. White accept the supernatural powers of the monkey's paw as a part of their reality. Could the truth be something different from the reality they perceive? What other explanation might there be for the story's events? In a brief essay, explain how the story's events could have happened without any supernatural causes.

Oral Response

15. Go back to question 2, 7, 8, or 9 or to the question your teacher assigns you. Take a few minutes to expand your answer and prepare an oral response. Find additional details in "The Monkey's Paw" that support your points. If necessary, make notes to guide your oral response.

"The Monkey's Paw" by W. W. Jacobs
Selection Test A

Critical Reading *Identify the letter of the choice that best answers the question.*

_____ 1. Why does Morris grow pale after he makes his third wish on the monkey's paw?
  A. The idea of magic frightens him.
  B. He is trying not to laugh as he fools his friends.
  C. He is remembering the horrible effects of his wishes.
  D. He is ashamed of believing in the monkey's paw.

_____ 2. Which detail foreshadows the effect of the first wish?
  A. There is a crashing sound from the piano, which Herbert is playing.
  B. Mr. White faints after the monkey's paw moves in his hand.
  C. Herbert urges his father to wish to be an emperor.
  D. Mr. White loses the chess game to his son.

_____ 3. How does the family feel in the morning after Morris's visit?
  A. relaxed and relieved
  B. anxious and upset
  C. angry and confused
  D. joyful and amazed

_____ 4. Which line foreshadows what happens to Herbert?
  A. "I don't see the money . . . and I bet I never shall."
  B. "Why, we're going to be rich, and famous, and happy."
  C. "If you only cleared the house, you'd be quite happy. . . ."
  D. "I expect you'll find the cash tied up in a big bag. . . ."

_____ 5. How do Mrs. White and Herbert regard Mr. White?
  A. as a hopeless romantic
  B. as a tiresome bore
  C. as a cruel tyrant
  D. as a lovable fool

_____ 6. What does the man from Maw and Meggins bring to the Whites?
  A. the body of their son
  B. two hundred pounds
  C. the monkey's paw
  D. a bill

____ 7. What fact about Mrs. White helps you predict what the second wish will be?
  A. She is a loving mother.
  B. She does not fear death.
  C. She does not believe in the monkey's paw.
  D. She is very angry.

____ 8. In "The Monkey's Paw," what is outside the door after the second wish?
  A. the man from Maw and Meggins
  B. Herbert's body, back from the dead
  C. the holy fakir
  D. Morris

____ 9. Which detail foreshadows the results of the third wish?
  A. The monkey's paw wriggles in Mr. White's grasp.
  B. Morris urges the Whites to burn the monkey's paw.
  C. Herbert goes off cheerfully to work.
  D. Mrs. White claims she could never fear the child she has nursed.

____ 10. What does this line spoken by Mr. White help you predict?
  "It seems to me I've got all I want."

  A. that he will wish for a large sum of money
  B. that the wishes can only change his life for the worse
  C. that his wife will force him to wish for something
  D. that he will regret it if he doesn't make a wish

Vocabulary and Grammar

____ 11. In what way is Mr. White much *maligned*?
  A. He is teased and criticized by his family.
  B. He is greatly praised by his son.
  C. He is ignored by his wife and son.
  D. He is treated with kindness by his wife.

____ 12. When Mrs. White reacts *apathetically*, what is she feeling?
  A. fascination
  B. deep confusion
  C. terrible fear
  D. lack of interest

___ **13.** Which sentence contains four common nouns?

    A. Mr. White looked up sharply, just in time to intercept a knowing glance between mother and son.

    B. He put down the empty glass, and sighing softly, shook it again.

    C. His manner was so impressive that his hearers were conscious that their light laughter jarred somewhat.

    D. Herbert sat alone in the darkness, gazing at the dying fire, and seeing faces in it.

Essay

14. In "The Monkey's Paw," many details foreshadow future events. In an essay, identify two examples of foreshadowing from the selection, and explain in detail the specific future events they suggest.

15. What might have happened if the Whites had opened the door when the knocking occurred? In an essay, explain your prediction. Identify details in "The Monkey's Paw" along with any prior knowledge of human nature or horror stories that helped you make the prediction.

16. Thinking About the Big Question: Is there a difference between reality and truth? In "The Monkey's Paw," both Mr. and Mrs. White believe that the monkey's paw has magical powers. But what if the paw isn't really magical? What other explanation might there be for the story's events? In a brief essay, explain how the story's events could have happened without any magic.

"The Monkey's Paw" by W. W. Jacobs
Selection Test B

Critical Reading *Identify the letter of the choice that best completes the statement or answers the question.*

_____ 1. What is "The Monkey's Paw" about?
   A. a retired sergeant major who brings a magical monkey's paw home from India
   B. an unsuspecting son who dies as a result of his mother's greed
   C. a monkey's paw that grants three wishes to three different people
   D. a magical but evil monkey's paw that ruins the quiet life of a family

_____ 2. Morris grows pale after his third wish on the monkey's paw because
   A. he is frightened by the idea of magic.
   B. he is trying not to laugh as he fools his easily tricked friends.
   C. he is recalling the horrible effects of his wishes.
   D. he is ashamed of believing in the power of the monkey's paw.

_____ 3. The man who Morris says wished for death probably did so because
   A. he had become very ill and was in great pain.
   B. his wishes had caused horrible things to happen.
   C. he had wished for everlasting life and did not really want it.
   D. he had killed everyone he loved with his wishes.

_____ 4. Which line helps you predict that the first wish will come true?
   A. "I don't know what to wish for, and that's a fact."
   B. "Never mind, though; there's no harm done."
   C. "As I wished it twisted in my hand like a snake."
   D. "I expect you'll find the cash tied up in a big bag in the middle of your bed."

_____ 5. The effect of the first wish is foreshadowed when
   A. there is a crash from the piano, which Herbert is playing.
   B. Mr. White faints.
   C. Herbert urges his father to wish to be an emperor.
   D. Mr. White loses the chess game to his son.

_____ 6. When a stranger comes to the Whites' door, Mrs. White first thinks that he has come to
   A. announce Herbert's death.
   B. give Mr. White 200 pounds.
   C. ask them for the monkey's paw.
   D. present a bill from the tailor.

_____ 7. Which aspect of Mrs. White's character helps you predict what the second wish will be?
   A. She is a loving mother.
   B. She has no fear of death.
   C. She does not believe in magic.
   D. She is very matter-of-fact.

_____ 8. Which line is an example of foreshadowing?
A. "When he went away he was a slip of a youth in the warehouse."
B. "I should like to see those old temples and fakirs and jugglers. . . ."
C. "[The monkey's paw] has caused enough mischief already."
D. "Did you give him anything for it, Father?"

_____ 9. Why is Mr. White afraid to wish a second time?
A. He does not believe the paw can grant wishes.
B. He is so grief-stricken that he forgets the paw.
C. He has become angry since Herbert's death.
D. He realizes his wishes can have bad consequences.

_____ 10. At the end of "The Monkey's Paw," what does Mrs. White realize just after she opens the door?
A. Her husband has made the third wish.
B. The monkey's paw killed her son.
C. She no longer wants her son to return.
D. The knocking sound is not Herbert.

_____ 11. The climax of "The Monkey's Paw" occurs when
A. Mr. White makes the first wish.
B. Mrs. White makes the second wish.
C. Mr. White makes the third wish.
D. Morris tries to burn the monkey's paw.

_____ 12. In the resolution of "The Monkey's Paw," what happens to Herbert?
A. He is killed in an accident.
B. He returns to the grave.
C. He mocks the monkey's paw.
D. He beats his father at chess.

_____ 13. In "The Monkey's Paw," which line spoken by Mr. White hints that the wishes can only change his life for the worse?
A. "And what is there special about it?"
B. "It seems to me I've got all I want."
C. "There's no harm done, but it gave me a shock all the same."
D. "The things happened so naturally. . . ."

Vocabulary and Grammar

_____ 14. In which sentence is the word *furtively* used correctly?
A. The sergeant major spoke furtively of his time in India.
B. The man from Maw and Meggins looked furtively at Mrs. White without speaking.
C. Mrs. White shouted furtively at her husband as the knocks on the door continued.
D. Herbert played the piano furtively as Mr. White made his wish.

_____ 15. Which statement shows that Mrs. White behaves *apathetically*?
   A. She stops speaking and sits disinterestedly all day long.
   B. She screams at her husband and begs him to wish for their son to live again.
   C. She struggles with her husband as she tries to open the door.
   D. She runs outside to view a quiet and deserted street.

_____ 16. Which sentence contains a proper noun?
   A. They sat down by the fire again while the two men finished their pipes.
   B. "I was to say that Maw and Meggins disclaim all responsibility."
   C. She caught her breath, and turning to her husband, laid her trembling old hand on his.
   D. The talisman fell to the floor, and he regarded it fearfully.

_____ 17. How many proper nouns are included in the following sentence?

   Without, the night was cold and wet, but in the small parlor of Laburnam Villa the blinds were drawn and the fire burned brightly.

   A. one
   B. two
   C. three
   D. four

Essay

18. In "The Monkey's Paw," many details foreshadow future events. In an essay, identify two examples of foreshadowing from the selection, and explain in detail the specific future events they suggest.

19. "The Monkey's Paw" is written from a third-person point of view. Write an essay in which you describe the events from Mr. White's point of view. Explain whether, assuming that you made the first wish, you would make the second wish. If so, how would you word the wish, and what do you predict would happen? If you would not make the second wish, why not?

20. **Thinking About the Big Question: Is there a difference between reality and truth?** In "The Monkey's Paw," both Mr. and Mrs. White accept the supernatural powers of the monkey's paw as a part of their reality. Could the truth be something different from the reality they perceive? What other explanation might there be for the story's events? In a brief essay, explain how the story's events could have happened without any supernatural causes.

"The Leap" by Louise Erdrich
Vocabulary Warm-up Word Lists

Study these words from "The Leap." Then, complete the activities that follow.

Word List A

anticipation [an tis uh PAY shuhn] *n.* expectation; looking forward to
Our <u>anticipation</u> increased in the final inning of the ball game.

associate [uh SOH see ayt] *v.* to connect in the mind
Many people <u>associate</u> spring with the color green.

carelessly [KAIR luhs lee] *adv.* without care; without paying attention
The cat ran out because I <u>carelessly</u> left the back door open.

collapsed [kuh LAPST] *v.* fell down; broke down suddenly
During the earthquake, several buildings <u>collapsed</u>.

culprit [KUL prit] *n.* offender; person guilty of a crime or action
The police caught the <u>culprit</u> responsible for the broken window.

drama [DRAH muh] *n.* exciting or tense events
There was plenty of <u>drama</u> when the test answers were stolen.

overcoming [oh ver KUM ing] *v.* conquering; mastering; getting over
The athlete is <u>overcoming</u> all of her opponents.

radiance [RAY dee uhns] *n.* bright, glowing light
After so many days of rain, I miss the sun's <u>radiance</u>.

Word List B

boredom [BAWR duhm] *n.* state of being bored or not interested
The loud yawns reflected the audience's <u>boredom</u>.

calculated [KAL kyuh lay tid] *v.* planned or schemed to make sure things work out the way one wants
We <u>calculated</u> the effects of changing our plans.

collide [kuh LYD] *v.* crash together forcefully
When two objects <u>collide</u>, they both usually change direction.

extension [ek STEN shuhn] *n.* a part that adds to or continues something else
The new <u>extension</u> to the library adds storage and a reading area.

precision [pri SIZH uhn] *n.* exactness; accuracy
The manufacturer produced the car engine with great <u>precision</u>.

sequence [SEE kwens] *n.* series of events
Pay attention to the <u>sequence</u> when you follow a recipe.

sequined [SEE kwind] *adj.* covered with sequins, which are small, shiny, metal discs
The <u>sequined</u> costume sparkles in the light.

version [VER zhuhn] *n.* distinct or particular form
The new <u>version</u> of the software is much better than the first one.

"The Leap" by Louise Erdrich
Vocabulary Warm-up Exercises

Exercise A *Fill in each blank in the paragraph below with an appropriate word from Word List A. Use each word only once.*

Before *Romeo and Juliet* began, you could sense the eager [1] _____

of the audience. When the curtain went up, stage lights cast their

[2] _____, and the actors began. However, the [3] _____

soon took an unexpected turn. One of the set walls [4] _____, nearly

hitting Romeo. Luckily, Juliet did a terrific job of [5] _____ the

problem. She simply pushed the wall back up and kept going. After the show,

the [6] _____ was discovered. One of the other actors had

[7] _____ leaned against the wall. The play was a hit, but everyone in

the audience will always [8] _____ *Romeo and Juliet* with falling walls.

Exercise B *Decide whether each statement below is true or false. Explain your answers.*

1. A <u>calculated</u> risk is one you take without thinking.
   T / F _____

2. It might take a long time to sew a <u>sequined</u> dress by hand.
   T / F _____

3. <u>Boredom</u> is a likely result if a movie plot is full of surprises.
   T / F _____

4. An <u>extension</u> ladder is a ladder that cannot be made longer.
   T / F _____

5. The written <u>version</u> of a story is always better than the movie.
   T / F _____

6. Making miniature models of buildings requires <u>precision</u>.
   T / F _____

7. Rearranging the <u>sequence</u> of an experiment can change the results.
   T / F _____

8. If two basketballs <u>collide</u>, only one is likely to move.
   T / F _____

"The Leap" by Louise Erdrich
Reading Warm-up A

Read the following passage. Pay special attention to the underlined words. Then, read it again, and complete the activities. Use a separate sheet of paper for your written answers.

On July 6, 1944, the sun's bright <u>radiance</u> lit up the afternoon sky in Hartford, Connecticut. More than 6,000 people decided to attend a matinee performance of the Ringling Brother and Barnum & Bailey Circus. Faces in the audience stared in eager <u>anticipation</u>, waiting for the next thrilling act. No one could have predicted that their happiness would soon turn to terror.

The circus was in progress when the <u>drama</u> shifted from the jugglers and gymnasts to the audience and the circus tent itself. Suddenly, a fire started. The flames spread with astonishing speed, becoming a raging inferno in moments. Why did the fire spread so quickly? One key factor was that the circus tent was painted with a mixture of wax and paraffin to make it waterproof.

The huge tent quickly <u>collapsed</u>, falling to the ground as it burned. People inside the tent rushed to the exits. "There was pushing and shoving, people just frantic to get out of there. It was a mass exodus," recalled Eunice Groark, who was six years old at the time.

Although the tragic fire caused the deaths of 100 children and 68 adults, its cause remains a mystery. Was it started by a <u>carelessly</u> tossed match or cigarette? Or did someone intentionally set the fire?

In 1950, Robert D. Segee of Circleville, Ohio, said he was the <u>culprit</u>, claiming to have set the fire himself. He was convicted, but later investigators have cast doubt on his confession. After reopening the investigation in 1991, the case was reclassified as undetermined.

In the years after the fire, many people in Hartford could only <u>associate</u> the circus with sadness and loss. <u>Overcoming</u> feelings of fear has been difficult for survivors and witnesses. "I am still terrified," says Groark. "When I go to the movies or am in a big crowd, I need to find the exit." Soon, a memorial will be built in Hartford to honor those lost in this frightening tragedy.

1. Underline the words that describe what the sun's <u>radiance</u> did. Then, tell what *radiance* means.

2. Underline the words that tell what the audience's <u>anticipation</u> was for. What might make you feel *anticipation*?

3. Underline the words that tell who and what the <u>drama</u> shifted to. Describe another situation with a lot of *drama*.

4. Underline the words that tell what happened to the tent when it <u>collapsed</u>. Tell what *collapsed* means.

5. Underline the words that name an action that might have been done <u>carelessly</u>. What can happen when an action is done *carelessly*?

6. Underline the words that tell what the <u>culprit</u> claimed. What is a *culprit*?

7. Circle two things that many people in Hartford <u>associate</u> with the circus. Then, tell something you *associate* with the circus.

8. Underline the words that tell what survivors had difficulty <u>overcoming</u>. Then, tell what *overcoming* means.

"The Leap" by Louise Erdrich
Reading Warm-up B

Read the following passage. Pay special attention to the underlined words. Then, read it again, and complete the activities. Use a separate sheet of paper for your written answers.

Modern circuses feature a huge variety of delights, from clowns and jugglers to trapeze artists in <u>sequined</u> costumes that sparkle and glisten in the light as they soar above our heads. With so many fascinating sights around us, <u>boredom</u> is out of the question.

The first circuses focused on just chariot racing. In Ancient Rome, chariot races took place in a circus, an oval track named after the Greek word for *circle*. The first circus in Rome was the Circus Maximus. Initially, there was no building, simply a flat, sandy track. The sport became so popular, however, that a huge building was constructed in the 6th century B.C. Archaeologists have <u>calculated</u> that the building was 620 meters long (678 yards) and about 150 meters (164 yards) wide. It could hold 150,000 spectators.

The circus was damaged in a terrible fire in A.D. 64 but was rebuilt. By A.D. 104, the most spectacular <u>version</u> of the circus was finished, complete with three tiers of seats. The efficient use of space in this vast building shows the <u>precision</u> of Roman engineering.

The audience for chariot races came from every part of Roman society, from slaves to emperors. Although the races were initially held only during religious festivals, the sport became so popular that the public demanded an <u>extension</u> to this limited schedule.

A day at the Circus Maximus always began with the same <u>sequence</u> of events. First, there was an elaborate parade led by the person who was sponsoring that day's race. He was followed by the chariot teams, musicians, dancers, and priests. Then, the races began. Each one covered seven full laps of the track.

Most charioteers began slowly in order to save energy for the long race. Because they tied the horse's reins around their waists, they were in danger when the chariots bumped together. When they would <u>collide</u>, the charioteers were often knocked out and dragged behind, sometimes to their death.

1. Circle the words that describe how the <u>sequined</u> costumes respond to light. Tell what *sequined* means.

2. Underline the words that explain why <u>boredom</u> is impossible at the circus. Describe a place where *boredom* is possible.

3. Underline the words that tell what archaeologists <u>calculated</u>. Then, explain what *calculated* means.

4. Tell which <u>version</u> of the circus you would like to have seen and explain why.

5. Underline the words that tell what part of the circus shows the <u>precision</u> of Roman engineers. Then, tell what *precision* means.

6. Circle the words that tell of what an <u>extension</u> was demanded. Tell what an *extension* is.

7. Circle the words that help you understand the <u>sequence</u> of events on race day. List the *sequence* of events at a modern sport.

8. Circle the word that is a synonym for <u>collide</u>. Then, describe two other objects that might *collide*.

"The Leap" by Louise Erdrich

Writing About the Big Question

Is there a difference between reality and truth?

Big Question Vocabulary

comprehend   concrete   confirm   context   differentiate
discern   evaluate   evidence   improbable objective
perception   reality   subjective uncertainty verify

A. *Use one or more words from the list above to complete each sentence.*

1. The events surrounding the election gave us a _____ in which to consider her remarks.

2. It is sometimes difficult to take a(n) _____ view of someone you know well.

3. Your personal feelings about your loved ones often lead to a _____ view of their actions.

B. *Follow the directions in responding to each of the items below.*

1. List a time when you learned that the reality you knew about a person was not the same as the truth about that person.

   _____

   _____

2. Write two sentences explaining your response in the preceding item. Use at least two of the Big Question vocabulary words.

   _____

   _____

   _____

   _____

C. *Complete the sentence below. Then, write a short paragraph in which you connect this situation to the Big Question.*

   The choices people make can have a variety of effects on _____

   _____

   _____

   _____

   _____

   _____

"The Leap" by Louise Erdrich
Literary Analysis: Plot

A **plot** is the sequence of related events that make up a story. A typical plot concerns a **conflict**—a struggle between opposing forces—and follows a pattern.

- In the **exposition,** the writer gives information about the characters and the situation.
- During the **rising action,** events occur that intensify the conflict.
- At the **climax,** the tension reaches its highest point because the outcome of the conflict is about to be revealed.
- The tension lessens during the **falling action.**
- The **resolution** is the final outcome of the conflict. It often involves a change or an insight.

Writers use various techniques to add tension to a story. One technique is **foreshadowing**—giving details that hint at coming events. For instance, when a character leaves a door unlocked in her haste, it may foreshadow a later event—a pet getting loose, for example.

Read the following passage from "The Leap."

When extremes of temperature collide, a hot and cold front, winds generate instantaneously behind a hill and crash upon you without warning.

Here, the author uses foreshadowing to hint at an event caused by weather later in the story.

DIRECTIONS: *Identify each passage below as* exposition, rising action, climax, falling action, *or* resolution. *Then, tell what each passage foreshadows.*

1. I would, in fact, tend to think that all memory of double somersaults and heart-stopping catches had left her arms and legs were it not for the fact that sometimes, as I sit sewing in the room of the rebuilt house where I slept as a child, I hear the crackle, catch a whiff of smoke from the stove downstairs, and suddenly the room goes dark, the stitches burn beneath my fingers, and I am sewing with a needle of hot silver, a thread of fire.

   Part of plot: _____ Foreshadows: _____

   _____

2. My mother once said that I'd be amazed at how many things a person can do within the act of falling.

   Part of plot: _____ Foreshadows: _____

   _____

3. That is the debt we take for granted since none of us asks for life. It is only once we have it that we hang on so dearly.

   Part of plot: _____ Foreshadows: _____

   _____

4. She has never upset an object or as much as brushed a magazine onto the floor. She has never lost her balance or bumped into a closet door left carelessly open.

   Part of plot: _____ Foreshadows: _____

   _____

"The Leap" by Louise Erdrich
Reading: Use Prior Knowledge to Make Predictions

A **prediction** is an idea about what will happen in a story. To make predictions, pay attention to story details and **use your prior knowledge.**

- Your knowledge of plot structure will help you predict that a character will experience difficulties. If you know other stories with similar plots, you might predict that similar things will happen.
- You can also use your prior knowledge of human nature. Think about how people you know react to events. Your insights into their behavior can help you predict how characters will act.

Read the following passage from "The Leap."

My mother is the surviving half of a blindfold trapeze act, not a fact I think about much even now that she is sightless, the result of encroaching and stubborn cataracts.

You can use your prior knowledge of the structure of short stories to predict that the story will tell about the death of the other half of the trapeze act.

DIRECTIONS: *Read each passage from the story. Make a prediction about what will happen based on the clues and your prior knowledge. List one clue and one piece of prior knowledge that helped you make each prediction.*

1. In one news account it says, "The day was mildly overcast, but nothing in the air or temperature gave any hint of the sudden force with which the deadly gale would strike."

   Prediction: _____

   Clue: _____

   Prior knowledge: _____

   _____

2. In the town square a replica tent pole, cracked and splintered, now stands cast in concrete.

   Prediction: _____

   Clue: _____

   Prior knowledge: _____

   _____

3. Outside, my mother stood below my dark window and saw clearly that there was no rescue.

   Prediction: _____

   Clue: _____

   Prior knowledge: _____

   _____

"The Leap" by Louise Erdrich
Vocabulary Builder

Word List

commemorates   constricting   encroaching   extricating   perpetually   tentative

A. DIRECTIONS: *Think about the meaning of each italicized word. Then, answer the question.*

1. If night is *encroaching* on daylight, what will happen in the next few minutes?

   _____

2. If a person takes a *tentative* step onto a diving board, what is he or she probably feeling?

   _____

3. If firefighters are involved in *extricating* people from a building, what are they doing?

   _____

4. If a statue in your city *commemorates* fire fighters, is it a serious or funny piece of art?

   _____

5. Would someone who *perpetually* trips be a good choice to carry trays of dishes?

   _____

B. WORD STUDY: The Latin root -*strict*- means "confine" or "squeeze." Answer the following questions using one of these words that contain the root -*strict*-: *district, restrict, stricture.*

1. If you won the spelling bee for your *district*, did you compete against students from across the country?

   _____

2. If you *restrict* your diet to apples, what are you eating?

   _____

3. When a team receives a *stricture* from the referee, should the team be worried?

   _____

Name _____ Date _____

"The Leap" by Louise Erdrich
Enrichment: Decisive Moments

In "The Leap," the narrator describes three events that resulted in her feeling that she owed her mother her existence. There are many such events in each person's life—events without which the person might not exist. Some are dramatic, and others are less so. Choose four of these events from your own life. Describe each event in the following chart, and explain why you might not exist without it.

Event	Why I Might Not Exist Without the Event

Name _____ Date _____

Integrated Language Skills: Grammar

Common and Proper Nouns

A **common noun** is a general name for any one of a group of people, places, or things. A **proper noun** names a particular person, place, or thing. A proper noun always begins with a capital letter.

Examples

Common Nouns: student, teacher, country, skyscraper, book

Proper Nouns: Will Fordham, Ms. Ruiz, Japan, Empire State Building, *The Outsiders*

A. DIRECTIONS: *In each of the following sentences from the selections, identify the underlined nouns as common or proper. For each common noun, name a proper noun that could take its place. For each proper noun, name a common noun that could take its place.*

1. <u>Mrs. White</u> drew back with a grimace.

   Type of noun: _____

   Substitute noun: _____

2. The <u>soldier</u> regarded him in the way that middle age is wont to regard presumptuous youth.

   Type of noun: _____

   Substitute noun: _____

3. "I was to say that <u>Maw and Meggins</u> disclaim all responsibility," continued the other.

   Type of noun: _____

   Substitute noun: _____

4. "You're afraid of your own <u>son</u>," she cried, struggling.

   Type of noun: _____

   Substitute noun: _____

B. DIRECTIONS: *Rewrite each of the following sentences by correcting any errors in capitalization. Make sure that proper nouns are capitalized.*

1. The narrator's Mother was one-half of a blindfolded Trapeze Act.

   _____

2. Mr. and mrs. white are horrified by the outcome of their Wishes.

   _____

3. Louise erdrich writes about a definitive moment in Her own life.

   _____

4. The Monkey's Paw brings bad luck to anyone who uses it.

   _____

57

Name _____ Date _____

Integrated Language Skills: Support for Writing a Sequel

Use the following flowchart to write the plot details for a sequel to the story you read.

Exposition:

⬇

Rising Action:

⬇

Climax:

⬇

Falling Action:

⬇

Resolution:

Now, use the details from your flowchart to write a sequel to "The Monkey's Paw" or "The Leap."

"**The Monkey's Paw**" by W. W. Jacobs
"**The Leap**" by Louise Erdrich

Integrated Language Skills: Support for Extend Your Learning

Listening and Speaking

Use the following lines to write five questions you could ask the Whites in your interview.

1. _____
2. _____
3. _____
4. _____
5. _____

Listening and Speaking

Use the following lines to write five questions you could ask the narrator of "The Leap" in your interview.

1. _____
2. _____
3. _____
4. _____
5. _____

"The Leap" by Louise Erdrich
Open-Book Test

Short Answer *Write your responses to the questions in this section on the lines provided.*

1. In the opening of "The Leap," the narrator tells us, "My mother is the surviving half of a blindfold trapeze act." What event in the mother's early life do these opening words help the reader predict? Think about what the words *surviving half* suggest about what happened to the other half of the act.

   _____

   _____

2. At the end of the second paragraph of "The Leap," the narrator describes a flashback she has when she hears the crackle of the stove downstairs and smells its smoke. What childhood event does the narrator's flashback help the reader predict?

   _____

   _____

3. Based on the opening paragraphs of "The Leap," how has the mother changed since her early years as a circus performer? Cite one detail from the second or third paragraph to support your conclusion.

   _____

   _____

4. In the third paragraph of "The Leap," the narrator says that she owes her existence to her mother three times. Then, she goes on to describe the first of these times. How can the narrator owe her existence to her mother's behavior in an accident that happened long before the narrator was born?

   _____

   _____

5. In describing the circus accident, the narrator of "The Leap" comments, "My mother once said that I'd be amazed at how many things a person can do within the act of falling." What future event in the narrator's life does this remark foreshadow? How is this event related to the mother's comment?

   _____

   _____

   _____

6. What traits does the mother in "The Leap" display with her circus performances and her actions when the accident takes place? Reread the relevant passages before you answer.

   _____

7. The narrator of "The Leap" says that in teaching her mother to read, her father offered "one form of flight for another." What does the narrator mean in this quotation?

_____

_____

8. The narrator of "The Leap" says that nobody asks for life; "It is only once we have it that we hang on so dearly." To which two people and events does the quoted sentence literally apply?

_____

_____

_____

9. What event would you identify as the climax of "The Leap"? Briefly explain why this event qualifies as the climax.

_____

_____

_____

10. In the incident near the end of "The Leap," why must the mother extricate her daughter from their home?

_____

Essay

Write an extended response to the question of your choice or to the question or questions your teacher assigns you.

11. Many details foreshadow future events in "The Leap." Write a brief essay in which you identify two examples of foreshadowing and explain the events they foreshadow. For example, consider the narrator's memory of the fire in the second paragraph. Why might the narrator include this detail? Use the following chart to help organize your thoughts.

Examples of Foreshadowing	Events They Foreshadow

12. In an essay of two or three paragraphs, write a brief character sketch of the mother in "The Leap." Discuss her personality traits, values, and attitude. As you write, consider the main changes in the course of her life. Use details from the story to support the general points you make about her character.

13. Write an essay about the significance of the story's title, "The Leap." Compare and contrast the two leaps that the mother makes and what they show about her character. Also discuss the narrator's leap and what it shows about her relationship with her mother.

14. **Thinking About the Big Question: What is the difference between reality and truth?** Write an essay about the characters' reality in "The Leap" and the more universal truths that the author also wants to convey. First, summarize two or three key events in the story. Then, explain how each event reflects more universal truths about human behavior.

Oral Response

15. Go back to question 1, 7, or 8 or to the question your teacher assigns you. Take a few minutes to expand your answer and prepare an oral response. Find additional details in "The Leap" that support your points. If necessary, make notes to guide your oral response.

"**The Leap**" by Louise Erdrich
Selection Test A

Critical Reading *Identify the letter of the choice that best answers the question.*

____ 1. Which line from "The Leap" foreshadows what happens during the storm?
A. I owe her my existence three times.
B. My mother is the surviving half of a blindfold trapeze act. . . .
C. There was time, before the storm, for three acts.
D. They loved to drop gracefully from nowhere, like two sparkling birds. . . .

____ 2. What fact about the narrator's mother in "The Leap" helps you predict that she will survive the storm?
A. She never lost her balance or upset an object.
B. She loved her husband.
C. She met the narrator's father in a hospital.
D. She lost a baby.

____ 3. In "The Leap," why was the Flying Avalons' trapeze act in the newspapers?
A. because their act was so daring
B. because they were so romantic during their act
C. because there was a terrible accident during their act
D. because there was a fire in their house after the act

____ 4. Why does the narrator of "The Leap" consider her sister a "less finished version" of herself?
A. because her mother loved the sister more than the narrator
B. because the sister was so much like the narrator when she died
C. because the sister never grew up to have a personality of her own
D. because the sister had the same name as the narrator

____ 5. In "The Leap," how did the narrator's mother and father meet?
A. at the circus during the high-wire act
B. at the hospital after the accident
C. during the fire
D. at the grave of the mother's dead daughter

____ 6. In "The Leap," what "form of flight" does the narrator's mother take up after she gives up the trapeze?
A. flying a plane
B. cooking
C. reading
D. hang gliding

_____ 7. Which detail from "The Leap" foreshadows the fire?

A. the story of the terrible storm

B. the description of the mother's blindness

C. the description of the changeable weather in New Hampshire

D. the narrator's memory of the smell of smoke and crackle of flame

_____ 8. Which phrase best describes the narrator's mother in "The Leap"?

A. hesitant and uncertain

B. graceful and daring

C. smart and cunning

D. stubborn and cautious

_____ 9. What prior knowledge can help you predict that the narrator's mother will try to save her in "The Leap"?

A. Trapeze artists are not afraid of fire.

B. Firefighters will not let people enter burning buildings.

C. Mothers will do whatever they can to save their children.

D. Children do not know how to escape from burning buildings.

_____ 10. In "The Leap," how does the narrator feel when she sees her mother outside the window of the burning house?

A. unsurprised

B. terrified

C. thrilled

D. angry

_____ 11. What event does this statement from "The Leap" foreshadow?

My mother once said that I'd be amazed at how many things a person can do within the act of falling.

A. the leap the mother makes with the narrator from the burning house

B. the leap the mother makes after lightning strikes

C. the father's terrible final fall

D. the mother's fall into love with the narrator's father

Vocabulary and Grammar

_____ 12. How might you feel about a person *encroaching* on you?

A. happy

B. relieved

C. disgusted

D. irritated

Name _____ Date _____

___ **13.** When the narrator takes a *tentative* step, how is she moving?
  A. confidently
  B. hesitantly
  C. awkwardly
  D. gracefully

___ **14.** Which sentence contains three common nouns?
  A. She has never upset an object or as much as brushed a magazine onto the floor.
  B. They bought their tickets and surrendered them in anticipation.
  C. The White Arabians of Ali-Khazar rose on their hind legs and waltzed.
  D. They made a romantic pair all right, especially in the blindfold sequence.

Essay

15. In "The Leap," many details foreshadow future events. In an essay, identify two examples of foreshadowing from the selection, and explain in detail the specific future events they suggest.

16. The narrator's mother's background as a trapeze artist in "The Leap" is her defining characteristic. How does her background affect the outcome of the three events described in the story? Write an essay in which you explain how the mother's background is essential to the development of the plot.

17. Thinking About the Big Question: Is there a difference between reality and truth? Sometimes writers use the experiences of their characters to make a general point about an important truth of all human experience. Choose one character in "The Leap." Describe two main events that happen to this character during the story. Then explain how these events might lead to a more universal truth about what all people experience or believe. Use details from the story to support your response.

Name _____   Date _____

"The Leap" by Louise Erdrich
Selection Test B

Critical Reading *Identify the letter of the choice that best completes the statement or answers the question.*

____ 1. What is "The Leap" about?
   A. a terrible accident at a circus
   B. a mother's actions that ensure the existence of her daughter
   C. the death of an infant and its repercussions
   D. the strange way in which two people meet and fall in love

____ 2. What do you learn about the narrator's mother in the exposition of "The Leap"?
   A. She had a daughter who died before the narrator was born.
   B. She was once a trapeze artist and is now going blind.
   C. She was married to two different men.
   D. She did not learn to read until she was an adult.

____ 3. Which phrase from "The Leap" best describes the narrator's mother?
   A. blind and smiling
   B. lives comfortably in extreme elements
   C. seven months and hardly showing
   D. a romantic pair

____ 4. What can you predict from this line in "The Leap"?
   In the town square a replica tent pole, cracked and splintered, now stands cast in concrete.
   A. There will be a terrible fire.
   B. The narrator's mother will be badly hurt.
   C. There will be an accident in the circus tent.
   D. The narrator's mother will save her daughter.

____ 5. Which line helps you predict that the narrator's mother will survive the high-wire accident?
   A. She has never lost her balance or bumped into a closet door left carelessly open.
   B. She has kept no sequined costume, no photographs, no fliers or posters. . . .
   C. There was time, before the storm, for three acts.
   D. They dropped gracefully from nowhere, like two sparkling birds. . . .

____ 6. Which line from "The Leap" is an example of foreshadowing?
   A. The catlike precision of her movements in old age might be the result of her early training. . . .
   B. I have lived in the West, where you can see the weather coming for miles. . . .
   C. I hear the crackle, catch a whiff of smoke from the stove downstairs, and suddenly the room goes dark. . . .
   D. It was while the two were in midair, their hands about to meet, that lightning struck the main pole. . . .

____ 7. In "The Leap," the Avalons' lips were destined "never to meet again" because
A. Mrs. Avalon fell in love with another man.
B. Mrs. Avalon was killed in the accident.
C. Mr. Avalon was killed in the accident.
D. Mrs. Avalon left her husband after the accident.

____ 8. In "The Leap," the narrator's mother saves herself by
A. trying to catch her husband.
B. letting herself fall into a net.
C. changing direction in midair.
D. lowering herself slowly to the ground.

____ 9. In "The Leap," what "form of flight" does the narrator's mother take up after she gives up the trapeze?
A. flying a plane   B. sewing   C. reading   D. hang gliding

____ 10. The climax of "The Leap" occurs when the narrator's mother
A. leaps from the window with her.
B. grasps the hot metal supports.
C. meets her husband.
D. loses her first child.

____ 11. In "The Leap," which line helps you predict that the mother will rescue her daughter?
A. From opposite ends of the tent they waved, blind and smiling, to the crowd below.
B. As soon as I awakened, in the small room that I now use for sewing, I smelled the smoke.
C. Outside, my mother stood below my dark window and saw clearly that there was no rescue.
D. She swung down, caught the ledge, and crawled through the opening.

____ 12. A central idea of "The Leap" is
A. mothers and daughters have an unbreakable bond.
B. it is important to find your true passion.
C. there is always another path to follow.
D. look before you leap.

____ 13. What event is foreshadowed by this line from "The Leap"?
   My mother once said that I'd be amazed at how many things a person can do within the act of falling.

A. the fall of the mother and narrator into the net during the fire
B. the fall of the mother's first husband to his death
C. the gradual fall of the mother into old age
D. the fall into love of the narrator's mother and father

Vocabulary and Grammar

_____ **14.** A *tentative* gesture conveys
   A. anger.
   B. joy.
   C. uncertainty.
   D. confidence.

_____ **15.** In which sentence is *extricating* used correctly?
   A. The rescuers had trouble extricating the woman from the rubble.
   B. The trapeze artists were extricating themselves toward each other.
   C. The woman met her husband while extricating in the hospital.
   D. The narrator's mother had extricating pain from her burns.

_____ **16.** Which sentence contains a proper noun?
   A. From opposite sides of the tent they waved, blind and smiling, to the crowd below.
   B. My mother once said that I'd be amazed at how many things a person can do within the act of falling.
   C. Anna was pregnant at the time, seven months and hardly showing, her stomach muscles were that strong.
   D. Once my father and mother married, they moved onto the old farm he had inherited but didn't care much for.

_____ **17.** How many proper nouns are in the following sentence?

   Anna Avalon had been to many of the places he longed to visit—Venice, Rome, Mexico, all through France and Spain.

   A. one
   B. three
   C. five
   D. six

Essay

18. In "The Leap," many details foreshadow future events. In an essay, identify two examples of foreshadowing from the selection, and explain in detail the specific future events they suggest.

19. What does the narrator in "The Leap" mean when she says she owes her mother her existence "three times"? Write an essay in which you explain the three events for which the narrator owes her mother her existence. What do you think she is saying about her mother in this statement? Include information from the story that supports your answer.

20. **Thinking About the Big Question: Is there a difference between reality and truth?**
   Write an essay about the characters' reality in "The Leap" and the more universal truths that the author also wants to convey. First, summarize two or three key events in the story. Then explain how each event reflects more universal truths about human behavior.

Study these words. Then, complete the activities that follow.

Word List A

alternatives [awl TER nuh tivz] *n.* other choices
   Kim found that organizing and cleaning were good <u>alternatives</u> to procrastinating.

buffer [BUHF er] *v.* to reduce shock or harm
   The padding on John's sneaker helped to <u>buffer</u> the impact of running.

corset [KAWR sit] *n.* a stiff undergarment that shapes the body
   The laces on the <u>corset</u> were pulled so tight, Lea could barely breathe.

fatigued [fuh TEEGD] *adj.* exhausted or very tired
   Ken felt <u>fatigued</u> after pitching all nine innings of the baseball game.

focused [FOH kuhst] *v.* concentrated on one person, place, or thing
   Julia, a pianist, <u>focused</u> her energy on getting into a music conservatory.

massive [MAS iv] *adj.* extremely large
   We couldn't see over the <u>massive</u> brick wall.

mechanically [muh KAN ik lee] *adv.* automatically; like a machine
   The actors went through the script <u>mechanically</u>, without emotion.

torso [TAWR soh] *n.* the trunk of the human body
   In Juan's drawing of the model, the <u>torso</u> was too short.

Word List B

compounding [kom POWN ding] *v.* adding to
   <u>Compounding</u> his problem, Tim argued with the teacher after failing his quiz.

exterior [ek STEER ee er] *adj.* outside part
   The <u>exterior</u> of the car was rusted and needed paint.

immersed [i MERST] *v.* covered completely in a liquid
   I <u>immersed</u> the dirty dishes in hot, soapy water.

inhaling [in HAYL ing] *v.* breathing in
   <u>Inhaling</u> too much dust made Ben cough.

prolonged [proh LAWNGD] *adj.* extended; made something last longer
   The <u>prolonged</u> hockey game left the children exhausted.

strait [STRAYT] *n.* a narrow waterway that joins two bodies of water
   The <u>strait</u> was the only connection from sea to sea.

swerved [SWERVD] *v.* changed direction, often suddenly
   The car <u>swerved</u> to avoid the oncoming truck.

tromping [TRAHMP ing] *v.* walking with a heavy step
   We could hear the children <u>tromping</u> off to school.

from **Swimming to Antarctica** by Lynne Cox
Vocabulary Warm-up Exercises

Exercise A *Fill in each blank in the paragraph below with an appropriate word from Word List A. Use each word only once.*

Lydia, an aspiring artist, grew [1] _____ after applying

paint to a [2] _____, oversized canvas for several hours. She

[3] _____ all of her energies on completing her painting. The

model, Elizabeth, wore a [4] _____, which covered most of her

[5] _____ and was very uncomfortable under her gown. Still,

neither Lydia nor Elizabeth could see any [6] _____ to finishing the

painting during this session. Though Lydia was afraid she was starting to paint

[7] _____, just going through the motions, her first exhibit opened the

following day. Elizabeth tried to [8] _____ her own discomfort by sitting

back against soft cushions.

Exercise B *Revise each sentence so that the underlined vocabulary word is used in a logical way. Be sure to keep the vocabulary word in your revision.*

Example: Mary took a nap, <u>compounding</u> her trouble with sleepiness.
Mary stayed up late, <u>compounding</u> her trouble with sleepiness.

1. The paint on the <u>exterior</u> of the house began to chip, so the bedroom looked awful.
   _____

2. When I <u>swerved</u> into oncoming traffic, I avoided a terrible driving mistake.
   _____

3. After Juan <u>immersed</u> the dumplings in water, they began to dry out.
   _____

4. The instructor explained how snorkels could be used for <u>inhaling</u> water.
   _____

5. After a <u>prolonged</u> soccer game, Bobby got home sooner than expected.
   _____

6. Only cars can travel on the <u>strait</u> that connects two waterways.
   _____

7. <u>Tromping</u> on thin ice is a good idea.
   _____

from **Swimming to Antarctica** by Lynne Cox
Reading Warm-up A

Read the following passage. Pay special attention to the underlined words. Then, read it again, and complete the activities. Use a separate sheet of paper for your written answers.

Young Graciela Herrera couldn't wait to begin her training for the marathon. Her friend Koji thought she was crazy. "Can't you find better <u>alternatives</u> to getting up at dawn and running for an hour, like maybe sleeping and eating?" Graciela, however, was single-minded in her devotion to running.

While the rest of her running friends would often stop to chat, Graciela <u>focused</u> determinedly on her training goals. When she found herself running <u>mechanically</u>, losing energy and enjoyment, she made up songs to keep herself going. Graciela even found ways to <u>buffer</u> the excruciating pain that came with long-distance running. Stretching exercises for her legs and the back muscles in her <u>torso</u> helped after she ran long distances.

Eventually, Graciela decided to run competitively. She ran her first half-marathon after six months of training. Finally, she felt ready for her first real marathon with a twenty-six mile course. Graciela was worried—even people who seem strong and in good physical shape sometimes had to be carried off a course by the end of the race. Still, she was ready to try.

The first thirteen miles were a breeze. Graciela ran in the middle of the pack; her running buddies shouted encouragement to one another, laughing as they ran. After that, runners started to slow down as the course took them up a steep, <u>massive</u> mountain. It seemed much more imposing to Graciela than it had during training. Some runners started to stagger, while others just gave up.

Graciela couldn't believe how <u>fatigued</u> she felt at the end of 22 miles, even though she had trained for nearly a year. It was so difficult to take a deep breath that she felt as if she was wearing a <u>corset</u> laced too tightly around her chest.

After what seemed an eternity, she saw a crowd cheering at the finish. She made it. Later, she would learn that her score was in the top ten percent of women runners.

1. Circle the two <u>alternatives</u> to morning runs that Koji names. Name other possible *alternatives*.

2. Circle the phrase that tells what Graciela <u>focused</u> on. Then, tell what *focused* means.

3. Circle the action Graciela did <u>mechanically</u>. Write a sentence about what it might feel like to do something *mechanically*.

4. Circle the phrase that tells what Graciela learned how to <u>buffer</u>. Then, tell what *buffer* means.

5. Circle the activity Graciela did to help the muscles in her <u>torso</u>. In addition to back muscles, what other muscles are located in the *torso*?

6. Circle the word that gives a clue to the meaning of <u>massive</u>. Explain why a steep, *massive mountain* would be difficult to run.

7. Underline the words that describe one sign that a runner is <u>fatigued</u>. Write about a time when you felt greatly *fatigued*.

8. Circle the words that describe how a <u>corset</u> might be worn. Tell what a *corset* is.

from **Swimming to Antarctica** by Lynne Cox
Reading Warm-up B

Read the following passage. Pay special attention to the underlined words. Then, read it again, and complete the activities. Use a separate sheet of paper for your written answers.

Born in 1917, Florence Chadwick was one of the greatest swimmers of all time. In 1950, Chadwick went <u>tromping</u> down the banks of Cap Gris Nez, France, to swim the formidable English Channel. She swam the 23 miles to Dover, England, in 13 hours and 28 minutes, breaking the record previously held by Gertrude Ederle, the first woman to cross the Channel.

In 1926, Ederle made the crossing with the <u>exterior</u> part of her body slathered in sheep's grease to insulate herself from the cold, rough waters. Ederle had to swim an extra twelve miles out of her way to avoid the rough currents. When Chadwick broke her record, Ederle suggested the comparison was unfair, claiming they swam under very different conditions.

Even so, Chadwick's achievement was undeniable. After her <u>prolonged</u> 23-mile swim, she emerged from the water prepared to swim back again.

In 1951, Chadwick got that chance. Once more, she <u>immersed</u> herself in the chilly waters of the Channel, swimming back from England to France. Because of the currents and weather, this was an even more arduous journey. Chadwick <u>swerved</u> as she swam, avoiding ice and making zigzags across the fog-covered Channel. When she made it to shore in 16 hours and 22 minutes, she became the first woman to swim both ways across the English Channel.

Florence Chadwick went on to other amazing feats. In the early 1950s, she swam both ways across the Dardanelles <u>Strait</u>, a narrow waterway connecting Europe to Asiatic Turkey. She also swam one way across the strait connecting the Black Sea to the Mediterranean.

In 1954, she was offered a prize of $10,000 to swim Lake Ontario but couldn't make it across. <u>Compounding</u> the physical difficulties of a marathon swim, choppy water made her seasick. <u>Inhaling</u> and exhaling became too difficult. Though she didn't get that prize, Florence Chadwick's triumphs greatly outnumbered her failures.

1. Underline the phrase that tells where Florence Chadwick went <u>tromping</u>. What does *tromping* mean?

2. Circle the words that tell what Gertrude Ederle had on the <u>exterior</u> part of her body. Tell what *exterior* is.

3. Explain why it was surprising that Florence said she felt fine after a <u>prolonged</u> swim.

4. Underline the phrase that tells where Florence <u>immersed</u> herself. What does *immersed* mean?

5. Circle the word that tells what Florence <u>swerved</u> to avoid. Write a sentence about something you *swerved* to avoid.

6. Circle the name of a <u>strait</u> that Florence swam. Explain what a *strait* is.

7. Write a sentence telling what was <u>compounding</u> Florence's difficulty in swimming Lake Ontario.

8. Circle the word that means the opposite of <u>inhaling</u>. Then, tell what might happen to a swimmer whose breathing pattern was disrupted.

Name _____ Date _____

from **Swimming to Antarctica** by Lynne Cox
Writing About the Big Question

Is there a difference between reality and truth?

Big Question Vocabulary

comprehend   concrete   confirm   context   differentiate
discern   evaluate   evidence   improbable   objective
perception   reality   subjective   uncertainty   verify

A. *Use one or more words from the list above to complete each sentence.*

1. _____ facts should be easy to believe, but they can obscure the truth.

2. Your physical senses can help you _____ what you *think* you know.

3. Facing _____ can make you doubt what is real.

4. People must face challenges in order to _____ the truth about what they can really do.

B. *Follow the directions in responding to each of the items below.*

1. List two different times when you learned the truth about what you could accomplish.

_____

_____

2. Write two sentences explaining one of the experiences you listed in your response, and describe the results. Use at least two of the Big Question vocabulary words.

_____

_____

_____

_____

C. *Complete the sentence below. Then, write a short paragraph in which you connect this situation to the Big Question.*

People often learn deep truths about themselves when facing _____

_____.

_____

_____

Name _____ Date _____

from **Swimming to Antarctica** by Lynne Cox
Literary Analysis: Author's Perspective

The **author's perspective** in a literary work includes the judgments, attitudes, and experiences the author brings to the subject.

- An author's perspective determines which details he or she includes. For example, a writer with firsthand experience of an event might report his or her own reactions as well as generally known facts. A writer with a positive view of a subject may emphasize its benefits.
- A work may combine several perspectives. For example, a writer may tell what it felt like to live through an event. In addition, the writer may express his or her present views of the experience.

In the following passage from *Swimming to Antarctica*, Lynne Cox states facts about her test swim in cold water and expresses her reactions to it.

I had mixed feelings about the test swim. In some ways, it had given me confidence; I now knew that I could swim for twenty-two minutes in thirty-three-degree water. But it had also made me feel uncertain.

DIRECTIONS: *For each of the following passages, write what facts the writer includes. Then, write the author's reactions.*

1. When I hit the water, I went all the way under. I hadn't intended to do that; I hadn't wanted to immerse my head, which could over-stimulate my vagus nerve and cause my heart to stop beating. Dog-paddling as quickly as I could, I popped up in the water, gasping for air. I couldn't catch my breath. I was swimming with my head up, hyperventilating. I kept spinning my arms, trying to get warm, but I couldn't get enough air. I felt like I had a corset tightening around my chest. I told myself to relax, take a deep breath, but I couldn't slow my breath.

Facts	Author's Reactions

2. I put my head down, and something suddenly clicked. Maybe it was because I knew shore was within reach, or maybe because I got a second wind; I don't know. But I was finally swimming strongly, stretching out and moving fluidly. My arms and legs were as cold as the sea, but I felt the heat within my head and contained in my torso and thrilled to it, knowing my body had carried me to places no one else had been in only a bathing suit.

Facts	Author's Reactions

Name _____ Date _____

from **Swimming to Antarctica** by Lynne Cox
Reading: Use Prior Knowledge to Make Predictions

As you read, **make predictions,** or educated guesses, about what will happen next based on your own experience and details in a text. **Verify,** or confirm, predictions by comparing the outcome you predicted to the actual outcome. **Revise,** or adjust, your predictions as you gather more information.

- **Strategy:** To help you make, verify, and revise predictions, **ask questions,** such as *Will the main character succeed?*
- For each question you ask, record your predictions and how they change with new information.

Read the following passage from the excerpt from *Swimming to Antarctica*.

The water temperature on the big swim would be a degree colder. Thirty-two degrees. That was a magic number, the temperature at which freshwater froze. I wondered if in thirty-two-degree water the water in my cells would freeze, if my body's tissues would become permanently damaged.

You can make a prediction about the rest of the selection by asking yourself a question such as this: *Will the one-degree difference make the swim impossible?*

DIRECTIONS: *Make a prediction about each of the following passages from the text. Write the details from the text and from your own experiences that helped you make your prediction.*

1. Dr. Block caught me at the top of the stairs, just before we stepped out the door and onto the ramp, and asked if I would sit down on a step so he could trace two veins on my hands with a blue Magic Marker. It was just a precaution, he said, in case I needed emergency assistance. . . . Why did he have to do this now, right before I swam? Didn't he realize this kind of stuff psyches people out?

Predict: Will the author be psyched out by the doctor's action? _____

_____

Details from the text that support my prediction: _____

_____

My own experiences that support my prediction: _____

_____

2. An icy wave slapped my face: I choked and felt a wave of panic rise within me. My throat tightened. I tried to clear my throat and breathe. My breath didn't come out. I couldn't get enough air in to clear my throat. I glanced at the crew. They couldn't tell I was in trouble. If I stopped, Dan would jump in and pull me out.

Predict: Will the author stop swimming? _____

Details from the text that support my prediction: _____

_____

My own experiences that support my prediction: _____

_____

from **Swimming to Antarctica** by Lynne Cox
Vocabulary Builder

Word List

abruptly   buffer   equilibrium   gauge   prolonged   venturing

A. DIRECTIONS: *Think about the meaning of each italicized word. Then, answer the question.*

1. If someone endures *prolonged* exposure to the sun, what will probably happen to him or her?

_____

2. If a dancer loses her *equilibrium* during a recital, what might happen?

_____

3. If a friend uses you to *buffer* himself from a group of other people, how does he probably feel about the other people?

_____

4. If your sister *abruptly* hung up the telephone during a conversation, how does she probably feel?

_____

5. If you want to *gauge* the warmth of a body of water, what should you do?

_____

B. WORD STUDY: The Latin prefix *pro-* means "forth" or "forward." Answer each of the following questions using one of these words containing *pro-*: pronounce, profess, project.

1. What are you doing if you *pronounce* your name?

_____

2. If you *profess* your support for your local animal shelter, do you support it?

_____

3. When actors *project* their voices, do they whisper?

_____

Name _____ Date _____

from **Swimming to Antarctica** by Lynne Cox
Enrichment: Preparing for a Task

When Lynne Cox decided to swim in Antarctic waters, she began a rigorous training schedule. She was already in very good shape, but she worked at weight-lifting (often balanced atop a big rubber ball), walking, and sprint-swimming, both in a pool and in the ocean. She changed the style of her swimming, learning to raise her head out of the water to keep as much body heat as possible. She put on twelve pounds for added insulation, and she grew her hair long so she could pile it against her head, trapping heat. After two years, she was ready.

DIRECTIONS: *Think of a difficult task that you would like to achieve. It can be a physical task, such as running a marathon or learning to skydive. It could also be a mental feat, such as competing in the National Spelling Bee or running for president of the United States. Use the following lines to write the things you would do to prepare for your task.*

What I Want to Do: _____

Physical Skills Needed: _____

_____

_____

Physical Preparations: _____

_____

_____

Mental Skills Needed: _____

_____

_____

Mental Preparations: _____

_____

_____

from **Swimming to Antarctica** by Lynne Cox
Open-Book Test

Short Answer *Write your responses to the questions in this section on the lines provided.*

1. As the selection from *Swimming to Antarctica* opens, Lynne Cox is returning to her cabin after her short test swim. At this point, what is Cox's attitude about making the longer swim? Cite details from the selection to support your response.

    _____

    _____

    _____

2. In the selection from *Swimming to Antarctica*, what seem to be Cox's main motives for making the long swim? List two motives.

    _____

    _____

    _____

3. In *Swimming to Antarctica*, which details help readers predict that the swim will be very difficult? Think about the dangers Cox will face. List two details from the first ten paragraphs of the selection.

    _____

    _____

    _____

4. In *Swimming to Antarctica*, what does Cox learn about what can happen when a person has *prolonged* exposure to thirty-two-degree water? Find where the word *prolonged* is used and read that passage again.

    _____

5. How would you describe the first few moments of Cox's mile-long swim to Antarctica? Cite one detail from the selection to support your description.

    _____

    _____

6. What does Cox do to regain her *equilibrium* in the early part of her swim to Antarctica?

    _____

7. In this selection from *Swimming to Antarctica*, how does the behavior of the people on the boat affect Cox's perspective as she swims?

_____

_____

_____

_____

8. In *Swimming to Antarctica*, why does Barry have Cox change the direction of her swim?

_____

_____

9. Near the end of the selection from *Swimming to Antarctica*, Cox shouts, "Barry, I'm swimming to Antarctica!" In the chart below, write two phrases to describe Cox's perspective before and after her exclamation. Then, on the line below, briefly explain how Cox's perspective changes.

Perspective Before Shouting	Perspective After Shouting

_____

10. List two details or events during this selection from *Swimming to Antarctica* that help you predict that Cox will succeed in the end.

_____

_____

Essay

Write an extended response to the question of your choice or to the question or questions your teacher assigns you.

11. As you read the selection from *Swimming to Antarctica*, did you predict that Cox would complete her swim successfully? Write a short essay about your prediction. State your prediction. Then, identify which details from the selection helped you make the prediction.

12. Cox has many character traits that help her succeed in her swim. In an essay, identify these character traits and explain how they help her achieve her goal. Include details from *Swimming to Antarctica* to illustrate the traits you identify.

13. Write an essay about the drive it takes for people to accomplish feats that few or no other people have done before. Discuss the motives behind great achievements. Also consider what kinds of people perform them. Use Cox as your main example. Cite details from *Swimming to Antarctica*, as well as one or two additional examples of heroes, to support your points.

14. **Thinking About the Big Question: What is the difference between reality and truth?** In a brief essay about *Swimming to Antarctica*, examine how Cox tries to create a safe reality in her mind instead of facing the full truth about the dangers of her Antarctic swim. Your essay should address these questions:
   - Before Cox begins her swim, of what dangers is she unaware? Why do you think she never fully investigates the danger?
   - How does Cox react when Dr. Block traces two veins on her hand? Why?
   - As she swims, how does Cox try to convince herself that she is safer than she truly is? Why does she do this?

Oral Response

15. Go back to question 2, 3, 5, or 10 or to the question your teacher assigns you. Take a few minutes to expand your answer and prepare an oral response. Find additional details in the selection from *Swimming to Antarctica* that support your points. If necessary, make notes to guide your response.

from **Swimming to Antarctica** by Lynne Cox
Selection Test A

Critical Reading *Identify the letter of the choice that best answers the question.*

____ 1. Why do you think Lynne Cox decided to swim a mile in Antarctic waters?
   A. to win a bet
   B. to prove that she could do it
   C. to improve her strength
   D. to qualify for the Olympics

____ 2. Which line from *Swimming to Antarctica* would logically lead a reader to predict that Lynne Cox's swim would be extremely difficult?
   A. I knew that the weather could suddenly change and the swim would be off.
   B. I wondered if in thirty-two-degree water the water in my cells would freeze. . . .
   C. Gabriella came in to take a core temperature; it was up to 100.4 degrees.
   D. In the protection of the Antarctic Peninsula, the wind dropped off and the sea grew calmer.

____ 3. How does Lynne Cox feel about the mile-long swim before she attempts it?
   A. She is certain she can do it.
   B. She is confident and carefree.
   C. She is nearly paralyzed with fear.
   D. She is fearful and excited.

____ 4. In *Swimming to Antarctica,* what goes wrong in the first moment of the swim?
   A. Lynne Cox's head goes under the water.
   B. Killer whales are sighted swimming nearby.
   C. Lynne Cox hurts her arm.
   D. Lynne Cox swims too slowly.

____ 5. Why does Lynne Cox have to change course as she swims?
   A. She needs to find warmer water.
   B. She is heading toward a pod of killer whales.
   C. There are icebergs in the way.
   D. The course she is on is not long enough.

____ 6. What does this reaction to her swim reveal about how Lynne Cox feels?

I lifted my head, took a big breath, and shouted, "Barry, I'm swimming to Antarctica!"

A. She is exhausted and wants to finish.

B. She is confused about what she is doing.

C. She is excited and determined to finish.

D. She knows she is in danger and is warning the others.

____ 7. When does Lynne Cox begin swimming strongly?

A. after fifteen minutes

B. after twenty-one minutes

C. when she first enters the water

D. in the last few seconds of the swim

____ 8. Which question can help you predict what will happen when Lynne Cox feels a second current pushing her into the inlet?

A. Why is there a current in the waters of the inlet?

B. Will the current change its direction?

C. Will she become too cold to keep swimming?

D. Is she strong enough to swim against the current?

____ 9. What does Lynne Cox learn later about her swim?

A. Someone else had already done it.

B. It could have caused permanent nerve damage.

C. Nobody thought that she would be able to do it.

D. She had not actually swum a whole mile.

____ 10. How does Lynne Cox feel after she completes her swim?

A. exhilarated

B. depressed

C. let down

D. unbelieving

Vocabulary and Grammar

____ 11. When does Lynne Cox achieve a state of *equilibrium*?

A. when she first enters the water

B. when she comes out of the water

C. when her fingers and toes are the same temperature as the water

D. when she begins swimming quickly toward the glacier

____ 12. Why is swimming to Antarctica a *novel* event?
   A. because no one has done it before
   B. because someone has written a book about it
   C. because it is extremely dangerous
   D. because it took a lot of training

____ 13. In which sentence is the underlined word an abstract noun?
   A. The next morning, Susan called me up to the <u>bridge</u>.
   B. I had mixed <u>feelings</u> about the test swim.
   C. Would my core <u>temperature</u> drop faster, more quickly than I could recognize?
   D. I rubbed <u>sunscreen</u> on my face, but not on my arms or legs.

Essay

14. Lynne Cox has many character traits that help her succeed in her swim. In an essay, explain what these character traits are. Tell how they help her achieve her goal. Include details from the selection that illustrate the traits you describe.

15. When she starts her swim, Lynne Cox doesn't know that her nerves are damaged and that she is in danger of doing permanent harm to herself. Do you think she would have changed her mind about the swim if she had known this? Write an essay in which you explain your answer. Use details about the author's perspective on her swim to support your answer.

16. **Thinking About the Big Question: Is there a difference between reality and truth?** In *Swimming to Antarctica*, Cox has to create a safe reality in her mind instead of facing the full truth about the dangers of her Antarctic swim. In a brief essay, answer the following questions: What is dangerous about Cox's swim? As she swims, how does Cox try to convince herself that she is safer than she really is? Why does she do this?

Name _____ Date _____

from **Swimming to Antarctica** by Lynne Cox
Selection Test B

Critical Reading *Identify the letter of the choice that best completes the statement or answers the question.*

_____ 1. Lynne Cox wanted to swim a mile in Antarctic waters because
   A. she wanted to win a bet.
   B. she wanted to prove that it could be done.
   C. she wanted to prove that women are as strong as men.
   D. she wanted to qualify for the Olympics.

_____ 2. Which question would help you predict whether Lynne Cox will finish her swim?
   A. How often does Lynne Cox swim?
   B. Has Lynne Cox trained enough in very cold water?
   C. What happens when the body becomes very cold?
   D. Why does Lynne Cox want to swim in Antarctic water?

_____ 3. What could you predict about Lynne Cox's swim from this line in *Swimming to Antarctica*?

   The water temperature on the big swim would be a degree colder. Thirty-two degrees.

   A. that Lynne Cox would find the swim very difficult
   B. that Lynne Cox would have no trouble with the swim
   C. that Lynne Cox would not be able to complete the swim
   D. that Lynne Cox would suffer permanent damage from the swim

_____ 4. In *Swimming to Antarctica*, when does the swim become difficult?
   A. in the first moment, when Lynne Cox's head goes under the water
   B. when killer whales are sighted
   C. partway through the swim, when Lynne Cox's arms become numb
   D. near the end of the swim, when Lynne Cox hits ice as she swims

_____ 5. Which line reveals Lynne Cox's feelings about her efforts?
   A. All I could do was go back to my room and wait.
   B. I picked out landmarks, places I could aim for, so I'd know if I was on or off course.
   C. I pulled my hands right under my chest so that I was swimming on the upper inches of the sea, trying to minimize my contact with the water.
   D. I lifted my head, took a big breath, and shouted, "Barry, I'm swimming to Antarctica!"

_____ 6. In this passage from *Swimming to Antarctica*, why does Mrs. Stokie think it is good for the captain to see what Lynne Cox is doing?

   The captain was watching you and he was shaking his head. He was an older man, and he had experienced everything. And now he was seeing something new. It was good for him.

   A. because he knew that he too could do the swim
   B. because he didn't think a woman could swim so far
   C. because his experience and knowledge were being tested
   D. because he learned that the swim could not be done

____ 7. Lynne Cox has to change course while she is swimming because
   A. she needs to find warmer water.
   B. she is heading toward a pod of killer whales.
   C. there are icebergs blocking her route.
   D. the course she is on is not a mile in length.

____ 8. Which question will help you predict what will happen when Lynne Cox feels a second current pushing her into the inlet?
   A. Why is there a current in the waters of the inlet?
   B. Will the current change its direction?
   C. Will Lynne Cox become too cold to continue swimming?
   D. Is Lynne Cox strong enough to swim against the current?

____ 9. What is Lynne Cox's perspective in this passage from *Swimming to Antarctica*?

   If you continue swimming, you're going to cool down even more. Remember how hard you shivered last time? Remember how much work it was? Remember how uncomfortable you were? This is the place where people make mistakes, when they're tired and cold and they push too far into the unknown.

   A. She has gone far enough.
   B. She should try to go on.
   C. She should never have started the swim.
   D. She should take a break.

____ 10. Lynne Cox is glad to see the penguins swimming beside her because
   A. they help push her along.
   B. it means that there are no killer whales nearby.
   C. they give her mental and emotional strength.
   D. they let her know she is near shore.

____ 11. Lynne Cox's perspective on her swim changes when she learns that
   A. someone had already completed that swim two years earlier.
   B. the swim could have caused permanent muscle and nerve damage.
   C. nobody had believed she could do it.
   D. she had not actually swum a whole mile.

____ 12. In *Swimming to Antarctica*, when Lynne Cox completes her swim she feels
   A. exhilarated.
   B. depressed.
   C. let down.
   D. disbelieving.

Vocabulary and Grammar

____ 13. A *prolonged* swim in cold water is dangerous because
    A. the body can't handle the pressure from deep water.
    B. the body is chilled for a long time.
    C. the edges of icebergs are very sharp.
    D. the shock of moving from cold to warm temperatures is intense.

____ 14. Lynne Cox needed a hand under her head to *buffer* her because
    A. the wind was blowing hard.
    B. ice had formed in her hair.
    C. her head was bouncing on the bottom of the boat.
    D. she was shivering too hard to stop.

____ 15. Identify an abstract noun in the following sentence.

    I stared across the icy water . . . and felt excitement building within me.

    A. icy
    B. water
    C. building
    D. excitement

____ 16. What number of concrete and abstract nouns does the following sentence include?

    I choked and felt a wave of panic rise within me.

    A. one concrete, two abstract
    B. two concrete, one abstract
    C. one concrete, one abstract
    D. three concrete, no abstract

Essay

17. Did you predict that Lynne Cox would complete her swim successfully? Write an essay in which you explain your prediction. Include details from the selection that helped you make the prediction.

18. Lynne Cox has many character traits that enable her to achieve her goal of swimming to Antarctica. In an essay, explain what these traits are and how they help her. Include details from the selection that illustrate the traits you describe.

19. **Thinking About the Big Question: Is there a difference between reality and truth?** In a brief essay about *Swimming to Antarctica,* examine how Cox tries to create a safe reality in her mind instead of facing the full truth about the dangers of her Antarctic swim. Your essay should address these questions:

• Before Cox begins her swim, of what dangers is she unaware? Why do you think she never fully investigates the danger?

• How does Cox react when Dr. Block traces two veins on her hand? Why?

• As she swims, how does Cox try to convince herself that she is safer than she truly is? Why does she do this?

Study these words. Then, complete the activities that follow.

Word List A

dwellings [DWEL ingz] *n.* places where people live
In some ancient villages, people's <u>dwellings</u> were built into the mountainside.

immediate [i MEE dee it] *adj.* happening right away, at once
Lou hoped for an <u>immediate</u> response to his letter asking for a raise.

indignation [in dig NAY shun] *n.* anger at a perceived injustice
We were filled with <u>indignation</u> when the burglar wasn't charged with a crime.

intellectual [in tuh LEC choo uhl] *adj.* involving thought and reason
Felix showed his <u>intellectual</u> ability as he presented his point of view in the debates.

suspicions [suh SPISH uhnz] *n.* thoughts that something is wrong
Maria had <u>suspicions</u> that the school election had been rigged.

proposal [pruh POHZ uhl] *n.* suggestion of a plan
Ali made a <u>proposal</u> that we should all look at the same colleges.

reveal [ri VEEL] *v.* show or make known
The writer could <u>reveal</u> his inner emotions only in his work.

tradition [truh DISH uhn] *n.* customs handed down through generations
My family has a <u>tradition</u> of celebrating birthdays with food instead of gifts.

Word List B

academic [ak uh DEM ik] *adj.* related to school or study
Gina had a superior <u>academic</u> record because she studied so hard.

comprehended [kahm pruh HEN did] *v.* understood
It took a while before I <u>comprehended</u> the complicated instructions for making bread.

contempt [kuhn TEMPT] *n.* a feeling of dislike and disrespect
She felt <u>contempt</u> for the players who cheated.

encountered [en KOWN terd] *v.* met with or was faced with
When Billy <u>encountered</u> difficulties in his work, he asked for help.

energetically [en er JET ik lee] *adv.* with much strength and activity
Rita ran <u>energetically</u> to impress her new coach.

gumption [GUMP shuhn] *n.* courage, nerve
Jo had the <u>gumption</u> to contradict the speaker, who was not pleased.

restricting [ri STRIK ting] *adj.* confining; keeping within limits
The <u>restricting</u> rules of the workplace made it difficult to leave the building.

resumed [ri ZOOMD] *v.* started again
Clara <u>resumed</u> playing the piano after she was interrupted by a phone call.

Name _____ Date _____

from **I Know Why the Caged Bird Sings** by Maya Angelou
Vocabulary Warm-up Exercises

Exercise A *Fill in each blank in the paragraph below with an appropriate word from Word List A. Use each word only once.*

Tim's family had a [1] _____ of discussing political issues at Sunday dinner. This started with Tim's grandmother, who was a teacher. She liked to encourage the family members to use their [2] _____ abilities. Others in the family harbored [3] _____ that she just liked to argue. Family members took turns deciding on a topic. As soon as someone made a [4] _____, others knew to make an [5] _____ trip to the library to learn what they could before Sunday. Often, family members wouldn't [6] _____ their own opinions on the issue until the discussion began. Sometimes they would get so angry and full of [7] _____ that people in nearby [8] _____ would be surprised by the loud voices.

Exercise B *Answer the questions with complete explanations.*

Example: If you were treated with <u>contempt</u>, would you be happy or upset?
I would probably be upset because <u>contempt</u> shows lack of respect.

1. If Mia had an excellent <u>academic</u> record, would you encourage her to go to college?
   _____

2. If your job has a <u>restricting</u> atmosphere, do you think you have a lot of freedom?
   _____

3. If you <u>comprehended</u> the difficult reading, would you ask a friend for help?
   _____

4. If Maria showed <u>gumption</u> when confronted with setbacks, would she be ashamed of her cowardice?
   _____

5. If a popular band <u>resumed</u> playing at a concert, what might the audience do?
   _____

6. If Seth continued his work <u>energetically</u>, how might his boss react?
   _____

7. If you <u>encountered</u> troubles in the past, would you be glad or sad?
   _____

Name _____ Date _____

from I Know Why the Caged Bird Sings by Maya Angelou
Reading Warm-up A

Read the following passage. Pay special attention to the underlined words. Then, read it again, and complete the activities. Use a separate sheet of paper for your written answers.

Julia Morgan broke with <u>tradition</u> when she tried to become the first woman ever to study architecture at the Ecole des Beaux-Arts, a world-famous school for architects in Paris. Morgan was born in 1872 in Oakland, California. Since she was young, she had shown great <u>intellectual</u> ability and did very well in school.

Julia studied engineering at the University of California at Berkeley. One of her teachers, a gifted architect named Bernard Maybeck, had studied at the Ecole des Beaux-Arts. When he heard that the school might allow women to apply, he made a <u>proposal</u> to Julia. He suggested that she try to enter the famous school.

Julia moved to Paris and tried to gain admittance to the school. However, authorities at Ecole des Beaux-Arts were not encouraging to students who weren't French, and they certainly were not encouraging to women. Julia did not give up. The following years would <u>reveal</u> her to be full of determination. There was no <u>immediate</u> step she could take to get in the school—she had to wait months to take the exam. When she finally got to take the test, it required metric measurement. Julia was not used to the system and made a mathematical error. It cost her admission to the school.

She had to wait months to retake the entrance exam. This time, her work was quite good but not among the top students. She was denied admission again. Some of Julia's peers had <u>suspicions</u> that Julia's exam received a lower grade than it deserved. Others might have felt great anger and <u>indignation</u>, but Julia persevered. On her third attempt, she scored very well on the exam, and the school had to let her in.

Julia Morgan was the first woman to gain admittance to the Ecole des Beaux-Arts. She went on to have a great career, designing everything from humble <u>dwellings</u> for friends to the famous Hearst Castle in California.

1. Circle the phrase that tells how Morgan broke with <u>tradition</u>. Explain what a *tradition* is.

2. Underline the phrase that tells how it was clear that Julia had <u>intellectual</u> ability. Then, tell what *intellectual* is.

3. Underline the sentence that tells what <u>proposal</u> Maybeck made to Julia. Tell, what a *proposal* is.

4. Circle the words that tell what the years would <u>reveal</u> Julia to be. Then, tell what *reveal* means.

5. Underline the phrase that explains why there was no <u>immediate</u> step Julia could take. Then, tell what *immediate* means.

6. Underline the phrase that tells what <u>suspicions</u> Julia's peers had. Why do you think they might have had these *suspicions*?

7. Circle the word that gives a clue to the meaning of <u>indignation</u>. Explain why some might have felt *indignation* at the way the school treated Julia.

8. Underline one of the famous <u>dwellings</u> Julia designed. Describe the *dwellings* on your street.

from I Know Why the Caged Bird Sings by Maya Angelou
Reading Warm-up B

Read the following passage. Pay special attention to the underlined words. Then, read it again, and complete the activities. Use a separate sheet of paper for your written answers.

Gumption and determination are two words that might describe Thurgood Marshall. Marshall had an exciting life in law, doing everything from arguing cases before the U.S. Supreme Court to serving as a justice on that same prestigious court. Like nearly everyone, Marshall encountered setbacks in his career. In his case, however, they had nothing to do with personal failures. The setbacks occurred simply because he was black.

Thurgood Marshall was born in 1908 in Baltimore, Maryland. At that time in the nation's history, African Americans did not have the same opportunities as white people. In fact, African Americans were kept separate from whites in many places and were often treated with contempt. Marshall quickly comprehended that he needed to make the most of the opportunities he had within this environment. For his undergraduate work, Marshall enrolled at a historically black college, Lincoln University. In 1930, Marshall applied to law school at the nearby University of Maryland but was rejected because he was an African American. Undeterred, Marshall resumed his efforts to enter law school and was admitted to Howard University that same year.

With a law degree in hand, Marshall turned the tables on the University of Maryland. In his first major court case, he sued the university for failing to admit a black candidate named Donald Gaines Murray. Murray had studied at a good college and had an excellent academic record. Why, was he being rejected? Marshall was able to prove that it was because of Murray's race. What a sweet victory when the court found for Murray! Marshall had ended the university's restricting admissions policy.

There were many such victories ahead for Thurgood Marshall. In his most famous case, *Brown* vs. *Board of Education of Topeka*, he energetically led the fight against segregation. The case put an end to the legal basis for separating students by race in public schools.

1. Circle the word that tells what Marshall encountered. Then, explain what *encountered* means.

2. Circle the words that tell who was treated with contempt. Describe how people might act when they treat others with *contempt*.

3. Underline the phrase that tells what Marshall comprehended. Tell what *comprehended* means.

4. In your own words, explain the setback Marshall experienced before he resumed his efforts.

5. Circle the words that tell where Murray obtained an excellent academic record. Then, tell about your own *academic* record.

6. In what way was the university's admission policy restricting? Tell what *restricting* means.

7. Underline the words that tell what Marshall did energetically. Define *energetically*.

8. Now that you have read the article, give one example of Marshall's gumption.

Name _____ Date _____

"Occupation: Conductorette" *from* I Know Why the Caged Bird Sings by Maya Angelou
Writing About the Big Question

Is there a difference between reality and truth?

Big Question Vocabulary

comprehend	concrete	confirm	context	differentiate
discern	evaluate	evidence	improbable	objective
perception	reality	subjective	uncertainty	verify

A. *Use one or more words from the list above to complete each sentence.*

1. When she finally stood at the podium, the _____ of the event was so overwhelming she lost her voice.

2. Discrimination is so puzzling that it is difficult to _____.

3. Sometimes people will not face the truth even when presented with _____ facts.

B. *Follow the directions in responding to each of the items below.*

1. List two different times when you encountered an unexpected and harsh reality.

   _____

   _____

   _____

   _____

2. Write two sentences explaining one of the experiences you listed in your response, and describe how you felt. Use at least two of the Big Question vocabulary words.

   _____

   _____

   _____

C. *Complete the sentence below. Then, write a short paragraph in which you connect this experience to the Big Question.*

People who see the truth behind problems in society must decide whether to

   _____

   _____

   _____

   _____

"Occupation: Conductorette" from I Know Why the Caged Bird Sings by Maya Angelou
Literary Analysis: Author's Perspective

The **author's perspective** in a literary work includes the judgments, attitudes, and experiences the author brings to the subject.

- An author's perspective determines which details he or she includes. For example, a writer with firsthand experience of an event might report his or her own reactions as well as generally known facts. A writer with a positive view of a subject may emphasize its benefits.
- A work may combine several perspectives. For example, a writer may tell what it felt like to live through an event. In addition, the writer may express his or her present views of the experience.

In the following passage from "Occupation: Conductorette," Maya Angelou recalls her reaction to being told that African Americans could not work on streetcars.

I would like to claim an immediate fury which was followed by the noble determination to break the restricting tradition. But the truth is, my first reaction was one of disappointment.

The author tells how she reacted at the time of the incident, and she also expresses her current attitude about the event.

DIRECTIONS: *For each of the following passages, write the author's reactions to the incident at the time and her present-day attitude toward the event.*

1. The next three weeks were a honeycomb of determination with apertures for the days to go in and out. The Negro organizations to whom I appealed for support bounced me back and forth like a shuttlecock on a badminton court. Why did I insist on that particular job? Openings were going begging that paid nearly twice the money. The minor officials with whom I was able to win an audience thought me mad. Possibly I was.

Author's Reaction at the Time	Author's Attitude Today

2. "I am applying for the job listed in this morning's *Chronicle* and I'd like to be presented to your personnel manager." While I spoke in supercilious accents, and looked at the room as if I had an oil well in my own backyard, my armpits were being pricked by millions of hot pointed needles.

Author's Reaction at the Time	Author's Attitude Today

Name _____ Date _____

"Occupation: Conductorette" from I Know Why the Caged Bird Sings by Maya Angelou
Reading: Use Prior Knowledge to Make Predictions

As you read, **make predictions,** or educated guesses, about what will happen next based on your own experience and details in a text. **Verify,** or confirm, predictions by comparing the outcome you predicted to the actual outcome. **Revise,** or adjust, your predictions as you gather more information.

- **Strategy:** To help you make, verify, and revise predictions, **ask questions,** such as *Will the main character succeed?*
- For each question you ask, record your predictions and how they change with new information.

Read the following passage from "Occupation: Conductorette."

In the offices of the Market Street Railway Company, the receptionist seemed as surprised to see me there as I was surprised to find the interior dingy and the décor drab. Somehow I had expected waxed surfaces and carpeted floors. If I had met no resistance, I might have decided against working for such a poor-mouth-looking concern.

You can make a prediction about the rest of the selection by asking yourself a question such as this: *Will the receptionist make it impossible for the author to get a job?*

DIRECTIONS: *Make a prediction about each of the following passages from the text. Write the details from the text and from your own experiences that helped you make your prediction.*

1. I wouldn't move into the streetcar but stood on the ledge over the conductor, glaring. My mind shouted so energetically that the announcement made my veins stand out, and my mouth tighten into a prune.

   I WOULD HAVE THE JOB. I WOULD BE A CONDUCTORETTE.

   Predict: Will the author keep trying to get the job? _____

   _____

   Details from the text that support my prediction: _____

   _____

   My own experiences that support my prediction: _____

   _____

2. On my way out of the house one morning she said, "Life is going to give you just what you put in it. Put your whole heart in everything you do, and pray, then you can wait." Another time she reminded me that "God helps those who help themselves."

   Predict: Will the author take her mother's advice? _____

   _____

   Details from the text that support my prediction: _____

   _____

   My own experiences that support my prediction: _____

   _____

"Occupation: Conductorette" from I Know Why the Caged Bird Sings by Maya Angelou
Vocabulary Builder

Word List

dexterous   dingy   hypocrisy   indignation   self-sufficiency   supercilious

A. DIRECTIONS: *Think about the meaning of each italicized word. Then, answer the question.*

1. If a friend wants to prove her *self-sufficiency* to you, what will she probably say when you offer to help her?

   _____

2. If an actor has a *supercilious* attitude during an interview, what might the interviewer write about him?

   _____

3. What needs to be done to a room that is *dingy*?

   _____

4. If someone's remarks cause you to feel *indignation*, what might that person have said?

   _____

5. What could a vegetarian do that would reveal his or her *hypocrisy*?

   _____

6. Your friend is very *dexterous* in language arts, so what does she probably like to do?

   _____

B. WORD STUDY: The Latin prefix *super-* means "above." Provide an explanation for your answer to each question containing a word with the prefix *super-: superfluous, supersede, superscript*

1. If you have *superfluous* paper in your backpack, do you need to save it?

   _____

2. If you want a new piece of your artwork to *supercede* the picture on the wall, what will you do?

   _____

3. When you write a *superscript* on a journal entry, what have you done?

   _____

Name _____ Date _____

Enrichment: Create a Resume

Maya Angelou did not have a resume when she applied for the streetcar job, but nowadays even a beginning worker is expected to have one. A resume lists your accomplishments, from education to work experience to community service. It helps an employer see your strengths at a glance.

DIRECTIONS: *Fill out the following resume with your own information or with the information of an imaginary student. Try to emphasize your strengths (or the imaginary student's) as a worker and a citizen.*

Resume

Name: _____

Address: _____

_____

Education (most recent grade completed): _____

School Name: _____

Previous Employment (position and dates):

Name of Employer: _____ Dates Employed: _____

Responsibilities: _____

_____

Name of Employer: _____ Dates Employed: _____

Responsibilities: _____

_____

Community Service: _____

_____

Computer Skills: _____

Hobbies: _____

_____

References Available from (name and address of two reference providers): _____

_____

_____

Name _____ Date _____

from **Swimming to Antarctica** by Lynne Cox
"Occupation: Conductorette" *from* **I Know Why the Caged Bird Sings** by Maya Angelou
Integrate Language Skills: Grammar

Concrete and Abstract Nouns

A **concrete** noun is a word that names a specific person, place, or thing that can be seen or recognized through any of the five senses. An **abstract noun** is a word that names an idea, an action, a condition, or a quality that cannot be seen, heard, smelled, tasted, or touched. The following are examples of concrete and abstract nouns.

Concrete nouns: desk, window, hallway, Tom, closet, wife, Times Square
Abstract nouns: tomorrow, conscience, deceit, intention, fear

A. DIRECTIONS: *Read the following sentences from the excerpt from* Swimming to Antarctica *and from "Occupation Conductorette." Underline the nouns. Write* **C** *above each concrete noun and* **A** *above each abstract noun.*

1. I had mixed feelings about the test swim.

2. I stared across the icy water at Neko Harbor's beach and felt excitement building within me.

3. She comprehended the perversity of life, that in the struggle lies the joy.

4. I choked and felt a wave of panic rise within me.

5. The next three weeks were a honeycomb of determination with apertures for the days to go in and out.

B. Writing Application: *Write a brief paragraph in which you summarize Lynne Cox's swim. Use a combination of abstract and concrete nouns, including at least four of the following words:* cold, water, exhaustion, penguins, excitement, beach.

_____

_____

_____

_____

_____

_____

from **Swimming to Antarctica** by Lynne Cox
"Occupation: Conductorette" *from* **I Know Why the Caged Bird Sings** by Maya Angelou

Integrated Language Skills: Support for Writing a Description

DIRECTIONS: *A description should appeal to the senses. Fill in the following chart with details you might observe in Antarctica or on a streetcar in the 1940s that appeal to each of the five senses. Use precise words.*

Details I Might See	
Details I Might Smell	
Details I Might Hear	
Details I Might Touch	
Details I Might Taste	

Now, use the details you have collected to write your description.

from **Swimming to Antarctica** by Lynne Cox
"Occupation: Conductorette" *from* **I Know Why the Caged Bird Sings** by Maya Angelou
Integrated Language Skills: Support for Extend Your Learning

Research and Technology

On the following lines, write the skills you will be charting, the state of your skills as you begin your journal, and the state of your skills at the end of the two weeks.

My Skills: _____

At Beginning of Two Weeks: _____

_____

_____

At End of Two Weeks: _____

_____

_____

Research and Technology

On the following lines, write the job you will be observing. Write your reasons for wanting the job. At the end of two weeks, write whether you still feel the same way about the job, and explain why or why not.

The Job I Will Observe: _____

Why I Want the Job: _____

_____

How I Feel About the Job at End of Two Weeks: _____

_____

_____

_____

Name _____ Date _____

"Occupation: Conductorette" by Maya Angelou
Open-Book Test

Short Answer *Write your responses to the questions in this section on the lines provided.*

1. In the beginning of "Occupation: Conductorette," how does Maya Angelou plan to achieve *self-sufficiency?* What will her life be like if her plan fails?

_____

_____

2. The events Angelou describes in "Occupation: Conductorette" take place during World War II. Based on the details in the second paragraph, what can you conclude about the effect of the war on American workers?

_____

_____

3. In "Occupation: Conductorette," what first attracts Angelou to the job of streetcar conductor? What are her new motivations to get the job after her mother says, "They don't accept colored people on the streetcars"? List Angelou's initial and new motivations by writing brief phrases in the appropriate lines below. Then, describe how Angelou's overall perspective on the job changes after her mother's comment.

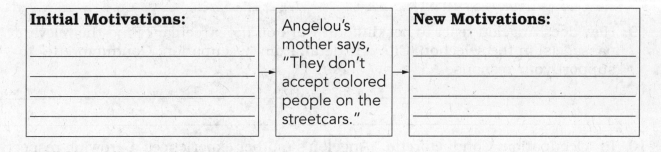

_____

4. In "Occupation: Conductorette," why does the receptionist at Market Street Railway Company tell Angelou that the company is only accepting applicants from agencies? Why does she also say that the personnel manager is out for the day?

_____

_____

_____

5. When Angelou goes to apply for the conductor job, she says, "If I had met no resistance, I might have decided against working for such a poor-mouth-looking concern." What can you predict about Angelou based on this statement from "Occupation: Conductorette"? Pay special attention to the words *If* and *might.*

_____

6. In "Occupation: Conductorette," what is Angelou's initial perspective on the Market Street Railway Company's receptionist? After she boards a streetcar, how does Angelou's attitude toward the receptionist change?

_____

_____

_____

_____

7. In "Occupation: Conductorette," as Angelou struggles to get the job of streetcar conductor, she finds that San Francisco becomes "alien and cold." Why does her perspective on the city change in this way?

_____

_____

_____

8. What details in "Occupation: Conductorette" help the reader predict that Angelou will get the job as a streetcar conductor? List two details.

_____

_____

_____

9. How does Angelou react to her difficult work on the streetcar? Find the relevant passage(s) in the selection. Cite one detail from "Occupation: Conductorette" to support your response.

_____

_____

10. In "Occupation: Conductorette," Angelou's mother experiences a growing respect and admiration for her daughter. Why? Think about Angelou's accomplishments.

_____

_____

Essay

Write an extended response to the question of your choice or to the question or questions your teacher assigns you.

11. Angelou states that as she tries for the job, "The struggle expanded. I was no longer in conflict only with the Market Street Railway but with the marble lobby of the building which housed its offices, and elevators and their operators." In a brief essay, explain what Angelou means. Against what obstacle is she really struggling in "Occupation: Conductorette"? Think about the larger social issues Angelou is facing.

12. In "Occupation: Conductorette," Angelou's mother gives Angelou advice in the form of aphorisms, or old sayings. Choose three of these aphorisms and write an essay discussing their relevance to Angelou's situation. Explain what the aphorisms mean and how they apply to Angelou. Then, state whether they help or harm her efforts in getting and keeping her job. Support your claims with details from the selection.

13. In "Occupation: Conductorette," Angelou lies about her age to get a job. Write an essay in which you evaluate her behavior. Do you consider her action completely wrong, or is it justified in any way? Examine both sides of the issue while stating your position. Use details from the selection to support your points.

14. **Thinking About the Big Question: What is the difference between reality and truth?** In "Occupation: Conductorette," Angelou describes her conversation with the streetcar-company receptionist as a "charade." In a brief essay, summarize this conversation and describe the false reality it creates. Then explain the truth behind this false reality. What is the main lie that Angelou and the receptionist are telling? Be sure to cite details from the selection to support your points.

Oral Response

15. Go back to question 3, 7, or 9 or to the question your teacher assigns you. Take a few minutes to expand your answer and prepare an oral response. Find additional details in "Occupation: Conductorette" that support your points. If necessary, make notes to guide your response.

"Occupation: Conductorette" *from* **I Know Why the Caged Bird Sings** by Maya Angelou
Selection Test A

Critical Reading *Identify the letter of the choice that best answers the question.*

____ 1. Why do you think Maya Angelou is so determined to be a streetcar conductor?

    A. She is desperate to find a way to make money.

    B. She knows her mother expects her to get the job.

    C. She wants to defy the powers that say she cannot have the job.

    D. She knows that the job will be a stepping-stone to a good career.

____ 2. Which question would help you predict that the author of "Occupation: Conductorette" would get the job as a conductor?

    A. Where would the author's streetcar go?

    B. What other jobs are available for the author?

    C. How much does the job pay?

    D. How much does the author want the job?

____ 3. Why doesn't Maya Angelou apply to work in an office?

    A. She has refused to learn office skills at school.

    B. African Americans were not allowed to work in offices at that time.

    C. Women were not allowed to work in offices at that time.

    D. She feels that office work will not pay enough.

____ 4. In "Occupation: Conductorette," what is the author's reaction to her mother's statement, "They don't accept colored people on the streetcars"?

    A. She is furious.

    B. She is disappointed.

    C. She is deeply hurt.

    D. She is amused.

____ 5. What can you predict about Maya Angelou based on this statement?

    If I had met no resistance, I might have decided against working for such a poor-mouth-looking company.

    A. She will give up trying to get the job.

    B. She will meet resistance and try even harder for the job.

    C. She will try to improve the looks of the company when she gets the job.

    D. She will quit the job after working for a few days.

____ 6. What does the receptionist tell Maya Angelou when she first asks about the conductor job?

A. The job is already filled.

B. They don't take women.

C. They don't take African Americans.

D. They only take applicants from agencies.

____ 7. How do Maya Angelou's feelings about the receptionist's treatment of her change over time?

A. She is angry at first, but then she begins to forgive the receptionist.

B. She is confused at first, but then she accepts the treatment.

C. She forgives the receptionist at first, but then she becomes very angry.

D. She tries to ignore the problem at first, but then she becomes depressed.

____ 8. Why does the author's attitude toward her city change, as the following passage from "Occupation: Conductorette" shows?

Downtown San Francisco became alien and cold, and the streets I had loved in a personal familiarity were unknown lanes that twisted with malicious intent.

A. She is visiting areas of the city she does not know.

B. She is struggling to learn all the streets of the city for her job.

C. She feels that the whole city has joined together to reject her.

D. She keeps getting lost when she goes to apply for jobs.

____ 9. Why does Maya Angelou's mother begin to admire her during the job search?

A. The mother believes her daughter will make a great conductor.

B. The mother is pleased that her daughter wants to make money.

C. The mother respects her daughter's perseverance and determination.

D. The mother wanted to be a conductor when she was a teenager.

____ 10. How does Maya Angelou react to her difficult work shifts on the streetcar?

A. She is resentful and often late.

B. She endures the hours ungraciously.

C. She ignores the difficulty and enjoys the job.

D. She is angry, but she struggles not to show it.

Vocabulary and Grammar

____ 11. Which place is most likely to look *dingy*?

    A. a new streetcar

    B. a run-down office

    C. a clean bedroom

    D. a marble lobby

____ 12. In which sentence is the underlined word an abstract noun?

    A. My intellectual <u>pride</u> had kept me from selecting typing.

    B. Mother was as <u>easy</u> as I had anticipated.

    C. I would go to work on the <u>streetcars</u> and wear a blue serge suit.

    D. The answer came to me with the suddenness of a <u>collision</u>.

Essay

13. In "Occupation: Conductorette," the author's mother gives her advice in the form of aphorisms, or old sayings. These include "Give it everything you've got," "Can't do is like Don't Care," "Nothing beats a trial but a failure," and "God helps those who help themselves." Determine what these aphorisms mean to the author. In an essay, explain whether the mother's comments help or harm the narrator's efforts to get the job. Support your claims with details from the selection.

14. The author's present-day perspective on her struggle for the conductor job in "Occupation: Conductorette" differs from the way she felt about the struggle at the time. In an essay, compare her current perspective to her perspective when the events happened. Use details from the selection to support your comparison.

15. **Thinking About the Big Question: Is there a difference between reality and truth?** In "Occupation: Conductorette," Angelou describes her conversation with the streetcar-company receptionist as a "charade." This means the conversation is just an act, and neither person is telling the truth. In a brief essay, summarize Angelou's conversation with the receptionist. Then explain why Angelou describes the conversation as a charade. What is the main lie that Angelou and the receptionist are telling? Provide details from the selection to support your points.

Name _____ Date _____

"Occupation: Conductorette" *from* **I Know Why the Caged Bird Sings** by Maya Angelou
Selection Test B

Critical Reading *Identify the letter of the choice that best completes the statement or answers the question.*

____ 1. In "Occupation: Conductorette," the author's mother does not try to prevent her from leaving school and getting a job because
   A. she badly needs the extra income.
   B. she knows the world and its rules are changing rapidly.
   C. she believes her daughter needs the experience.
   D. she believes her daughter should be part of the war effort.

____ 2. Which question will best help you predict whether Maya Angelou will keep trying after her first rejection for the job of conductor?
   A. What does the receptionist say to the narrator?
   B. What does the job mean to the narrator?
   C. What other jobs can the narrator get?
   D. What is the personnel manager's attitude?

____ 3. Maya Angelou is determined to get a job as a streetcar conductor because
   A. she desperately needs to make money for her education.
   B. she wants to please her mother by finding a job.
   C. she wants to defy the powers that say she cannot have that job.
   D. she knows that the job will be a stepping-stone to a good career.

____ 4. In "Occupation: Conductorette," when the author's mother says, "They don't accept colored people on the streetcars," what is the author's reaction?
   A. fury
   B. disappointment
   C. hurt
   D. amusement

____ 5. Based on the following statement from "Occupation: Conductorette," what prediction can you make about the narrator?
   > If I had met no resistance, I might have decided against working for such a poor-mouth-looking concern.

   A. She will give up trying to get the job.
   B. She will meet resistance and try even harder for the job.
   C. She will apply at a more prosperous-looking company.
   D. She will quit the job after a few days.

____ 6. What does this statement reveal about Maya Angelou's perspective today?
   > I would like to claim an immediate fury which was followed by the noble determination to break the restricting tradition. But the truth is, my first reaction was one of disappointment.

   A. She still feels the same disappointment she felt at the time.
   B. She now feels amused about the situation.
   C. She now feels she should have been angry about the situation.
   D. She now feels angry about her earlier feeling of disappointment.

____ 7. When Maya Angelou goes to organizations for help in getting a job at the streetcar company, they tell her she should
A. look for a different job.
B. insist on an interview.
C. go back to school.
D. ask for more money.

____ 8. In "Occupation: Conductorette," the narrator is forgiving of the receptionist at first. How does her attitude change over time?
A. She forgives the receptionist completely.
B. She becomes more and more confused.
C. She becomes very angry.
D. She becomes very depressed.

____ 9. Based on this passage from "Occupation: Conductorette," what do you predict will happen?
On my way out of the house one morning she said, "Life is going to give you just what you put in it. Put your whole heart in everything you do, and pray, then you can wait."
A. No matter what the author does, she won't get the job.
B. If the author keeps trying, she will get the job.
C. The author will have to wait for years before she gets the job.
D. The author will have to lie to get the job.

____ 10. The author's mother begins to admire her in "Occupation: Conductorette" because
A. the mother believes the daughter will make a great conductor.
B. the mother is pleased that her daughter wants to make money.
C. the mother respects her daughter's perseverance.
D. the mother once had a dream of being a conductor herself.

____ 11. How does Maya Angelou react to her difficult work shifts on the streetcar?
A. She is resentful and often late.
B. She endures the hours ungraciously.
C. She ignores the difficulty and enjoys the job.
D. She is angry, but she struggles not to show it.

____ 12. Why does the author's mother in "Occupation: Conductorette" drive her to work and pick her up after work?
A. She wants her daughter to get some rest.
B. She fears her daughter might get lost.
C. She is afraid of buses and streetcars.
D. She doesn't trust taxi drivers.

Vocabulary and Grammar

____ 13. Which of the following is an example of *hypocrisy*?
A. an environmentalist who litters
B. a person who is afraid of dogs
C. a thief who steals jewelry
D. an athlete who becomes a coach

_____ 14. Which character(s) in "Occupation: Conductorette" behave in a *supercilious* manner?
   A. the receptionist and the narrator
   B. the narrator's mother and the narrator
   C. the personnel manager
   D. the owner of the streetcar company

_____ 15. Maya Angelou is surprised to see that the streetcar office is *dingy*; she had thought it would be
   A. crowded.
   B. larger.
   C. elegant.
   D. dirtier.

_____ 16. Identify an abstract noun in the following sentence.

   The Negro organizations to whom I appealed for support bounced me back and forth like a shuttlecock on a badminton court.

   A. court
   B. badminton
   C. shuttlecock
   D. support

_____ 17. What number of concrete and abstract nouns does the following sentence include?

   Later my room had all the cheeriness of a dungeon and the appeal of a tomb.

   A. three concrete, two abstract
   B. two concrete, three abstract
   C. four concrete, one abstract
   D. two concrete, two abstract

Essay

18. In "Occupation: Conductorette," the author's perspective on her struggle for the job as conductor changes over time. In an essay, compare her perspective on the events at the time they happened with her perspective as an adult looking back. Use details from the selection to support your comparison.

19. Maya Angelou states that as she tried for the job, "The struggle expanded. I was no longer in conflict only with the Market Street Railway but with the marble lobby of the building which housed its offices, and elevators and their operators." What does she mean by this statement? In an essay, explain her meaning. What is she struggling against?

20. **Thinking About the Big Question: Is there a difference between reality and truth?** In "Occupation: Conductorette," Angelou describes her conversation with the streetcar-company receptionist as a "charade." In a brief essay, summarize this conversation and describe the false reality it creates. Then explain the truth behind this false reality. What is the main lie that Angelou and the receptionist are telling? Be sure to cite details from the selection to support your points.

Vocabulary Warm-up Word Lists

Study these words. Then, complete the activities that follow.

Word List A

critics [KRIT iks] *n.* people who write reviews of plays, books, or concerts
The critics hated the musical version of Shakespeare's *Macbeth*.

debut [day BYOO] *n.* first public appearance by a performer or group of performers
After its very first performance, the dance company got rave reviews for its debut.

enthusiastically [en thoo zee AS tik lee] *adv.* showing lots of excitement and interest
The crowd roared enthusiastically when the home team got a home run.

outstanding [out STAND ing] *adj.* very good
The concert pianist did an outstanding job of performing a complicated concerto.

prejudice [PREJ uh dis] *n.* unfair attitudes toward a group of people
It showed prejudice when a black woman was asked to sit at the back of a bus.

publicity [puhb LIS uh tee] *n.* information given out to get the public's attention
The newspaper headlines were great publicity for the candidate.

racial [RAY shuhl] *adj.* happening between races of people
There was no racial prejudice against minorities in the small town.

recordings [ri KAWR dingz] a permanent copy of sounds, such as a compact disc
Recordings of big-band music from the 1920s had lots of background noise.

Word List B

accommodations [uh kahm uh DAY shuhnz] *n.* places to stay
The hotel has accommodations for more than five hundred guests.

canopied [KAN uh peed] *adj.* covered or sheltered
Dense leaves created a dark cover across the canopied forest floor.

diesel [DEE zuhl] *adj.* of a kind of fuel used in some cars, trucks, and buses
The diesel engine on the bus made lots of noise.

financial [fi NAN shuhl] *adj.* having to do with money
The financial building housed banks, businesses, and government offices.

fumes [FYOOMZ] *n.* gas, smoke, or vapor
The fumes from the fire made my eyes burn.

pharmacy [FAHR muh see] *n.* store where prescription drugs are sold
The pharmacy was out of the medicine I needed.

privileged [PRIV uh lijd] *adj.* having the right or advantage
Leo was privileged to hear the famous author speak about her work.

spiritual [SPEER i choo uhl] *n.* religious folk music, usually African American
As I sang the spiritual with the choir, I felt my heart soar.

"Marian Anderson, Famous Concert Singer" by Langston Hughes
"Tepeyac" by Sandra Cisneros

Vocabulary Warm-up Exercises

Exercise A *Fill in each blank in the paragraph below with an appropriate word from Word List A. Use each word only once.*

The music [1] _____ for several newspapers and magazines wrote

[2] _____, praising the [3] _____ that had just been

released. The compact disc was another "best of" the Wiley Jones Trio and included

only the most [4] _____ selections from their long career.

[5] _____ surrounding the release of the CD mentioned the time when the

band made its [6] _____ in New York City. That was nearly eighty years

ago, and there was still a great deal of [7] _____ against people of color,

even in the music industry. The [8] _____ situation between minorities

and whites was worse then than it is today. Still, the music survived and can now be

enjoyed by a whole new generation.

Exercise B *For each item, use a word from Word List B to replace the underlined word or phrase without changing its meaning. Write your answers as complete sentences.*

Example: After we found <u>a place to stay</u>, we still needed to rent a car.
After we found <u>accommodations</u>, we still needed to rent a car.

1. Maria was <u>lucky</u> to have purchased the last ticket for the band's final concert.
   _____

2. I needed to get to the <u>place where prescription drugs are sold</u> before it closed to buy cough medicine.
   _____

3. When Cecee sang a <u>type of religious folk music</u>, she felt a strong connection with her ancestors.
   _____

4. The truck's engine ran on <u>special fuel</u>, which the truck driver needed to buy.
   _____

5. The <u>covered</u> bed was Nancy's favorite part of early American bedroom furniture.
   _____

6. The family works with their accountant on all <u>money</u> matters, including their taxes.
   _____

7. We keep a fan on to air out the <u>vapors</u> from the cleaning products.
   _____

Name _____ Date _____

"Marian Anderson, Famous Concert Singer" by Langston Hughes
"Tepeyac" by Sandra Cisneros
Reading Warm-up A

Read the following passage. Pay special attention to the underlined words. Then, read it again, and complete the activities. Use a separate sheet of paper for your written answers.

When James Reese Europe enlisted in the army during World War I, he didn't have plans to work as a musician. Fame followed him into the army, however. Europe had already gained <u>publicity</u> as a composer and a bandleader. The army wanted to use Europe's talents both to recruit other men and to boost morale overseas. Europe was hugely successful on both counts.

James Reese Europe had become famous before the war by organizing the first concert of African American musicians at Carnegie Hall in New York City. Europe's band made its <u>debut</u> in 1912, and the audience loved the show. Newspaper <u>critics</u> expressed their admiration for the talented bandleader.

When the United States entered World War I, Europe believed that it was important for black men to prove that they could be good soldiers. He put his career on hold. Europe became a lieutenant in the army and worked both as a bandleader and as the leader of a machine-gun company. Remarkably, Europe did this during a time when black servicemen had to deal with <u>racial</u> discrimination. Because of <u>prejudice</u> against African Americans, white men did not fight alongside black men. (Women didn't fight at all.) Europe didn't let this hold him back. He organized one of the greatest military bands in the history of the United States Army.

Those who got to hear this band felt that they were hearing a whole new kind of music. Europe brought jazz to military music, adding a syncopated rhythm to marching tunes. Audiences cheered <u>enthusiastically</u>. Everyone thought the band was <u>outstanding</u>. In fact, James Reese Europe was one of the first to popularize jazz in France.

After serving in combat, Europe made <u>recordings</u> with his military band. He seemed to be destined for a great career. Sadly, his life was cut short. Europe was murdered by one of his own band members soon after the war ended.

1. For which talents did Europe gain <u>publicity</u>? Circle the words. Then, tell what *publicity* is.

2. Circle the time when Europe's band made its <u>debut</u>. Then, explain what a *debut* is.

3. Underline the phrase that tells what <u>critics</u> thought about James Reese Europe. Then, tell what *critics* are.

4. Circle the words that tell who had to deal with <u>racial</u> discrimination. Do you believe that *racial* discrimination exists in the U. S. today? Explain.

5. Underline an example of what happened in the army due to <u>prejudice</u>. Tell what *prejudice* is.

6. Circle the word that tells what was done <u>enthusiastically</u>. Write about the last time you applauded *enthusiastically* for someone or something.

7. Rewrite the sentence with the word <u>outstanding</u>, replacing *outstanding* with a synonym.

8. Underline the phrase that tells who made <u>recordings</u> along with Europe. Name your three favorite *recordings* today.

"Marian Anderson, Famous Concert Singer" by Langston Hughes
"Tepeyac" by Sandra Cisneros
Reading Warm-up B

Read the following passage. Pay special attention to the underlined words. Then, read it again, and complete the activities. Use a separate sheet of paper for your written answers.

When Daniel thought of his grandfather, he felt underline{privileged} to be his grandson and lucky to know him. Because they lived three thousand miles apart, he hadn't been able to see Granddad in a few years. When he was little, though, he had spent a couple of months with his grandparents in Florida every summer.

Sometimes, Daniel snuggled into the old <u>canopied</u> bed that once belonged to his mother. More often, though, Granddad set up special sleeping <u>accommodations</u> for Daniel on the screened-in porch, where he put a cozy sleeping bag on an army cot. At night, Granddad and Grandma would sing an old <u>spiritual</u> to Daniel; he loved listening to the song as he drifted off to sleep.

Granddad liked to take Daniel on errands in his old car with the <u>diesel</u> engine. Though the diesel <u>fumes</u> sometimes made Daniel feel queasy as he sat in the backseat, he never said no to these outings. Granddad might take Daniel to the grocery store, letting him pick out some favorite foods while he rode in the cart. He might take Daniel to the library, where he filled his arms with books for both of them; or he might take Daniel to the <u>pharmacy</u> where he got his own medicine. He let Daniel sit on the floor and play with toys while he chatted with the pharmacist and waited for his prescriptions. Of course, Daniel was too old to sit on the floor playing with toys, but he remembered those times fondly.

Granddad taught him the names of plants and trees and how to fly a kite. He tried to teach Daniel to swing a bat, too, but Daniel never got very good at that. Grand-dad didn't mind. Often they would just take walks together, and they had wonderful talks.

Now that Granddad was sick, Daniel wanted to see him again more than anything. Though he didn't usually ask for money, he really hoped his parents had the <u>financial</u> means to help him get there. He needed to have a few more wonderful talks with Granddad.

1. Underline the words that tell in what way Daniel felt <u>privileged</u>. Then, tell what *privileged* means.

2. Describe a <u>canopied</u> bed. What else can be *canopied*?

3. Underline the words that tell about Daniel's sleeping <u>accommodations</u>. Then, explain what *accommodations* are.

4. What particular kind of song is a <u>spiritual</u>? Why might a *spiritual* make a good lullaby?

5. Underline the phrase that tells where <u>diesel</u> is used. Explain what *diesel* is.

6. Write a sentence about <u>fumes</u> that you have been exposed to.

7. Underline the phrase that tells what Granddad got at the <u>pharmacy</u>. Then, tell what a *pharmacy* is.

8. Circle the word that helps explain "<u>financial</u> means." Why would Daniel's parents need *financial* means to send him to Florida?

"Marian Anderson, Famous Concert Singer" by Langston Hughes
"Tepeyac" by Sandra Cisneros

Writing About the Big Question

Is there a difference between reality and truth?

Big Question Vocabulary

comprehend	concrete	confirm	context	differentiate
discern	evaluate	evidence	improbable	objective
perception	reality	subjective	uncertainty	verify

A. *Circle the word or phrase that is closer in meaning to the underlined word.*

1. **evaluate:** judge; increase

2. **verify:** to make real; to prove

3. **discern:** to see something concealed; to reject

4. **comprehend:** to capture; to understand

5. **uncertainty:** being in doubt; unaltered

B. *Follow the directions in responding to each of the items below.*

1. Describe a memory from childhood that you believed was real until you later found out it was not a true memory.

_____

_____

_____

_____

2. In one or two sentences, explain how the memory you described above was different from the truth.

_____

_____

_____

_____

C. *Complete the sentence below. Then, write a short paragraph in which you connect this experience to the Big Question.*

One person's idea of the truth can be challenged when _____

_____

_____

_____

Name _____ Date _____

"Marian Anderson, Famous Concert Singer" by Langston Hughes
"Tepeyac" by Sandra Cisneros
Literary Analysis: Style

A writer's **style** consists of the features that make his or her expression of ideas distinctive. Writers may write on the same topic, or even tell the same story, in very different styles. Two important elements of style are diction and syntax.

Diction, or word choice, is the type of words the writer uses. One writer might like to use everyday words, while another might prefer scholarly ones. In "Marian Anderson," for example, Langston Hughes writes that the singer *broke* her ankle rather than *fractured* it. This word choice reflects the author's straightforward style.

Syntax is the way an author arranges words into sentences. A single sentence might express one distinct thought, or it might express several related ones. In "Tepeyac," Cisneros weaves words and phrases together to form rich, rolling sentences that overflow with ideas and images.

A. DIRECTIONS: *Read each of the following passages. Then, answer the questions.*

from "Tepeyac" by Sandra Cisneros

Green iron gates that arabesque and scroll like the initials of my name, familiar whine and clang, familiar lacework of ivy growing over and between except for one small clean square for the hand of the postman whose face I have never seen, up the twenty-two steps we count out loud together— *uno, dos, tres*—to the supper of *sopa de fideo* and *carne guisada*. . . .

from "Marian Anderson, Famous Concert Singer" by Langston Hughes

Marian Anderson's mother was a staunch church worker who loved to croon the hymns of her faith about the house, as did the aunt who came to live with them when Marian's father died. Both parents were from Virginia. Marian's mother had been a schoolteacher there, and her father a farm boy.

1. **A.** Which author's style is more direct and down-to-earth? _____

   B. Identify two words in the passage that contribute to this style. _____

   _____

2. **A.** Which author's style is more descriptive and poetic? _____

   B. Identify two words in the passage that contribute to this style. _____

   _____

   _____

3. Compare the kinds of sentences each author uses. Consider sentence length and the number of ideas expressed in each sentence. _____

   _____

   _____

B. DIRECTIONS: *A writer's style can be affected by his or her **purpose,** or reason for writing. Choose one of the works in this pair. On a separate sheet of paper, state one purpose the author might have had for writing the work. Explain how this purpose influenced the author's style.*

"Marian Anderson, Famous Concert Singer" by Langston Hughes
"Tepeyac" by Sandra Cisneros
Vocabulary Builder

Word List

arabesques	canopied	debut	dimpled
irretrievable	lucrative	repertoire	staunch

A. DIRECTIONS: *Complete each sentence so that it makes sense.*

1. Isabel received two job offers. She decided to accept the more *lucrative* one because
   _____

2. I am glad our patio is *canopied* because _____
   _____

3. The toddler's *repertoire* consisted of _____
   _____

4. The *irretrievable* balloon _____

5. A *staunch* fan of the football team, Jackson _____
   _____

6. An hour before her *debut*, Ava felt _____ because _____
   _____

7. Her handwriting looked like a series of *arabesques*. It_____
   _____

8. My little brother's face becomes *dimpled* when he_____
   _____

B. DIRECTIONS: *Circle the letter of the word or phrase closest in meaning to the vocabulary word.*

1. canopied
   A. folded   B. shredded   C. covered   D. decorated

2. staunch
   A. firm   B. hostile   C. disappointed   D. cheerful

3. repertoire
   A. old clothes   B. small books   C. odd beliefs   D. ready songs

4. irretrievable
   A. unclear   B. lost   C. astonishing   D. careful

"Marian Anderson, Famous Concert Singer" by Langston Hughes
"Tepeyac" by Sandra Cisneros
Support for Writing to Compare Literary Works

Before you draft your essay evaluating the effectiveness of each author's style, complete the following graphic organizer.

> **Cisneros's Purpose:**
> _____

Examples of Style Elements That Help Achieve Purpose

Diction:

Syntax:

Examples of Style Elements That Get in the Way

Diction:

Syntax:

> **Hughes's Purpose:**
> _____

Examples of Style Elements That Help Achieve Purpose

Diction:

Syntax:

Examples of Style Elements That Get in the Way

Diction:

Syntax:

Now, use your notes to write an essay that evaluates how well each author's style advances his or her purpose.

"Marian Anderson, Famous Concert Singer" by Langston Hughes
"Tepeyac" by Sandra Cisneros
Open-Book Test

Short Answer *Write your responses to the questions in this section on the lines provided.*

1. Langston Hughes opens "Marian Anderson, Famous Concert Singer" with an account of Anderson's childhood. What types of support did Anderson receive from her community as she grew up? Provide two examples to back up your answer.

   _____

   _____

   _____

2. According to "Marian Anderson, Famous Concert Singer," what are two problems that Anderson had to overcome to become a famous singer?

   _____

   _____

   _____

3. In "Marian Anderson, Famous Concert Singer," Hughes describes a time when the Daughters of the American Revolution refused to let Anderson sing at Constitution Hall. What does this incident and its aftermath show about American culture in 1939?

   _____

   _____

   _____

4. In "Tepeyac," Sandra Cisneros recalls evening walks home from the market with her grandfather. She uses a great deal of detail to describe these walks. What does the level of detail suggest about Cisneros's memories?

   _____

   _____

5. In "Tepeyac," is Cisneros's style more like that of a news report or that of a journal entry? Explain your answer.

   _____

   _____

   _____

6. Hughes's diction, or word choice, in "Marian Anderson, Famous Concert Singer" is very different from Cisneros's diction in "Tepeyac." Whose diction is simpler and more like everyday speech? Explain your answer briefly.

   _____

   _____

7. What is similar about the topics of "Marian Anderson, Famous Concert Singer" and "Tepeyac"? How are the authors' attitudes toward their subjects similar?

_____

_____

_____

8. Compare and contrast the kinds of details that the authors supply in "Marian Anderson, Famous Concert Singer" and "Tepeyac." How does each type of detail reveal the author's purpose? Fill in the chart. Then, on the lines below, explain how the two authors' overall purposes are different.

	Type of Detail	**Author's Purpose**
Hughes		
Hughes		
Cisneros		
Cisneros		

_____

_____

9. Why is the phrase "wandering in a maze" a good description of Cisneros's syntax in "Tepeyac"? Does the phrase also apply to Hughes's syntax in "Marian Anderson, Famous Concert Singer"? Why or why not?

_____

_____

_____

_____

10. When Anderson made her *debut* in Berlin, Germany, had she sung in that city before? Use your knowledge of the meaning of the word *debut* and information in "Marian Anderson, Famous Concert Singer" to help explain your answer.

_____

_____

Essay

Write an extended response to the question of your choice or to the question or questions your teacher assigns you.

11. Hughes and Cisneros, the authors of "Marian Anderson, Famous Concert Singer" and "Tepeyac," use very different styles. In a brief essay, discuss whose style you liked most and why. Write about the author's diction, or word choice, as well as his or her syntax, or sentence structure. Also consider the author's purpose in writing the selection. Provide examples from the selection to support your response.

12. Hughes and Cisneros, the authors of "Marian Anderson, Famous Concert Singer" and "Tepeyac," use unique styles that help to achieve a central purpose. In a brief essay, identify each author's main purpose. Then, describe each author's style and tell how it helps the author achieve that purpose.

13. Imagine that Langston Hughes were telling the life story of the grandfather in "Tepeyac." How would his style be different from Cisneros's? Which details would he probably change or eliminate, and what kinds of details would he probably add? Answer these questions in an essay. Demonstrate your understanding of both Hughes's and Cisneros's styles.

14. **Thinking About the Big Question: What is the difference between reality and truth?** In a brief essay, apply the Big Question to either of the two selections. If you write about "Marian Anderson, Famous Concert Singer," contrast the truth of Anderson's achievement with the reality of opportunities for many African Americans in Anderson's day. If you write about "Tepeyac," contrast the truth that Cisneros realizes in the end of the selection with the childhood reality that she describes early in the selection. Provide details from the selection to support your points.

Oral Response

15. Go back to question 1, 2, or 9 or to the question your teacher assigns you. Take a few minutes to expand your answer and prepare an oral response. Find additional details in "Marian Anderson, Famous Concert Singer" and/or "Tepeyac" that support your points. If necessary, make notes to guide your oral response.

"Marian Anderson, Famous Concert Singer" by Langston Hughes
"Tepeyac" by Sandra Cisneros
Selection Test A

Critical Reading *Identify the letter of the choice that best answers the question.*

____ 1. Which is the best summary of "Tepeyac"?
  A. The author remembers wooden booths and shoeshine stands in the Tepeyac marketplace.
  B. The author recalls a boy named Arturo closing up the hardware shop.
  C. The author remembers evening walks home with her grandfather through the marketplace.
  D. The author recalls climbing twenty-two steps to her childhood apartment.

____ 2. In "Tepeyac," what is the author's main feeling toward her grandfather?
  A. fear
  B. affection
  C. concern
  D. anger

____ 3. When Cisneros returns to her old neighborhood as an adult, what does she realize?
  A. that her childhood was precious
  B. that her grandfather was dishonest
  C. that her home never existed
  D. that Tepeyac is still beautiful

____ 4. Reading "Tepeyac" is *most* like which of these?
  A. wandering in a maze
  B. following a recipe
  C. playing a game
  D. viewing a photograph

____ 5. In "Marian Anderson, Famous Concert Singer," why does the author describe Anderson's youth?
  A. to show how popular church music was at that time
  B. to show why Anderson became a singer rather than a violinist
  C. to show why African Americans had not yet succeeded as concert singers
  D. to show how Anderson's community supported her growth as a singer

____ 6. Which is true of Marian Anderson's career?

    A. She succeeded first in Europe, then in America.

    B. She never succeeded in America.

    C. She succeeded first in America, then in Europe.

    D. She never succeeded in Europe.

____ 7. Why were so many Americans angry when Marian Anderson was not allowed to sing at Constitution Hall?

    A. because Anderson was such a famous singer

    B. because the previous owners of the hall had opened its doors to everyone

    C. because the decision went against national values

    D. because the story made newspaper headlines

____ 8. What is the main idea of "Marian Anderson, Famous Concert Singer"?

    A. Concert performers are the most talented singers.

    B. Musical talent is not limited to a single race.

    C. Europeans are the best judges of good music.

    D. A good manager is the key to success in the concert business.

____ 9. Which word in this sentence is the best example of Hughes's "ordinary folks" diction?

    She propped herself in a curve of the piano before the curtains parted, and gave her New York concert standing on one foot!

    A. *propped*

    B. *the*

    C. *New York*

    D. *standing*

____ 10. Which idea is expressed in both "Tepeyac" and "Marian Anderson, Famous Concert Singer"?

    A. It is painful to lose someone dear to you.

    B. Our actions should match our beliefs.

    C. There is nothing to learn from the distant past.

    D. Childhood helps shape who we later become.

____ 11. What do "Tepeyac" and "Marian Anderson, Famous Concert Singer" have in common?

    A. They are both written in a simple, direct style.

    B. They both tell about someone important to the author.

    C. They both describe the author's childhood neighborhood.

    D. They are both addressed to a single person.

_____ 12. How are Cisneros's sentences different from Hughes's?

    A. They are generally shorter.

    B. They are simpler.

    C. They contain fewer ideas.

    D. They are generally longer.

_____ 13. Which phrase is the best example of "ordinary folks" diction?

    A. comes down in an ink of Japanese blue

    B. born in a little red brick house

    C. establish a trust fund

    D. familiar whine and clang

Vocabulary

_____ 14. What does the word *staunch* mean in the following sentence?

    Marian Anderson's mother was a staunch church worker who loved to croon the hymns of her faith. . . .

    A. loyal   C. harsh

    B. casual   D. sad

_____ 15. What does the word *dimpled* mean in the following sentence?

    I take Abuelito's hand, fat and dimpled in the center like a valentine, and we walk past the basilica. . . .

    A. decorated   C. dented

    B. red   D. pointed

Essay

16. The authors of "Tepeyac" and "Marian Anderson, Famous Concert Singer" use very different styles. In a short essay, explain what style is. Then, tell what you liked most about each author's style.

17. In their essays, the authors of "Tepeyac" and "Marian Anderson, Famous Concert Singer" paint a portrait of another person. In a short essay, describe each portrait. Whom do the portraits show? What does each author want the reader to know about his or her subject? Use examples from each essay to support your ideas.

18. **Thinking About the Big Question: Is there a difference between reality and truth?** Sometimes people miss out on the truth because they are living in their own version of reality. According to Langston Hughes's "Marian Anderson, Famous Concert Singer," Anderson achieved greatness as a singer even though she faced unfair treatment as an African American. However, the reality in Anderson's time was that many African Americans did not have the same opportunities as white people. In an essay, explain why you think Anderson was able to succeed even though she faced the reality of society's unfair treatment. Provide details from the selection to support your points.

"Marian Anderson, Famous Concert Singer" by Langston Hughes
"Tepeyac" by Sandra Cisneros
Selection Test B

Critical Reading *Identify the letter of the choice that best answers the question.*

____ 1. Which is the best summary of "Tepeyac" by Sandra Cisneros?
A. The author compares the Tepeyac of today with the Tepeyac of long ago.
B. The author catalogues the items her grandfather sold in his shop in Tepeyac.
C. The author recalls evening walks home with her grandfather through Tepeyac.
D. The author describes the vendors who sell their wares in the Tepeyac marketplace.

____ 2. Which is the best interpretation of this sentence from "Tepeyac"?
Who would've guessed, after all this time, it is me who will remember when everything else is forgotten, you who took with you to your stone bed something irretrievable. . . .
A. The author is angry that her grandfather died without confiding in her.
B. The author is surprised that her grandfather, who so impressed her, now lives only in her own memories.
C. The author's grandfather regrets that Cisneros does not appreciate her childhood.
D. The author's grandfather does not understand Cisneros's need to remember.

____ 3. When Cisneros returns to Tepeyac as an adult, her old neighborhood
A. has become foreign to her.
B. is now a busy marketplace.
C. is just as she remembers it.
D. has become a thriving suburb.

____ 4. Cisneros's style in "Tepeyac" is most like that of
A. a movie script.
B. an e-mail message.
C. a news report.
D. a journal entry.

____ 5. Which word best describes both Cisneros's syntax and her memories themselves?
A. diluted
B. unforgiving
C. wandering
D. generous

____ 6. The central idea of "Marian Anderson, Famous Concert Singer" is that
A. concert performers are the best trained musical vocalists.
B. publicity is the key to success in the music business.
C. Europeans are the best judges of good music.
D. musical talent knows no racial or national boundary.

____ 7. Why does Hughes begin "Marian Anderson" with a discussion of black singers?
A. to describe the development of black music in America
B. to examine major influences on Marian Anderson's singing style
C. to compare different forms of black musical expression
D. to explain the significance of Marian Anderson's achievements

____ 8. The author's account of Marian Anderson's youth in Philadelphia shows
   A. why African Americans had not yet succeeded on the concert stage.
   B. how Anderson's community supported her musical development.
   C. why Anderson became a singer rather than a violinist.
   D. how popular church music was at that time in history.

____ 9. Which of the following best explains why so many Americans were angered when the Daughters of the American Revolution refused to allow Marian Anderson to sing?
   A. Anderson was a world-renowned vocal artist.
   B. Previous proprietors of the hall had made it available to everybody.
   C. The action violated basic national values.
   D. The Daughters of the American Revolution was not a popular organization.

____ 10. Which word in this sentence best shows Hughes's "ordinary folks" diction?
   She propped herself in a curve of the piano before the curtains parted, and gave her New York concert standing on one foot!
   A. *propped*
   B. *piano*
   C. *New York*
   D. *one*

____ 11. In which sentence is Hughes's style poetic?
   A. "When Marian Anderson again returned to America, she was a seasoned artist."
   B. "'Ah,' he said, "a Negro singer with a Swedish name! . . ."
   C. "A coast-to-coast American tour followed."
   D. "Sometimes her neighbors across the fields can hear the rich warm voice that covers three octaves . . . ."

____ 12. What do the essays by Hughes and Cisneros have in common?
   A. They are both written in a style that is simple and direct.
   B. They both recall the life of someone important to the author.
   C. They both lament the difficulties of life in the mid-1900s.
   D. They are both written for a small, specialized audience.

____ 13. Which idea do Cisneros and Hughes both explore in their essays?
   A. It is painful to lose someone dear to you.
   B. We should take actions that reflect our deepest convictions.
   C. There is little value in attempting to recall the distant past.
   D. Our childhood experiences help shape who we later become.

____ 14. What is one purpose Hughes and Cisneros both had for writing their essays?
   A. to express intense emotions
   B. to move their readers to action
   C. to preserve a piece of history
   D. to celebrate racial differences

_____ 15. What is a major difference between Hughes's and Cisneros's sentences?
  A. Cisneros's are more complex.
  B. Cisneros uses traditional syntax.
  C. Hughes's are longer.
  D. Hughes experiments with syntax.

_____ 16. The first word in each pair below is from Cisneros's essay, and the second is from Hughes's. Which pair could best be described as examples of "everyday" diction?
  A. *basilica, stereotype*
  B. *paintbrushes, cubby holes*
  C. *Juan Diego, "Black Patti"*
  D. *arabesque, schoolteacher*

Vocabulary

_____ 17. When Cisneros remembers the "red-*canopied* thrones of the shoeshine stands," what is she remembering?
  A. painted statues
  B. brightly lit booths
  C. raised benches
  D. covered seats

_____ 18. Cisneros's writing style could best be compared to
  A. a *repertoire.*
  B. something *irretrievable.*
  C. *arabesques.*
  D. something *lucrative.*

Essay

19. Cisneros and Hughes both use a style that helps them achieve their central purpose. In an essay, identify each author's main purpose. Then, describe each author's style and tell how it helps the author accomplish that purpose.

20. Analyze your response to each work by answering the following questions: Which aspect of each author's style did you most enjoy? Which aspect of each author's style did you least enjoy? Which essay appealed more to your intellect, and which to your emotions? How do you explain this difference?

21. **Thinking About the Big Question: Is there a difference between reality and truth?** In a brief essay, apply the Big Question to either of the two selections. If you write about "Marian Anderson, Famous Concert Singer," contrast the truth of Anderson's achievement with the reality of opportunities for many African Americans in Anderson's day. If you write about "Tepeyac," contrast the truth that Cisneros realizes in the end with the childhood reality that she describes early in the selection. Provide details from the selection to support your points.

Name _____ Date _____

Writing Workshop
Autobiographical Narrative

Prewriting: Gathering Details

Create a character and setting chart by thinking about the people and places you will describe in your story and listing your ideas in the following chart.

Settings Jot down physical details to use in your descriptions.	**Characters** Include facts like name, age, and physical descriptions, and note personality, habits, and this person's role in the story.

Drafting: Shaping Your Writing

Use the following plot diagram to list the events of your story in a logical order.

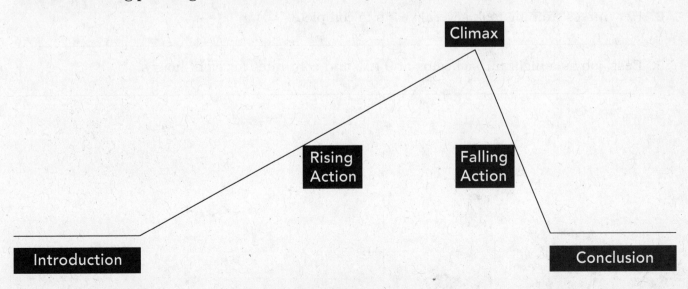

Writing Workshop
Autobiographical Narrative: Integrating Grammar Skills

Using Possessive Nouns Correctly

Possessive nouns show possession or ownership. They actually function as adjectives in sentences, modifying other nouns. Follow these rules to form possessive nouns:

- For singular nouns, add an apostrophe and *s*.
  the book of my sister ⇒my *sister's* book
  the signature of her boss ⇒her *boss's* signature
- For plural nouns that end in *s* or *es*, add just an apostrophe.
  the performance of the dancers ⇒the *dancers'* performance
  the bells of the churches ⇒the *churches'* bells
- For plural nouns that do not end in *s*, add an apostrophe and *s*.
  the choice of the people ⇒the *people's* choice
  the clothing department of the women ⇒the *women's* clothing department

Identifying Correct Possessive Nouns

A. DIRECTIONS: *Circle the correct form of the noun in parentheses.*

1. (James's, Jameses) cousin Ali got tickets for Saturday.
2. Ali and James are going to see the (women's, womens') soccer team.
3. The (coaches, coaches') uniforms are the same colors.

Fixing Incorrect Possessive Nouns

B. DIRECTIONS: *On the lines provided, rewrite these sentences using possessive nouns correctly.*

1. My sister Bess works at a childrens' hospital near the city's oldest park.

   _____

2. Her nurses training took several year's to complete.

   _____

3. Bess' job as a night nurse begins at 9 P.M. and continues for eight hour's.

   _____

Unit 1: Fiction and Nonfiction
Benchmark Test 1

MULTIPLE CHOICE

Literary Analysis: Plot and Foreshadowing

1. Which part of a story introduces the characters and setting?
   A. exposition
   B. rising action
   C. falling action
   D. resolution

Read the selection. Then, answer the questions that follow.

(1) In the summer, Camille went to the town pool with her little brother Fred nearly every day. (2) Few adults used the pool—except for Mrs. Ramos. (3) She came to the pool almost daily, but always alone. (4) Mrs. Ramos complained if Camille and her friends splashed too much when diving; she complained when Fred and his friends made too much noise. (5) In revenge, Camille made fun of Mrs. Ramos behind her back. (6) One day, Fred, who was still learning how to swim, was walking by the deep end of the pool and slipped, falling in. (7) Camille heard one of Fred's friends shout for help, so she ran over. (8) Mrs. Ramos, however, had already jumped out of her chair and dived into the pool—even before the lifeguard saw what had happened! (9) Mrs. Ramos plunged through the water with ease, grabbed Fred, and pulled him to the surface. (10) Camille helped lift her brother out of the water. (11) Fred was shaken, but otherwise fine. (12) As she wrapped the little boy in a towel, Camille knew that she would never again make fun of Mrs. Ramos.

2. Around what conflict do the events of the story center?
   A. Camille's struggle to take care of her brother
   B. Camille's struggle with Mrs. Ramos
   C. Fred's struggle to learn to swim
   D. Mrs. Ramos's struggle to understand noisy kids

3. Which part of the plot is sentence 4?
   A. the rising action
   B. the climax
   C. the falling action
   D. the resolution

4. Where does the climax of the story take place?
   A. in sentences 1 through 4
   B. in sentences 4 through 5
   C. in sentences 5 through 6
   D. in sentences 6 through 9

5. What key change or insight does the resolution of the story contain?
   A. Mrs. Ramos realizes that she has been too grouchy.
   B. Fred learns not to walk too close to the pool.
   C. Camille revises her opinion of Mrs. Ramos.
   D. Camille realizes that she needs to pay more attention to her brother.

Literary Analysis: Author's Perspective; Style

6. In a literary work, what is the author's perspective?
   A. the structure in which the author organizes ideas or events
   B. the artful language that the author chooses to use
   C. the particular sound of the author's words on the page
   D. the judgments, attitudes, and experiences the author brings to the subject

Read this excerpt from an autobiographical essay. Then, answer the questions that follow.

When I was a young girl, my favorite relative was my mother's father, whom I called Abuelito. We talked about all sorts of things—he in his broken English and me in my not-so-perfect Spanish. Still, I did not talk to him as much as I could have. I was busy with school, with sports, and with friends. He seemed to understand; he always encouraged me to enjoy life. Now Abuelito is long gone—he died more than twenty years ago. I regret not having spent more time with him, and I wish I knew more about his life.

7. How does the author's perspective change in this selection?
   A. It moves from a child's perspective to an adult's.
   B. It moves from an adult's perspective to a child's.
   C. It moves from a beginner's perspective to an expert's.
   D. It moves from an expert's perspective to a beginner's.

8. What did the author rely on most to create this selection?
   A. firsthand experience   C. technical knowledge
   B. historical research   D. fictional events

Answer the following question.

9. How would your diction on a postcard to a friend be different from your diction in a letter to the editor of a local newspaper?
   A. The diction on the postcard would be less formal and might contain slang.
   B. The diction on the postcard would be more flowery and poetic.
   C. The diction on the postcard would be more precise and technical.
   D. The diction on the postcard would be more formal and polite.

Reading Skill: Make Predictions

10. Which of the following strategies would most effectively help you make predictions while reading?
   A. Make an outline of the work.
   B. Use context to determine the meanings of unfamiliar words.
   C. Read each word closely, being careful not to skip any details.
   D. Combine details in the text with your own knowledge and experiences.

11. What is the best way to verify predictions you make when reading?
    A. change your predictions as you gather more information
    B. ask a classmate if your predictions seem valid
    C. compare the outcome you predicted to the actual outcome
    D. consider your background knowledge and experiences

Read the passage, and answer the questions that follow.

(1) The mountain was volcanic, but it had not erupted for over a hundred years. (2) Then, one morning in March, there was a great rumbling beneath it. (3) Seismographs registered a 4.1 magnitude earthquake. (4) A week later, a plume of ash spouted from the mountain. (5) Then, a few days later, an explosion blasted a wide crater in the mountain's peak. (6) People fled their homes, expecting a full-fledged eruption at any time. (7) They were mistaken. (8) The mountain quieted down, although smoke sometimes streamed from the summit. (9) New-fallen snow quickly melted at the peak. (10) Surprisingly, tourism is now thriving in towns near the foot of the volcano.

12. What prediction is most logical to make after reading sentence 2?
    A. People will want to visit the volcano to take pictures.
    B. People will be concerned, thinking that the volcano will erupt.
    C. People will try to ignore the volcano.
    D. People will think that the dormant volcano is about to die out.

13. What prediction would you most likely make after reading only as far as sentence 5?
    A. There will be a full-fledged volcanic eruption on the mountain.
    B. People will ignore the danger signs and will therefore be killed when the volcano erupts.
    C. There will not be a full-fledged volcanic eruption on the mountain.
    D. People will heed the danger signs and be annoyed when the volcano fails to erupt.

14. What background knowledge would be most helpful in predicting what happens later in the narrative?
    A. knowledge about the behavior of volcanoes
    B. knowledge about earthquakes
    C. knowledge about the causes of snow on high mountains
    D. knowledge about the weather

15. Which sentence makes you revise your initial prediction about what is going to happen to the mountain?
    A. sentence 5   B. sentence 6   C. sentence 7   D. sentence 9

16. If the passage were to include an eleventh sentence, which of the following choices would most logically follow sentence 10?
    A. Volcanoes are beautiful, but dangerous.
    B. Science will never help us understand volcanoes.
    C. Perhaps it is simply human nature to ignore danger when there is a chance to turn a profit.
    D. People tried to plant crops in the rich volcanic soil, but their efforts were unsuccessful.

Reading Skill: Analyze Structure and Format

17. What is the usual function of a main heading?
    A. It provides an overview of content.
    B. It entertains readers with inessential information.
    C. It calls attention to supporting details.
    D. It communicates visually through illustration.

18. What is the usual function of a subheading?
    A. It provides a visual illustration of what the text says in words.
    B. It identifies and introduces a specific aspect of the main topic.
    C. It introduces a topic unrelated to the main topic.
    D. It calls attention to a small detail within a text.

Vocabulary: Roots and Prefixes

19. The root -cred- means "believe." In the following sentence, what does the word *credible* mean?

    The jury thought the witness was credible because he remembered many details from the crime scene.

    A. unbelievable   C. reliable
    B. virtuous   D. amazing

20. The word root -strict- means "confine" or "squeeze." Using this knowledge, what can you conclude is an example of something that *constricts* movement?
    A. an empty warehouse
    B. loose, baggy clothing
    C. a comfortable pair of shoes
    D. a cast set around a broken foot

21. The words *progress, propel,* and *project* share the prefix *pro-*. Using this knowledge, choose the answer that best states the meaning of *pro-*.
    A. small   C. equal
    B. forward   D. within

22. The prefix *super-* means "above." Using this knowledge, determine the meaning of *supervise* in the following sentence.

    Li's summer job was to supervise the morning activities of third-grade campers.

    A. oversee   C. develop
    B. understand   D. improve

Grammar: Nouns

23. How many proper nouns are in the following sentence?

Last May, Mark and his parents visited a museum in New York City.

    A. two   **C.** four

    B. three   **D.** five

24. In which of the following sentences is the capitalization of nouns correct?

    A. In most States, students start School in September, but in Arizona, they start in August.

    B. In most states, students start school in September, but in Arizona, they start in August.

    C. In most states, students start school in September, but in arizona, they start in August.

    D. In most States, students start school in september, but in Arizona, they start in August.

25. Which of the following words is a concrete noun?

    A. science   **C.** fascination

    B. astronomy   **D.** telescope

26. How many common nouns are there in the following sentence?

After buying a house, Josh moved his family, pets, and possessions from Iowa to Ohio.

    A. two   **C.** four

    B. three   **D.** seven

27. Which of the following words is an abstract noun?

    A. happiness   **C.** window

    B. computer   **D.** lake

28. Which of the following sentences contains a possessive noun?

    A. Ron's going to the party tonight.   **C.** Ron has three horses in the corral.

    B. Are you going to Ron's party tonight?   **D.** The three horses in the corral are his.

29. How many abstract nouns does the following sentence contain?

Love can bring sorrow, joy, smiles, and tears.

    A. one   **B.** three   **C.** four   **D.** five

30. Which of the following answer choices shows the correct possessive case of a singular noun?

    A. Evitas bike

    B. Evitas' bike

    C. Evita's bike

    D. Evitas's bike

31. Which of the following sentences uses possessive nouns correctly?
    A. The two brothers' contribution to the family's garage sale was a box of children's toys.
    B. The two brother's contribution to the familys' garage sale was a box of childrens' toys.
    C. The two brothers' contribution to the families garage sale was a box of children's toys.
    D. The two brother's contribution to the family's garage sale was a box of childrens' toys.

WRITING

32. Think of the plot of a book or story that you really liked. Then, write a brief sequel that is structured by a plot. Begin with an exposition that briefly sums up the key characters, events, and settings of the original book or story. Continue your sequel including these elements: rising action, a climax, and a resolution.

33. Think of a place that has made a lasting impression on you. It might be a place you visited personally or a place you saw in a movie or on TV. Then, write a brief description of the place.

34. Recall an incident in your life that you found especially humorous or interesting. Then, recount the event in a brief autobiographical narrative. Convey your perspective through the details you include, as well as your general statements about the incident.

Unit 1: Fiction and Nonfiction Skills Concept Map—2

Is there a difference between reality and truth?

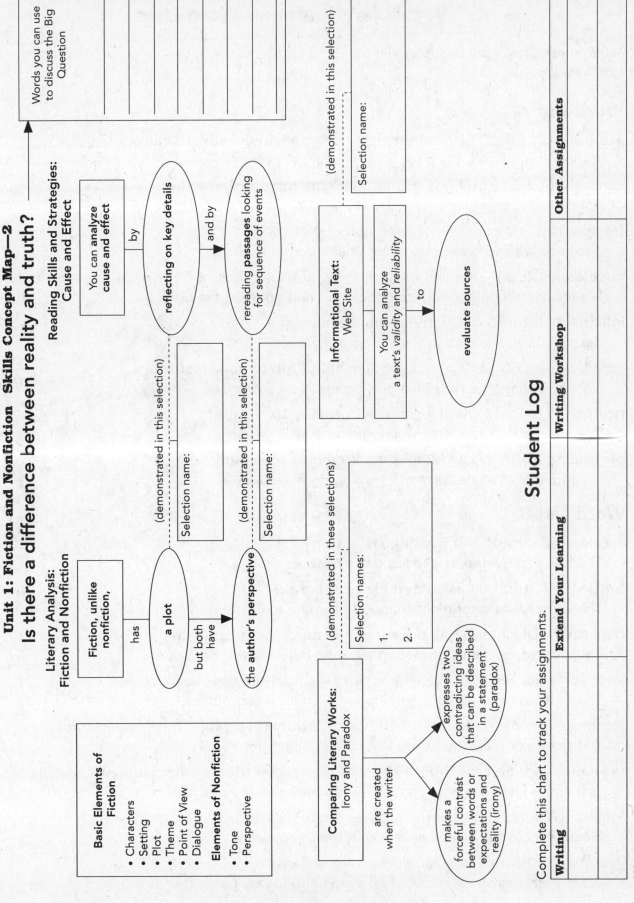

**Literary Analysis:
Fiction and Nonfiction**

**Reading Skills and Strategies:
Cause and Effect**

You can analyze cause and effect

by

reflecting on key details

and by

rereading **passages** looking for sequence of events

(demonstrated in this selection)

Selection name:

Informational Text:
Web Site

You can analyze a text's *validity and reliability*

to

evaluate sources

(demonstrated in this selection)

Selection name:

Fiction, unlike nonfiction,

has

a plot

but both have

the author's perspective

(demonstrated in this selection)

Selection name:

(demonstrated in this selection)

Selection name:

Basic Elements of Fiction

- Characters
- Setting
- Plot
- Theme
- Point of View
- Dialogue

Elements of Nonfiction

- Tone
- Perspective

Comparing Literary Works:
Irony and Paradox

are created when the writer

expresses two contradicting ideas that can be described in a statement (paradox)

makes a forceful contrast between words or expectations and reality (irony)

(demonstrated in these selections)

Selection names:

1.
2.

Words you can use to discuss the Big Question

Student Log

Complete this chart to track your assignments.

Writing	Extend Your Learning	Writing Workshop	Other Assignments

Study these words from "Contents of the Dead Man's Pocket." Then, apply your knowledge to the activities that follow.

Word List A

astonishingly [uh STAHN ish ing lee] *adv.* amazingly; surprisingly
   Although it is small, the book is <u>astonishingly</u> heavy.

comical [KAHM i kuhl] *adj.* humorous; causing amusement
   The clown's <u>comical</u> act earned many laughs.

fragments [FRAG mints] *n.* broken pieces; parts
   The vase fell and broke into many small <u>fragments</u>.

hopelessly [HOHP luhs lee] *adv.* in a way showing lack of hope or of a reason to hope
   My test was <u>hopelessly</u> difficult because I had not read the book.

infinite [IN fuh nit] *adj.* without limit; endless
   People's lives are filled with <u>infinite</u> possibilities.

intention [in TEN shuhn] *n.* aim; determination to do something
   My firm <u>intention</u> is to write a play before New Year's Eve.

postponed [pohst POHND] *v.* put off until later; delayed
   The baseball game was <u>postponed</u> due to rain.

protruding [pruh TROO ding] *v.* sticking out; projecting
   I snagged my sweater on a nail <u>protruding</u> from the wall.

Word List B

accelerated [ak SEL uh ray tid] *v.* sped up
   The ball <u>accelerated</u> as it rolled down the steep hill.

brittle [BRIT uhl] *adj.* hard and likely to break
   The branch was so <u>brittle</u> it snapped off when a bird landed on it.

duplicated [DOO pluh kay tid] *v.* copied; made happen again
   I <u>duplicated</u> my aunt's tasty soup by using her recipe at home.

impossibly [im PAHS uh blee] *adv.* not possible; not able to be done
   The problem was <u>impossibly</u> complex, even for a computer.

incomprehensible [in kahm pri HEN suh buhl] *adj.* unable to be understood
   The speaker's quiet mumbling was totally <u>incomprehensible</u>.

revelation [rev uh LAY shuhn] *n.* new information that is surprising or valuable
   Last night, I had a <u>revelation</u> that helped me solve the problem.

utmost [UT mohst] *adj.* to the highest degree; extremely
   Please handle the injured animal with the <u>utmost</u> care.

yearning [YERN ing] *n.* strong desire for something
   When I am away from home, I feel a <u>yearning</u> for my family.

"Contents of the Dead Man's Pocket" by Jack Finney
Vocabulary Warm-up Exercises

Exercise A *Fill in each blank in the paragraph below with an appropriate word from Word List A. Use each word only once.*

The jigsaw puzzle looked easy but was [1] _____ difficult. The box said there were 2,500 pieces, but the number of combinations seemed [2] _____. My family worked together with the [3] _____ of finishing the puzzle in an afternoon. Ha! It was several days before small [4] _____ of the picture began to appear. When we were almost done, we even [5] _____ going to the movies so we could finish the job. At last, we had just one piece to go. It was [6] _____ over the edge of the table. Oh no! My baby brother put it in his mouth. The piece was [7] _____ ruined. Now it seems [8] _____, but you should have seen our faces at the time.

Exercise B *Write a complete sentence to answer each question. For each item, use a word from Word List B to replace each underlined word or group of words without changing its meaning.*

1. What is something for which most people feel a strong <u>desire</u>?
   _____

2. Is a tree branch more <u>breakable</u> when it is living or dead?
   _____

3. Do you know someone whose handwriting is <u>not understandable</u>?
   _____

4. What sport would be <u>hopelessly</u> difficult for someone with no training?
   _____

5. How might visitors react if they found out that a museum's artwork was actually <u>copied</u> and not original?
   _____

6. What is one goal that you tried your <u>hardest</u> to achieve and did?
   _____

7. What is something that came as a complete <u>surprise</u> to you?
   _____

8. What might happen if Earth <u>sped up</u> in its orbit?
   _____

"Contents of the Dead Man's Pocket" by Jack Finney
Reading Warm-up A

Read the following passage. Pay special attention to the underlined words. Then, read it again, and complete the activities. Use a separate sheet of paper for your written answers.

I finally reached the top of the hill and was rewarded with a view so <u>astonishingly</u> beautiful that I could only stop and stare. The valley spread out below my feet like a vast green blanket. Standing atop the hill, I felt the limitless sky cradle my shoulders and stretch an <u>infinite</u> distance up into the galaxies.

My original plan was to walk down and have lunch near a stream I had passed on my way up. When I felt the power of this magnificent place I immediately <u>postponed</u> my return.

I decided to take a few pictures, but when I opened my backpack, I couldn't find my camera. Then, I remembered the sad truth. I had taken it out to recharge the battery and had forgotten to put it back. Disappointed, I picked up my backpack to put it on. That's when I noticed the corner of my journal <u>protruding</u> from the inside. I took it out.

My original <u>intention</u> was to jot down a brief description, but soon I discovered that I was writing a poem. My first ideas came in <u>fragments</u>, incomplete ideas and words. Yet the scene was so inspiring that within half an hour, these pieces had come together in a finished poem. I tore out the page, placed it in my pocket, and headed for home.

When I reached the stream again, I had a snack, took out my poem, and started to read it aloud. I was nearly done when a sharp wind swept the paper out of my hand. I stared <u>hopelessly</u> as my poem was carried up into the trees. Finally, it got stuck in a high clump of branches.

I dropped my backpack and started up the tree, even though I am a poor climber. Inching my way up, I felt almost confident until another gust of wind grabbed the poem. I watched sadly as my poem was carried out of the trees and into the infinite sky. Meanwhile, I was a mere five feet off the ground, hugging the tree like it was a giant teddy bear. I'm sure I made quite a <u>comical</u> picture, though I didn't feel like laughing.

1. Circle words that tell what the narrator did because the view was <u>astonishingly</u> beautiful. Tell what *astonishingly* means.

2. Circle the word that is a synonym for <u>infinite</u>. Write about something that you think is *infinite*.

3. Underline the words that tell you what the narrator <u>postponed</u>. Then, write about another event that could be *postponed*.

4. Circle the words that tell what was <u>protruding</u> from the backpack. Then, write what *protruding* means.

5. Underline the words that explain the narrator's <u>intention</u>. Then, tell what *intention* means.

6. Underline the words that describe the <u>fragments</u>. Tell what *fragments* are.

7. Circle the words that tell what the narrator stared at <u>hopelessly</u>. Write about something that would make you stare *hopelessly*.

8. Underline the words that describe the <u>comical</u> picture. Describe an event that you would find *comical*.

"Contents of the Dead Man's Pocket" by Jack Finney
Reading Warm-up B

Read the following passage. Pay special attention to the underlined words. Then, read it again, and complete the activities. Use a separate sheet of paper for your written answers.

Most buildings in the nineteenth century were no more than six stories tall. Their height was limited by building methods of that period. An engineer in 1850 would probably have found the idea of a skyscraper <u>incomprehensible</u>. Nonetheless, builders dreamed of creating magnificent structures, and that <u>yearning</u> became reality due to several important inventions.

One key <u>revelation</u> was the discovery that steel could be used to create a strong supporting skeleton for buildings. The main weight-bearing elements in earlier buildings were the walls. In 1889, inventor George Fuller changed architectural history when he designed the Tacoma Building in Chicago. This was the first building in which the weight was supported not by the walls but by an interior system of steel cages.

Fuller's methods have been <u>duplicated</u> around the world. Architects copied his design and used it in buildings from the 102-story Empire State Building in New York City (1931) to the 108-story Sears Tower in Chicago (1974).

The invention of a new building material also <u>accelerated</u> the development of skyscrapers. Reinforced concrete, inspired by an accidental discovery by a French gardener in 1860, contains steel bars. Plain concrete is too <u>brittle</u> to support the stress and tension of a building. When it is reinforced with steel rods, the resulting material is both strong and flexible. Reinforced concrete is a combination of materials that acts as a single substance.

Using a steel framework and reinforced concrete, designers could create buildings that soared ten or twenty stories in the air. Who would want to walk up all those stairs, however? The problem of finding a way to take people up and down these tall buildings had to be handled with the <u>utmost</u> care. Fortunately, Elisha Otis's invention of the elevator in 1853 provided the essential solution.

"Skyscraper" once referred to the tall mast on a large sailing ship. Today skyscrapers are the giant buildings at heights that once seemed <u>impossibly</u> ambitious.

1. Describe something else that people in 1850 would find *incomprehensible* about our modern world.

2. Circle the word that tells what the <u>yearning</u> became for builders. Then, tell what *yearning* means.

3. Circle the word that is a synonym for <u>revelation</u>. Then, tell what *revelation* means.

4. Circle the word that is a synonym for <u>duplicated</u>. Then, describe another invention that people *duplicated*.

5. Describe how a recent invention has *accelerated* change.

6. Circle the words that tell what plain concrete is too <u>brittle</u> to do. Identify another *brittle* substance.

7. What do you think is the <u>utmost</u> problem facing inventors today?

8. Write about a goal that seems *impossibly* ambitious today, but might be possible in 100 years.

"Contents of the Dead Man's Pocket" by Jack Finney

Writing About the Big Question

Is there a difference between reality and truth?

Big Question Vocabulary

comprehend	concrete	confirm	context	differentiate
discern	evaluate	evidence	improbable	objective
perception	reality	subjective	uncertainty	verify

A. *Write the word from the list above that best fits each definition.*

1. the part of a passage, in which a word is used, that defines that word's meaning _____

2. to detect or see something that is concealed _____

3. to see or show the difference between two or more things _____

4. not based on emotion or prejudice _____

5. personal, or taking place within an individual's mind _____

B. *Follow the directions in responding to each of the items below.*

1. Write one or two sentences describing a time or an event in people's lives that might make them look at the reality about themselves and change their perception about what is really important.

   _____

   _____

   _____

2. Write a sentence describing how the perceptions or attitudes of people you described above might have changed. Use one or two Big Question vocabulary words.

   _____

   _____

   _____

C. *Complete the sentence below. Then, write a short paragraph in which you connect this experience to the Big Question.*

   The most important thing in life is _____

   _____

   _____

   _____

"Contents of the Dead Man's Pocket" by Jack Finney
Literary Analysis: Conflict and Resolution

Conflict is the struggle between two forces. In an **external conflict,** a character struggles against an outside force, such as an element of nature or another character. In an **internal conflict,** a character struggles with his or her own opposing desires, beliefs, or needs. A **resolution** occurs when the conflict is settled or resolved.

Writers use **suspense,** a rising curiosity or anxiety in readers, to build interest in a conflict. To accomplish this, writers may hint at events to come or "stretch out" action that leads up to an important moment in the story.

A. DIRECTIONS: *Answer the following questions about conflict and suspense in "Contents of the Dead Man's Pocket."*

1. Both internal conflict and external conflict are present in "Contents of the Dead Man's Pocket." Find one sentence in the story that shows internal conflict and one that shows external conflict and write them on the following lines.

   Internal conflict: _____

   _____

   External conflict: _____

   _____

2. If Finney had chosen to focus only on the external conflict and had not included internal conflict at all, how would the story have been affected? _____

   _____

   _____

3. How does the title "Contents of the Dead Man's Pocket" contribute to the story's suspense?

   _____

   _____

B. DIRECTIONS: *Write a brief alternative ending for "Contents of the Dead Man's Pocket" in which Tom Benecke's internal conflict is resolved differently than it was in Finney's version.*

_____

_____

_____

_____

_____

_____

_____

Name _____ Date _____

Reading: Reflect on Key Details to Analyze Cause and Effect

A **cause** is an event, an action, or a situation that produces a result. An **effect** is the result produced. To better follow a story, **analyze causes and effects** as you read, determining which earlier events lead to which later events. To analyze causes and effects, **reflect on key details**, details that the writer spends time explaining or describing.

Example of a cause-and-effect sequence from "Contents of the Dead Man's Pocket":

Cause: As he picks up the paper, Tom looks down between his legs and sees the street far below.

Effect 1:   He instantly becomes terrified and loses his deftness.

Effect 2:   The trip back to the window is much more difficult than the trip to the paper had been.

A. DIRECTIONS: *Complete the following organizer by filling in the boxes with the events that resulted from Tom Benecke's decision to go out on the ledge.*

Cause

Tom decides to go out on the ledge to get the yellow paper.

⇩

Effect 1

⇩

Effect 2

⇩

Effect 3

B. DIRECTIONS: *Describe three future effects that may result from Tom's realizations about his wife and his job at the end of the story.*

_____

_____

_____

_____

_____

_____

_____

_____

Name _____ Date _____

Vocabulary Builder

Word List

convoluted   deftness   imperceptibly   interminable   reveling   verified

A. DIRECTIONS: *For each of the following items, think about the meaning of the italicized word, and then answer the question in a complete sentence.*

1. Which is more likely to be *convoluted:* a pebble or a seashell? Why?

   _____

2. If a factory worker completes her tasks with *deftness,* how do you think her supervisor feels about her work?

   _____

3. What is an example of something that happens *imperceptibly?*

   _____

4. If your wait in a doctor's reception area is *interminable,* was the doctor prompt in seeing you? Why or why not?

   _____

5. Why is it important that your identity be *verified* when you are cashing a check?

   _____

6. Do you think you would be *reveling* if you received a perfect score on a test? Why or why not?

   _____

B. WORD STUDY: The Latin root *-ver-* means true. Define each word showing how *-ver-* contributes to the meaning.

1. **verity:**

   _____

2. **veracious:**

   _____

3. **very:**

   _____

Name _____ Date _____

"Contents of the Dead Man's Pocket" by Jack Finney
Enrichment: Making Decisions

What led Tom to risk his life for a piece of paper? Ambition motivates people to work hard, achieve goals, and improve themselves. Ambition can lead to success, but, as Tom learned, it can also cloud judgment. Good decisions are based on an analysis of the problem—exploring one's purpose, possible choices, and probable outcomes.

A. DIRECTIONS: *Analyze Tom's decision about whether or not he should go out on the ledge to retrieve the paper. Answer the following questions on the lines provided.*

1. What is the reason for, or purpose of, this decision?

   _____

   _____

2. What is one possible solution to the problem?

   _____

   _____

3. What, if anything, could go wrong with this solution?

   _____

   _____

4. What is an alternative choice he could make and its probable outcome?

   _____

   _____

B. DIRECTIONS: *Analyze a decision of your own on the following lines.*

Decision _____

   _____

Purpose of or Reason for Decision

   _____

   _____

One Possible Choice and Its Probable Outcome

   _____

   _____

An Alternative Approach and Its Probable Outcome

   _____

   _____

Final Course of Action

   _____

   _____

Name _____ Date _____

"Contents of the Dead Man's Pocket" by Jack Finney
Open-Book Test

Short Answer *Write your responses to the questions in this section on the lines provided.*

1. At the beginning of "Contents of the Dead Man's Pocket," what does Tom seem to think is the most important thing in his life? Provide a detail that leads you to your conclusion.

_____

_____

_____

2. In the second paragraph of "Contents of the Dead Man's Pocket," Tom has a hard time opening his window. How does this detail cause trouble later in the story?

_____

_____

3. Early in "Contents of the Dead Man's Pocket," Clare mentions that by leaving just after seven o'clock, she will be able to make the first feature at the movies. How does this seemingly unimportant detail become a key detail as the story progresses? What do Clare's plans cause Tom to do when he is in danger?

_____

_____

_____

4. What incident in "Contents of the Dead Man's Pocket" sets in motion the chain of cause and effect that puts Tom in danger? Read and complete the diagram. Then, on the line below, identify a character trait that causes Tom to get into a dangerous situation.

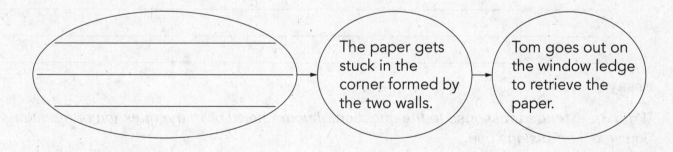

The paper gets stuck in the corner formed by the two walls.

Tom goes out on the window ledge to retrieve the paper.

_____

5. In "Contents of the Dead Man's Pocket," why is the yellow slip of paper valuable to Tom?

_____

_____

6. Which of Tom's actions in "Contents of the Dead Man's Pocket" require *deftness?* List one action.

_____

_____

7. How does Jack Finney create suspense in "Contents of the Dead Man's Pocket"? Provide one detail that adds to the suspense. Then explain your answer.

_____

_____

_____

_____

8. What is the main external conflict that Tom faces in "Contents of the Dead Man's Pocket"? What is the resolution of that conflict?

_____

_____

_____

9. As Tom resolves his internal conflict in "Contents of the Dead Man's Pocket," what does he realize about his job and his life so far?

_____

_____

_____

_____

10. In "Contents of the Dead Man's Pocket," after Tom returns to his apartment, the yellow paper flies out the broken window once again. Why does Tom burst into laughter when this happens?

_____

_____

_____

Essay

Write an extended response to the question of your choice or to the question or questions your teacher assigns you.

11. "Contents of the Dead Man's Pocket" contains both internal and external conflicts. In internal conflict, a character struggles with his or her own desires, beliefs, and needs. In external conflict, a character struggles with something outside himself or herself. In an essay, describe a conflict from the story and state whether it is internal or external. Then, explain how the conflict is resolved.

12. Consider how the title of Finney's story, "Contents of the Dead Man's Pocket," relates to its central conflicts and themes. Who is the dead man, and why is he called dead? What do the contents of his pocket help him realize about his life? Address these questions in a brief essay about the significance of the story's title.

13. In an essay, examine the ways in which Finney builds suspense in "Contents of the Dead Man's Pocket." Show how Finney prompts questions to form in readers' minds and makes them feel compelled to find the answers by reading further. Then, discuss how he maintains suspense throughout the story with the words and phrases he chooses and the details he provides.

14. **Thinking About the Big Question: What is the difference between reality and truth?** What is Tom's reality at the beginning of "Contents of the Dead Man's Pocket"? What truth does he learn in the course of the story? Answer these questions in a brief essay about the change that takes place in Tom's goals and values.

Oral Response

15. Go back to question 3, 5, or 8 or to the question your teacher assigns to you. Take a few minutes to expand your answer and prepare an oral response. Find additional details in "Contents of the Dead Man's Pocket" that support your points. If necessary, make notes to guide your oral response.

"Contents of the Dead Man's Pocket" by Jack Finney
Selection Test A

Critical Reading *Identify the letter of the choice that best answers the question.*

____ 1. At the beginning of the story, what seems to be the most important thing in Tom Benecke's life?
   A. opening the window that always sticks
   B. going to the movies with his wife
   C. getting paid at the end of the week
   D. getting a promotion at work

____ 2. Which of the following events happened first in "Contents of the Dead Man's Pocket"?
   A. Tom thought about what the police would find in his pockets.
   B. Tom dropped coins from his pockets to the street below.
   C. Tom watched his wife get ready to go out alone.
   D. Tom smashed his fist through the window.

____ 3. Which of the following events causes Tom to go out on the ledge?
   A. Tom does research on store displays.
   B. Clare goes to the movies alone.
   C. Tom's paper flies out the window.
   D. Tom puts on his coat.

____ 4. Which event in "Contents of the Dead Man's Pocket" causes Tom to panic?
   A. His wife goes to the movies.
   B. He sees the street below him.
   C. He thinks about the contents of his pockets.
   D. He sees a man reading a newspaper across the street.

____ 5. Which of the following is a moment of high suspense in the story?
   A. Clare leaves.
   B. Tom looks down and panics.
   C. Tom stares through the window into his living room.
   D. Tom sees the yellow paper fly out the window a second time.

____ 6. Why doesn't Tom simply wait for his wife to come home and help him?
   A. He thinks she probably would not notice him out on the ledge.
   B. She will become very angry if she comes home and finds him on the ledge.
   C. She had left early to see the second feature and would not be home for hours.
   D. He wants to get off the ledge and join her at the movies.

___ 7. Why does Tom change his attitude toward life?

   A. His wife goes to the movies alone.

   B. He almost falls off the ledge and dies.

   C. He smashes his fist through the window.

   D. The paper flies out the window again.

___ 8. Often, a seemingly minor detail mentioned early in a short story becomes very important later. Which of the following details later becomes important to Tom's efforts to get back into his apartment?

   A. The window is hard to open.

   B. It is hot in the apartment.

   C. Clare is slender and pretty.

   D. Tom puts on his jacket.

___ 9. Which of the following is an example of internal conflict in "Contents of the Dead Man's Pocket"?

   A. Tom's efforts to open the window

   B. Tom's struggle to stay on the ledge

   C. Tom's attempts to get someone's attention

   D. Tom's struggle to overcome his fear

___ 10. What does Tom decide the contents of his pockets would say about him if he were to fall and die?

   A. His life had been wasted.

   B. He did not love his wife.

   C. He should have gotten a promotion.

   D. He was a selfish and foolish man.

___ 11. In "Contents of the Dead Man's Pocket," Tom has an important realization during his terrible experience on the ledge. What is this realization?

   A. He will never get ahead at work.

   B. He hasn't put enough effort into his work.

   C. He wants to spend more time with his wife.

   D. He is going to fall off the ledge and die.

___ 12. What is "Contents of the Dead Man's Pocket" mostly about?

   A. a man and the contents of his pockets

   B. a man who does not think about his actions

   C. a man and woman who go to the movies

   D. a man whose desire for a promotion at work nearly kills him

Vocabulary and Grammar

___ 13. If Tom hits the window with even _____ less force than is needed to break it, the recoil will send him hurtling to his death.

    A. interminably   **C.** imperceptibly

    B. suspensefully   **D.** instantaneously

___ 14. Moving along the ledge requires _____, which means that Tom must use his hands and feet with great skill in order to avoid slipping and falling.

    A. calmness   **C.** sophistication

    B. courage   **D.** deftness

___ 15. Identify the third-person personal pronouns in the following sentence.

    He watched her walk down the hall, flicked a hand in response as she waved, and then he started to close the door, but it resisted for a moment.

    A. down, in, for   **C.** hall, hand, door, moment

    B. He, her, she, he, it   **D.** watched, flicked, waved, started

Essay

16. In an essay, identify what Tom values the most at the beginning of "Contents of the Dead Man's Pocket." Then, state what is most important to him at the end of the story. Explain why Tom's experience on the ledge changed his values.

17. "Contents of the Dead Man's Pocket" contains both internal and external conflicts. In an essay, describe a conflict from the story and state whether it is an internal or external conflict. Then, tell how the conflict is resolved in the story.

18. **Thinking About the Big Question: Is there a difference between reality and truth?** People sometimes fail to see the truth because they are trapped in their own version of reality. For example, at the beginning of "Contents of the Dead Man's Pocket," Tom thinks that work is the most important part of his life. This reality keeps him from seeing the deeper truth about what is valuable. In an essay, write about how Tom learns the truth in the course of the story. How do the events of the story help him discover what is really important? What are his new goals and values by the end of the story?

Name _____ Date _____

"Contents of the Dead Man's Pocket" by Jack Finney
Selection Test B

Critical Reading *Identify the letter of the choice that best completes the statement or answers the question.*

_____ 1. At the beginning of the story, what seems to be the most important thing in Tom Benecke's life?
   A. his research on past shopping trends
   B. going to the movies with his wife
   C. getting paid at the end of the week
   D. his long-term professional goals

_____ 2. Which of the following events happened first in "Contents of the Dead Man's Pocket"?
   A. Tom contemplated what the police would find in his pockets.
   B. He counted customers passing by displays in the grocery store.
   C. He watched his wife get ready to go out alone.
   D. He sat down to write a memo about store displays.

_____ 3. Which event in "Contents of the Dead Man's Pocket" causes Tom to panic?
   A. He thinks about the contents of his pockets.
   B. He sees the street below him.
   C. The paper flies out the window.
   D. He realizes he has no more coins to drop.

_____ 4. Which of the following is the event that sets the story's cause-and-effect chain in motion?
   A. Tom does research on store displays.
   B. Clare goes to the movies alone.
   C. Tom's paper flies out the window.
   D. Tom climbs out on the ledge.

_____ 5. To Tom, the contents of his pockets represent
   A. his love for his wife.
   B. the accomplishments of his life.
   C. his next paycheck.
   D. all of his personal possessions.

_____ 6. In "Contents of the Dead Man's Pocket," what does Tom struggle with the most?
   A. his neighbors
   B. his wife
   C. his fear
   D. his job

_____ 7. Often, a seemingly minor detail mentioned early in a short story becomes very important later. Which of the following is a good example of such a detail?
   A. The window is hard to open.
   B. It is hot in the apartment.
   C. Clare goes out for the evening.
   D. Tom puts on his coat to go out.

_____ 8. At the beginning of the story, Tom's wife Clare goes to the movies alone. Which of the following events from the story is a direct effect of Clare's being at the movies?
   A. Tom goes out on the ledge to retrieve the paper that had flown out the window.
   B. Tom thinks about what the police would find in his pockets if he falls to his death.
   C. Tom realizes that Clare is more important to him than his job.
   D. Tom realizes Clare won't come home in time to help him, so he tries to catch other people's attention.

_____ 9. "Contents of the Dead Man's Pocket" is mostly about
   A. the risks Tom Benecke takes to save his job.
   B. the contents of Tom Benecke's pockets.
   C. a man and woman who go to the movies.
   D. a man whose ambitions nearly kill him.

_____ 10. Why is the following passage from "Contents of the Dead Man's Pocket" suspenseful?
   For a single moment he knelt, knee bones against stone on the very edge of the ledge, body swaying and touching nowhere else, fighting for balance. Then he lost it, his shoulders plunging backward, and he flung his arms forward, his hands smashing against the window casing on either side; and—his body moving backward—his fingers clutched the narrow wood stripping of the upper pane.
   A. Tom is in a dangerous spot.
   B. It makes readers think Tom is going to fall.
   C. Tom finally falls from the ledge.
   D. The author doesn't tell what happens.

_____ 11. Which of the following is an example of internal conflict in "Contents of the Dead Man's Pocket"?
   A. Tom's efforts to get a promotion at work
   B. Tom's struggle to stay on the ledge
   C. Tom's attempts to get someone's attention
   D. Tom's struggle to overcome his fear

_____ 12. After Tom makes it safely back into his apartment, the yellow paper flies out the broken window once again. Tom bursts into laughter. What is the most likely cause for his reaction?
   A. He is simply relieved to be alive and expresses his joy in laughter.
   B. He is glad to see this symbol of the job he no longer cares for fly out of his life.
   C. He imagines someone will find it and be completely confused by his notations.
   D. He sees the irony of losing the paper for which he had almost died.

_____ 13. In "Contents of the Dead Man's Pocket," a moment of high or intense suspense occurs when
   A. Clare leaves.
   B. Tom looks down and panics.
   C. Tom stares through the window into his living room.
   D. Tom sees the yellow paper fly out the window a second time.

Name _____ Date _____

____ 14. Which of the following contributes the most to the suspense in "Contents of the Dead Man's Pocket"?
A. Tom's thoughts about falling
B. descriptions of the pain Tom experiences
C. the actions of the man in the window across the street
D. waiting to see if anyone responds to the coins Tom dropped

Vocabulary and Grammar

____ 15. How many personal pronouns are in the following passage?
He took a half dollar from his pocket, and struck it against the window. . . .
A. one
B. two
C. three
D. four

____ 16. Tom loses the *deftness* in his hands, which means he loses
A. the ability to move his hands skillfully.
B. the ability to move his hands suddenly.
C. all feeling in his hands.
D. all the warmth in his hands.

____ 17. Tom moves "almost imperceptibly" along the ledge. *Imperceptibly* means that he is moving
A. backwards.
B. so slowly that the movement can hardly be seen.
C. hand over hand.
D. with an extremely careful, shuffling motion.

Essay

18. In an essay, describe Tom's goals and values at the beginning of "Contents of the Dead Man's Pocket." Then, state what his values seem to be at the end of the story. Explain why Tom's experience altered his values.

19. "Contents of the Dead Man's Pocket" contains both internal and external conflicts. In an essay, briefly describe one example of each of these conflicts and how they are resolved in the story. Then, evaluate the story's resolution by considering the following questions. Do you feel the story's ending was an effective resolution to the internal and external conflicts? What message did this resolution convey to readers?

20. **Thinking About the Big Question: Is there a difference between reality and truth?**
What is Tom's reality at the beginning of "Contents of the Dead Man's Pocket"? What truth does he learn in the course of the story? Answer these questions in a brief essay about the change that takes place in Tom's goals and values.

Vocabulary Warm-up Word Lists

Study these words from "Games at Twilight." Then, complete the activities that follow.

Word List A

arid [A rid] *adj.* very dry; barren
  The <u>arid</u> desert stretched for miles without water or plants.

looting [LOOT ing] *v.* stealing; plundering
  The pirates are <u>looting</u> the gold from the sinking ship.

misery [MIZ uh ree] *n.* condition of great suffering, sorrow, or pain
  You could see signs of pure <u>misery</u> in the flood victims' faces.

passion [PASH uhn] *n.* strong emotion; enthusiasm
  The bright red shirt showed her <u>passion</u> for strong colors.

recognizable [REK uhg ny zuh buhl] *adj.* able to be identified
  Hilary was easily <u>recognizable</u> even though she wore a disguise.

skittering [SKIT uhr ing] *v.* skipping along quickly
  The stone was <u>skittering</u> across the surface of the lake.

stifled [STY fuhld] *v.* suppressed; stopped
  The brave child <u>stifled</u> a sob when I stepped on her toe.

successfully [suhk SES fuh lee] *adv.* effectively; in a favorable way
  We <u>successfully</u> finished the obstacle course.

Word List B

congratulation [kuhn GRACH uh lay shuhn] *n.* good wishes on-another's success
  We gave a hearty <u>congratulation</u> to the winning swimmer.

crucial [KROO shuhl] *adj.* of the highest importance; critical
  If you go hiking, it is <u>crucial</u> that you carry water.

elude [ee LOOD] *v.* to avoid; to escape notice
  Many animals <u>elude</u> their enemies by running away.

emerged [ee MURJD] *v.* came out from behind or under something
  I was surprised when my sister <u>emerged</u> from under the blanket.

jubilation [joo buh LAY shuhn] *n.* joy; a happy celebration
  Even though I didn't win, I felt <u>jubilation</u> because I ran my best.

legitimate [luh JIT uh mit] *adj.* following recognized rules or laws
  Does the king have a <u>legitimate</u> claim to the throne?

refrain [ri FRAYN] *n.* repeated phrase or verse
  I could not get the song's catchy <u>refrain</u> out of my head.

wholly [HOH lee] *adv.* to a complete extent; entirely
  The witness's account was <u>wholly</u> believable.

Name _____ Date _____

Exercise A *Fill in each blank in the paragraph below with an appropriate word from Word List A. Use each word only once.*

The recent drought caused [1] _____ conditions, which contributed to the sudden power failure and citywide blackout. Because people lacked light and electricity, a feeling of [2] _____ quickly spread through town. This sad mood was [3] _____ in our sad, candlelit faces. Only someone with a [4] _____ for disorder could have enjoyed those tense times. Police worried that people might begin [5] _____ products from downtown stores. Fortunately, the looters [6] _____ from neighborhood to neighborhood were effectively [7] _____ by alert shopkeepers. After two days of failure, electricity was [8] _____ restored on the third day.

Exercise B *Answer the questions with complete explanations.*

Example: What would you do if a wolf suddenly <u>emerged</u> from behind a tree?
I would run away if a wolf suddenly <u>emerged</u> from behind a tree.

1. How would you treat a guest who is <u>wholly</u> welcome?
   _____

2. What is one thing you can do to <u>elude</u> cold weather?
   _____

3. Do you think rhymes help make a <u>refrain</u> memorable?
   _____

4. What are the <u>crucial</u> pieces of equipment for playing basketball?
   _____

5. How can you tell if a crowd's roar expresses <u>jubilation</u> or outrage?
   _____

6. Do you think there is ever a <u>legitimate</u> reason to lie?
   _____

7. How would you give a sign of <u>congratulation</u> to a friend who had won a race?
   _____

"Games at Twilight" by Anita Desai
Reading Warm-up A

Read the following passage. Pay special attention to the underlined words. Then, read it again, and complete the activities. Use a separate sheet of paper for your written answers.

After two weeks without rain, the playground was an <u>arid</u> plain covered in dust. Mahesh kicked up a dusty cloud as he shuffled his feet in a bored dance. It was too hot and uncomfortable, but Mahesh had nowhere else to go. He exhaled a deep sigh but cut it off sharply when he noticed someone approaching. At first, she was too far away to be <u>recognizable</u>, but as she got closer, Mahesh's eyes lit up. He wasn't happy to see Lona, but he was thrilled to see the bag of marbles she was carrying. Mahesh had a strong <u>passion</u> for marbles and decided right away he would trick Lona out of hers. He knew that <u>looting</u> toys from a younger child was unfair, but when he saw a new bag of marbles, his morals drifted away.

"I could show you how to play," offered Mahesh, with an irresistible smile. Lona nodded. One by one, he flicked the marbles with his thumb. They <u>skittered</u> along the ground, making dusty puffs as they bounced.

Mahesh was patient, spending more than half an hour helping Lona learn to control the arc and roll. After <u>successfully</u> earning the young girl's trust, he made a casual suggestion. "We could play for keeps if you want to." Lona happily agreed. She didn't seem to notice that Mahesh added no marbles of his own.

In less than ten minutes, Mahesh had won all the marbles. He barely <u>stifled</u> a laugh as he captured the last one, stuffed all the marbles into his pockets, and started to leave. He had taken only a few steps when he heard a soft sound.

Lona wasn't crying. She was laughing. When she saw Mahesh's puzzled face, she laughed even louder.

"I saw you all alone here on the playground," she explained, "so I thought I would end your <u>misery</u>. My brother told me you like marbles. I don't think they're much fun." As Mahesh stomped away, he had to agree. Suddenly marbles seemed a lot less fun.

1. Underline the words that describe why the playground was <u>arid</u>. Then, tell what *arid* means.

2. Underline the words that tell why Lona was not <u>recognizable</u> at first. Then, tell what *recognizable* means.

3. Underline the words that tell what Mahesh did because he had a <u>passion</u> for marbles. Describe something you have a *passion* for.

4. Circle what Mahesh plans to be <u>looting</u>. Then, tell what *looting* means.

5. Underline the words that tell how the marbles moved when they <u>skittered</u>. Then, tell what *skittered* means.

6. Circle the words that tell what Mahesh <u>successfully</u> earned. Write about something you have done *successfully*.

7. Circle the word that tells what Mahesh <u>stifled</u>. Then, describe a time when you might have *stifled* the same thing.

8. Underline the words that explain why Lona thought Mahesh was in <u>misery</u>. Then, tell what *misery* means.

"Games at Twilight" by Anita Desai
Reading Warm-up B

Read the following passage. Pay special attention to the underlined words. Then, read it again, and complete the activities. Use a separate sheet of paper for your written answers.

Psychologists report that the game of hide-and-seek provides a lot more than just fun. Play is not just a frivolous treat. It is a <u>legitimate</u> tool that helps children expand their understanding of themselves and the world. Play gives children opportunities to experiment with a wide variety of roles and situations.

Hide-and-seek is played by children around the world. The specific rules and details of play vary from region to region. However, the <u>crucial</u> elements remain the same. One or more players hide, trying to <u>elude</u> a seeker, the player who is "it." Older players often take the adult role of teacher when they explain the rules to younger players.

Playing hide-and-seek is a social event, too. The fun of the game involves being part of a group. Simply hiding is not fun. Hiding when someone is looking for you, however, can be a source of delight and <u>jubilation</u>. Players must trust that the seeker will try to find them. Indeed, a game of hide-and-seek will be <u>wholly</u> disappointing if the seeker gives up too easily.

Some observers suggest that the thrill of the game also lies in presenting a safe model of dangerous situations. This allows children to work out feelings of anxiety and fear. Hiding players are the pursued. The seeker, who represents the figure out to catch them, is the pursuer. In other words, children play the roles of the hunter and the hunted. Once all the players have <u>emerged</u> from their hiding places, the tension is released.

In many regions, the end of the game is signaled with a gleeful <u>refrain</u>, "Ollie Ollie Oxen free!" The origin of this repeated phrase probably comes from a German phrase, "Alle, alle auch sind frei," which means "everyone, everyone also is free." This refrain is used to call in the remaining hiders, marking the end of the silent hiding. The hiders come out, revealing their secret positions, and the other players give shouts of <u>congratulation</u> as the small community begins another round of serious fun.

1. Circle the word that is an antonym for <u>legitimate</u>. Then, tell what *legitimate* means.

2. Underline the words that describe the elements that are *not* <u>crucial</u>. Then, describe the *crucial* elements of your favorite activity.

3. Write a sentence about something you might try to *elude*.

4. Circle a word that has a similar meaning to <u>jubilation</u>. Then, tell when you might feel *jubilation*.

5. Tell something that you would find *wholly* enjoyable.

6. Circle the words that tell where the players have <u>emerged</u> from. Then, tell what *emerged* means.

7. Underline the words that define a <u>refrain</u>. Then, tell where you can hear a *refrain*.

8. Tell why someone might send you a card of <u>congratulation</u>.

"Games at Twilight" by Anita Desai

Writing About the Big Question

Is there a difference between reality and truth?

Big Question Vocabulary

comprehend	concrete	confirm	context	differentiate
discern	evaluate	evidence	improbable	objective
perception	reality	subjective	uncertainty	verify

A. *Write the word from the list above that best completes each sentence.*

1. Ravi felt it was _____ that he would be found in his hiding place.

2. He had feelings of _____ while waiting to be found.

3. Ravi could not _____ that he could be so easily forgotten.

4. In the dim twilight, it was difficult to _____ the faces of the children.

5. Ravi looked for some _____ in their faces that they were glad to see him.

B. *Follow the directions in responding to each of the items below.*

1. Write two sentences describing two ways in which a person might not see the reality of his or her own limitations.

   _____

   _____

2. In one or two sentences, describe a situation in which the person described above might learn the truth about himself or herself. Use one or two Big Question vocabulary words.

   _____

   _____

C. *Complete the sentence below. Then, write a short paragraph in which you connect this situation to the Big Question.*

You can tell how people really see you when _____

_____

_____

_____

_____

_____

Name _____ Date _____

"Games at Twilight" by Anita Desai
Literary Analysis: Conflict and Resolution

Conflict is the struggle between two forces. In an **external conflict,** a character struggles against an outside force, such as an element of nature or another character. In an **internal conflict,** a character struggles with his or her own opposing desires, beliefs, or needs. A **resolution** occurs when the conflict is settled or resolved.

Writers use **suspense,** a rising curiosity or anxiety in readers, to build interest in a conflict. To accomplish this, writers may hint at events to come or "stretch out" action that leads up to an important moment in the story.

A. DIRECTIONS: *Answer the following questions about conflict and suspense in "Games at Twilight."*

1. Both an internal and an external conflict are present in "Games at Twilight." Find one sentence in the story that shows internal conflict and one that shows external conflict and write them on the following lines.

   Internal conflict: _____

   _____

   External conflict: _____

   _____

2. If Desai had chosen to focus only on the external conflict and had not included internal conflict at all, how would the story have been affected? _____

   _____

   _____

3. Identify a moment of great suspense in the story. How does this suspenseful moment help to build your interest in the conflict? _____

   _____

   _____

B. DIRECTIONS: *Write a brief alternative ending for "Games at Twilight" in which Ravi's internal conflict is resolved differently than it was in Desai's version.*

_____

_____

_____

_____

_____

_____

Name _____ Date _____

Reading: Reflect on Key Details to Analyze Cause and Effect

A **cause** is an event, an action, or a situation that produces a result. An **effect** is the result produced. To better follow a story, **analyze causes and effects** as you read, determining which earlier events lead to which later events. To analyze causes and effects, **reflect on key details**, details that the writer spends time explaining or describing.

Example of a cause-and-effect sequence from "Games at Twilight":

Cause: Ravi hides in the shed to escape Raghu.

Effect 1: Raghu does not find him and moves away.

Effect 2: Ravi is encouraged by Raghu's inability to find him and becomes excited about the idea of winning the game.

A. DIRECTIONS: *Complete the organizer by filling in the boxes with the events that resulted from Ravi's decision to run to the "den" to win the game.*

Cause

| Ravi runs to the veranda in tears. |

Effect 1

Effect 2

Effect 3

B. DIRECTIONS: *Describe three possible future effects that may result from Ravi's new awareness of his own insignificance.*

_____

_____

_____

_____

_____

_____

Name _____ Date _____

"Games at Twilight" by Anita Desai
Vocabulary Builder

Word List

   defunct   dejectedly   dogged   elude   intervened   livid

A. DIRECTIONS: *For each of the following items, think about the meaning of the italicized word, and then answer the question.*

1. If Sara's father's face becomes *livid* upon seeing her report card, what kind of grades do you think she made?

   _____

2. What should you do with a *defunct* television?

   _____

3. If Gilberto runs a marathon in a *dogged* way, is he likely to finish the course? Why or why not?

   _____

4. What might you do if your best friend is behaving *dejectedly*?

   _____

5. If your parent *intervened* in an argument between you and your sister, how would you feel? Why?

   _____

6. Why might a person try to *elude* someone?

   _____

B. WORD STUDY: The Latin root *-ven-* means "come" or "go." Define each word showing how *-ven-* contributes to the meaning.

1. **convent:**

   _____

2. **ventilate:**

   _____

3. **convene:**

   _____

Unit 1 Resources: Fiction and Nonfiction
159

Name _____ Date _____

Enrichment: Science Connection

The climate in India, where "Games at Twilight" takes place, ranges seasonally from extremely hot and dry to monsoons (heavy rains and flooding). As the story opens, the author makes it clear how hot it is and how being shut inside the stifling house affects the children.

What is the climate like where you live? How would "Games at Twilight" have been different if it were set in your community in the present? What aspects of the story could remain the same? Use the following graphic organizer to help you think about these questions. Then, on a separate piece of paper, rewrite the first few paragraphs of "Games at Twilight" to show what the story would be like if it were set in your community in the present.

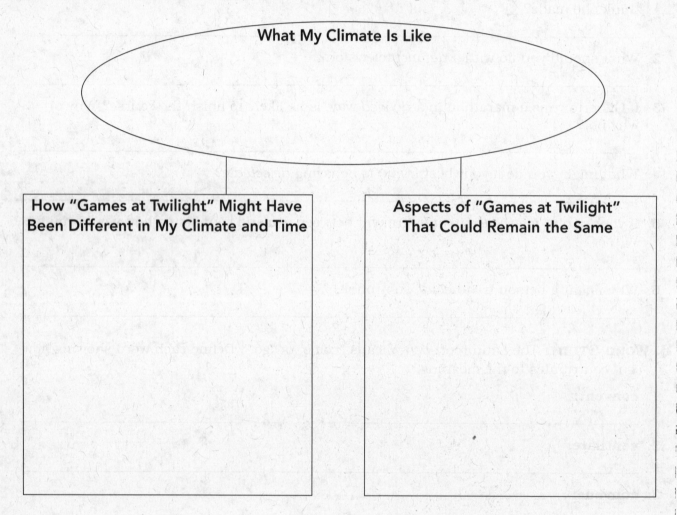

What My Climate Is Like

How "Games at Twilight" Might Have Been Different in My Climate and Time

Aspects of "Games at Twilight" That Could Remain the Same

Name _____ Date _____

"Contents of the Dead Man's Pocket" by Jack Finney
"Games at Twilight" by Anita Desai
Integrated Language Skills: Grammar

Personal Pronouns

A **pronoun** is a word that is used in place of a noun or in place of words that work together as a noun. The most commonly used pronouns are personal pronouns, which refer to the person speaking (first-person pronouns), the person spoken to (second-person pronouns), or the person, place, or thing spoken about (third-person pronouns).

Personal Pronouns

	Singular	**Plural**
First Person	I, me, my, mine	we, us, our, ours
Second Person	you, your, yours	you, your, yours
Third Person	he, him, his, she, her, hers, it, its	they, them, their, theirs

A. PRACTICE: *The following sentences are taken from "Contents of the Dead Man's Pocket" or "Games at Twilight." Circle each first-person pronoun, draw a box around each second-person pronoun, and underline each third-person pronoun.*

Example: Tom looked regretful when she kissed him good-bye. "I wish I could go with you," he said, "but I have to work."

1. "What are you doing here?" she whispered, surprised to see him as he sat down next to her in the dark theater. He smiled at her and kissed her cheek, "I just missed you, Clare."

2. When they returned to their apartment, she was very surprised to see the broken glass. It was all over the living room floor.

3. "You were acting like such a baby, Ravi," she said later. "I was embarrassed for you."

4. The next time they played hide-and-seek, he did not play. He claimed his head was hurting, but it really wasn't.

5. It would bother him for many years. How could they have forgotten him?

B. Writing Application: *Rewrite each of the following sentences. Replace each underlined word or group of words with an appropriate personal pronoun.*

1. Tom did not want to lose the paper because Tom had worked on the paper for months.

   _____

2. Tom tried to get the neighbors' attention, but none of the neighbors noticed Tom out on the ledge.

   _____

161

"Contents of the Dead Man's Pocket" by Jack Finney
"Games at Twilight" by Anita Desai

Integrated Language Skills: Support for Writing an Anecdote with an Ironic Ending

For your anecdote with an ironic ending, use the following graphic organizer to help you come up with a character, a conflict, an expected outcome, and an unexpected outcome. Use the bottom portion of the organizer to brainstorm details to set your reader up for the expected outcome and hints that could explain the unexpected outcome.

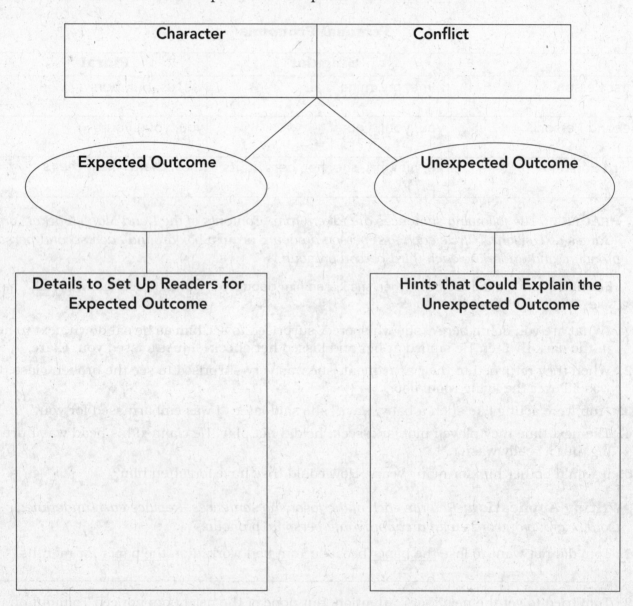

Character	Conflict

Expected Outcome

Unexpected Outcome

Details to Set Up Readers for Expected Outcome	Hints that Could Explain the Unexpected Outcome

Now, use your notes to write an anecdote with an ironic ending.

"Contents of the Dead Man's Pocket" by Jack Finney
"Games at Twilight" by Anita Desai

Integrated Language Skills: Support for Extend Your Learning

Listening and Speaking: "Contents of the Dead Man's Pocket"

While your group discusses possible solutions to Tom's problem of retrieving the paper, record each person's solution—including your own—in the following chart. Then, write one positive aspect and one negative aspect of each proposed solution.

Solution	Positive Aspect	Negative Aspect

Listening and Speaking: "Games at Twilight"

While your group discusses possible solutions to Ravi's problem of earning others' respect, record each person's solution—including your own—in the following chart. Then, write one positive aspect and one negative aspect of each proposed solution.

Solution	Positive Aspect	Negative Aspect

Name _____ Date _____

"Games at Twilight" by Anita Desai
Open-Book Test

Short Answer *Write your responses to the questions in this section on the lines provided.*

1. In the beginning of "Games at Twilight," why are the children so eager to go outside and play? Provide one detail from the story to support your answer.

   _____

   _____

   _____

2. How does the setting of "Games at Twilight" affect the rules governing the children's play?

   _____

   _____

   _____

3. At the beginning of the third section of "Games at Twilight," Raghu approaches Ravi while Ravi is still on the flower pot. Ravi wishes he were taller and bigger. Based on the narrator's details in this section, how does Ravi feel about Raghu? Provide one detail to support your answer.

   _____

   _____

   _____

4. In "Games at Twilight," what causes Ravi to leave the upturned flower pot and go into the shed even though he has never gone inside it before? What causes him to stay there even though it is scary? Fill in the cause-and-effect diagram. Then, on the line below, describe Ravi's behavior during these events.

Cause	**Effect**	**Cause**	**Effect**
_____ _____ _____ _____	Ravi hides in the shed.	_____ _____ _____ _____	Ravi stays in the shed.

   _____

   _____

5. Which details about the inside of the shed help create suspense in "Games at Twilight?" List two details, and explain how they help create suspense.

_____

_____

_____

_____

6. In "Games at Twilight," why is Ravi so determined to win the game of hide-and-seek? Support your answer with a detail from the story.

_____

_____

_____

7. In "Games at Twilight," Ravi is *dogged* in his determination to win the game of hide-and-seek. What does this show about his personality?

_____

_____

8. In "Games at Twilight," what internal conflict does Ravi experience while he is hiding?

_____

_____

9. What is the main external conflict that Ravi faces in "Games at Twilight"?

_____

_____

10. When Ravi finally leaves the shed, how do the other children treat him? Provide two details from "Games at Twilight" to support your answer.

_____

_____

_____

_____

Essay

Write an extended response to the question of your choice or to the question or questions your teacher assigns you.

11. Put yourself in Ravi's place. Would you have behaved and reacted as he did during the game of hide-and-seek? Why or why not? Answer these questions in a short essay about "Games at Twilight." Provide details from the story to support your answer.

12. Why is Ravi so determined to win the game of hide-and-seek in "Games at Twilight"? Does his plan work out the way he hoped? Why or why not? Address these questions in an essay that explores Ravi's motives and feelings throughout the story.

13. At the end of "Games at Twilight," how is Ravi's conflict with the other children resolved? Write an essay in which you describe the story's resolution, focusing on Ravi's conflict with the other children. Also discuss whether you find the resolution satisfying, and explain why or why not.

14. **Thinking About the Big Question: What is the difference between reality and truth?** In "Games at Twilight," Ravi is a child whose impressions of the world are not always accurate. How is his view of Raghu different from the way the older children see Raghu? How is his view of the hide-and-seek game different from the truth he discovers after he leaves the shed? Answer these questions in a brief essay that examines the difference between reality as Ravi sees it and the true situation.

Oral Response

15. Go back to question 1, 5, 6, or 10 or to the question your teacher assigns to you. Take a few minutes to expand your answer and prepare an oral response. Find additional details in "Games at Twilight" that support your points. If necessary, make notes to guide your oral response.

"Games at Twilight" by Anita Desai
Selection Test A

Critical Reading *Identify the letter of the choice that best answers the question.*

_____ 1. Why are the children so eager to go outdoors and play at the start of "Games at Twilight"?

    A. They are beginning to argue and feel they need their own space.

    B. Their faces are turning red and they are having trouble breathing.

    C. They have been in the house all day and they are feeling restless.

    D. It will be a refreshing change from the heat of the house.

_____ 2. Why does Ravi enter the shed in "Games at Twilight"?

    A. He hopes that Raghu will be too afraid to look for him in the shed.

    B. He knows that he can easily slip back out and find another hiding place.

    C. He is proud of himself because he has considered something so bold.

    D. He fears that his brother Raghu will find him on the flower pot.

_____ 3. What is it about the shed that scares Ravi?

    A. It is filled with broken furniture, spiders, and rats.

    B. It is old and rickety, and he is afraid it might fall apart.

    C. He is afraid that once he gets inside, he will not be able to get back out.

    D. It is not a very good hiding place; Raghu could easily find him.

_____ 4. What is the main internal conflict for Ravi while he is hiding?

    A. Ravi wants to go back inside where it is cooler.

    B. Ravi worries that he has been forgotten.

    C. Ravi feels something tickling his neck and works up the courage to find out what it is.

    D. Ravi struggles to decide if his desire to win the game is greater than his fear of the shed.

_____ 5. At one point, Ravi almost decides to leave the shed. What causes him to stay?

    A. He sees Manu get caught.

    B. He realizes it has gotten dark outside.

    C. He hears Raghu catch one of the girls.

    D. He wants to wait for the gardener to wet the ground.

_____ 6. Which of the following is an example of external conflict in "Games at Twilight"?

    A. Ravi wants very badly to win the game of hide-and-seek.

    B. Ravi tries to decide if he is more afraid of Raghu or the shed.

    C. Ravi charges into the group of children, crying that he won.

    D. Ravi is crushed by his terrible feeling of being unimportant.

___ 7. Which of the following is a moment of suspense in "Games at Twilight"?

A. The children are released from the house to play.

B. Ravi imagines creatures are watching him in the dark shed.

C. Ravi squashes a spider that had been tickling his neck.

D. The children continue playing their funeral game.

___ 8. When Ravi finally comes out of the shed, he is stumbling, sobbing, and shouting. What effect does his behavior have on his family?

A. They are relieved and happy to see him.

B. They are amused, distracted, and a little angry.

C. They are amazed, confused, and a little worried.

D. They are distracted and do not notice his arrival.

___ 9. At the end of "Games at Twilight," the other children invite Ravi to

A. play a funeral game with them.

B. play another game of hide-and-seek.

C. sit on the veranda and "share a loot of mulberries."

D. run through the water falling from the hosepipe.

___ 10. What is "Games at Twilight" mostly about?

A. a boy's realization of his insignificance

B. a boy's fear of a dark, unfamiliar place

C. India's unbearable hot season

D. a game of hide-and-seek

Vocabulary and Grammar

___ 11. Near the beginning of "Games at Twilight," the author describes the bougainvillea as hanging "purple and magenta in <u>livid</u> balloons." How do the flowers look?

A. pale   C. bruised

B. dead   D. delicate

___ 12. Anita Desai describes the furniture in the shed as "defunct" because it was discarded. What is another word for *defunct*?

A. dirty   C. thriving

B. dead   D. empty

___ 13. Ravi is *dogged* in his determination to win. What does this show about his personality?

A. He is rude and obnoxious.   C. He likes to be in control.

B. He does not give in easily.   D. He is easily persuaded.

___ **14.** Identify the personal pronoun in the following sentence from "Games at Twilight."

> Ravi had once got locked into the linen cupboard and sat there weeping for half an hour before he was rescued.

   A. Ravi   **C.** hour

   B. sat   **D.** he

___ **15.** How many personal pronouns appear in the following sentence from "Games at Twilight"?

> He tore himself out of his mother's grasp and pounded across the lawn into their midst, charging at them with his head lowered so that they scattered in surprise.

   A. 6   **C.** 3

   B. 5   **D.** 1

Essay

16. At the end of "Games at Twilight," is Ravi's conflict with the other children resolved? Write an essay in which you describe the story's resolution. Focus on Ravi's conflict with the other children. Do you feel the resolution is satisfying? Why or why not?

17. Put yourself in Ravi's place. In what ways might you have behaved and reacted the same way as Ravi? In what ways might you have behaved and reacted differently? Explain your answers.

18. Thinking About the Big Question: Is there a difference between reality and truth? In "Games at Twilight," Ravi is a child whose impressions of the world are not always accurate. In a brief essay, write about how Ravi's impressions—his version of reality—are different from the truth in some situations. In the body of your essay, write one paragraph about each of the following questions: How is Ravi's view of Raghu different from the way the older children see Raghu? How is his view of the hide-and-seek game different from the way the older children view the game? Provide examples from the story to support your response.

Name _____ Date _____

"**Games at Twilight**" by Anita Desai

Selection Test B

Critical Reading *Identify the letter of the choice that best completes the statement or answers the question.*

____ 1. What does the narrator mean by "worthier prey" in the following passage from "Games at Twilight"?

"You're dead," he said with satisfaction, licking the beads of perspiration off his upper lip, and then stalked off in search of worthier prey, whistling spiritedly so that the hiders should hear and tremble.

A. children he dislikes

B. children who will not be easily caught

C. children who have chosen poor hiding places

D. children he will be able to find quickly

____ 2. What initially motivates Ravi to enter the shed in "Games at Twilight"?

A. his certainty that he will win the game if he hides in there

B. knowing that he can easily slip back out and find another hiding place

C. his amusement that he would consider something so bold

D. his fear that his brother Raghu will find him on the flower pot

____ 3. In "Games at Twilight," why would the children's games "become legitimate" in the evening?

A. Their parents would sit on the lawn and watch them.

B. They would play games that their parents chose for them.

C. The gardener would moisten the ground, making it easier to run.

D. The weather would cool down, making it safe to play outdoors.

____ 4. Which of the following statements reflects Ravi's feelings toward Raghu?

A. He admires Raghu's gentle and compassionate nature.

B. He is intimidated by Raghu, but he also admires him.

C. He thinks Raghu is a bully and has no respect for him.

D. He thinks Raghu is weak and cowardly.

____ 5. What is it about the shed that makes Ravi apprehensive?

A. It is filled with broken furniture, spiders, and rats.

B. It is old and rickety, and he is afraid it might fall apart.

C. He is afraid that once he gets inside, he will not be able to get back out.

D. It is not a very good hiding place; Raghu could easily find him.

____ 6. What is the main internal conflict for Ravi while he is in the shed?

A. Ravi jumps when he hears Raghu hit the side of the shed with his stick.

B. Ravi struggles to decide if his desire to win the game is greater than his fear of the shed.

C. Ravi hears Raghu catch one of the girls and decides to wait a bit longer.

D. Ravi feels something tickling his neck and works up the courage to find out what it is.

_____ 7. Why is Ravi so determined to win the game of hide-and-seek in "Games at Twilight"?
   A. Raghu always wins, and Ravi wants to show that he can win, too.
   B. He wants to prove something to the other children because they always tease him about his size.
   C. He believes that defeating the older, bigger children would be thrilling beyond imagination.
   D. He feels that the other children do not take him seriously.

_____ 8. At one point, Ravi almost decides to leave the shed. What causes him to almost leave, and what causes him to stay?
   A. He wants to be in the light; he hears Raghu catch one of the girls.
   B. He feels a spider on his neck; he sees Manu get caught.
   C. He is uncomfortable sitting on the bathtub; he realizes it has become dark.
   D. He thinks about an uncle who bought him chocolate; he is too afraid of Raghu.

_____ 9. What causes Ravi to finally leave the shed in "Games at Twilight"?
   A. He hears the other children calling for him to join them.
   B. He remembers that he must touch the "den" in order to win.
   C. He is feeling confined and overheated in the stuffy shed.
   D. He wants to smell the "intoxicating scent of water on dry earth."

_____ 10. Which of the following is an example of external conflict in "Games at Twilight"?
   A. Ravi wants very badly to win the game of hide-and-seek.
   B. Ravi tries to decide if he is more afraid of Raghu or the shed.
   C. Ravi charges into the group of children, bawling that he won.
   D. Ravi feels crushed by his terrible feeling of insignificance.

_____ 11. In "Games at Twilight," a moment of high suspense occurs when
   A. the children are released from the house to play.
   B. Ravi squashes a spider that had been tickling his neck.
   C. Ravi bursts out of the shed to run sobbing to the "den."
   D. Ravi thinks about how thrilled he would be if he won the game.

_____ 12. Which of the following is a detail from the story that indicates why Ravi is so upset when he realizes the other children have forgotten him?
   A. Ravi hears Raghu whistling and becomes brave enough to enter the shed.
   B. Ravi remembers being locked in a linen cupboard for half an hour.
   C. Ravi smiles to himself while thinking about his victory.
   D. Ravi stumbles on his way to the den because his legs had become numb.

_____ 13. How do the other children feel about Ravi after he charges at them?
   A. They feel bad that they never found him.
   B. They are angry at him for interfering with their game.
   C. They had completely forgotten about him and are not sure why he is upset.
   D. They are happy to see him because they were worried about him.

____ 14. At the end of "Games at Twilight," the other children invite Ravi to
   A. play a funeral game with them.
   B. play another game of hide-and-seek.
   C. sit on the veranda and "share a loot of mulberries."
   D. run through the water falling from the hosepipe.

Vocabulary and Grammar

____ 15. Which of the following is another way to describe the "livid balloons" of the bougainvillea at the beginning of "Games at Twilight"?
   A. pale   C. purple
   B. green   D. dried-up

____ 16. A synonym for the word *defunct* is
   A. dirty.   C. thriving.
   B. dead.   D. empty.

____ 17. If someone is *dogged*, he or she
   A. is rude and obnoxious.   C. likes to be in control.
   B. does not give in easily.   D. is easily swayed.

____ 18. Identify the personal pronouns in the following sentences from "Games at Twilight."
   They all turned to stare at him in amazement. Their faces were pale and triangular in the dusk.
   A. They, him, Their   C. amazement, faces, dusk
   B. turned, stare, were   D. pale, triangular

Essay

19. Put yourself in Ravi's place. In what ways might you have behaved and reacted the same way as Ravi? In what ways might you have behaved and reacted differently? Explain your answers.

20. In an essay, trace the cause-and-effect chain of events in "Games at Twilight" that led Ravi to hide in the shed and stay there for so long.

21. **Thinking About the Big Question: Is there a difference between reality and truth?** In "Games at Twilight," Ravi is a child whose impressions of the world are not always accurate. How is his view of Raghu different from the way the older children see Raghu? How is his view of the hide-and-seek game different from the truth he discovers after he leaves the shed? Answer these questions in a brief essay that examines the difference between reality as Ravi sees it and the true situation.

Study these words. Then, complete the activities that follow.

Word List A

crevices [KRE vi siz] *n.* narrow openings
When it rains, deep <u>crevices</u> in a rock surface can fill with water.

dwellers [DWEL erz] *n.* those who make their home in a place
The only <u>dwellers</u> in the remote cave are bats and mice.

fragile [FRA juhl] *adj.* easily broken
Though the glass looked very <u>fragile</u>, it did not break when I dropped it.

ominous [AH mi nus] *adj.* threatening; suggesting something bad will happen
The sky was dark and <u>ominous</u> so we assumed there would be a storm.

sensation [sen SAY shuhn] *n.* physical or general feeling
As I entered the sauna, the <u>sensation</u> of damp heat hit me like a wave.

varied [VAR eed] *adj.* of many different kinds
My <u>varied</u> collection of stamps includes examples from all over the world.

visibly [VI zuh blee] *adv.* able to be seen
The speaker was <u>visibly</u> nervous, trembling slightly as she gave the speech.

vital [VY tuhl] *adj.* relating to life; full of life
Our peppy new puppy is certainly a <u>vital</u> force in our house.

Word List B

conceivable [kuhn SEE vuh buhl] *adj.* able to be imagined or believed
It is <u>conceivable</u> that she will win the race, but it is not likely.

evaporation [i vap uh RAY shuhn] *n.* the process of changing from a liquid to vapor
The hot sun caused the <u>evaporation</u> of water from the tide pools.

exquisite [ek SKWI zit] *adj.* very beautiful; of highest quality
The <u>exquisite</u> meal took my father many hours to prepare.

inorganic [in or GAN ik] *adj.* not living; not animal or vegetable
Plastic, metal, and polyester are examples of <u>inorganic</u> materials.

intricate [IN tri kit] *adj.* full of many details
The instructions were so <u>intricate</u> that they filled six pages.

receded [ri SEED id] *v.* went out; moved back
After the flood <u>receded</u>, we began to clean up the mess it left behind.

revelation [re vuh LAY shuhn] *n.* surprising discovery or understanding
A gasp was heard in the courtroom after the <u>revelation</u> of the new evidence.

worldwide [WERLD wyd] *adj.* throughout the world
The <u>worldwide</u> population of tigers has decreased dramatically.

"The Marginal World" by Rachel Carson
Vocabulary Warm-up Exercises

Exercise A *Fill in each blank in the paragraph below with an appropriate word from Word List A. Use each word only once.*

Sabina was in a hurry to get home from the mountains before sunset. She was
[1] _____ nervous, moving quickly and without much care. When she
dropped her compass over a small ledge, she felt a strong [2] _____ of
cold fear. She knew that it was very [3] _____ and could easily break.
She climbed down and found the compass, but it was stuck in one of the ledge's many
tight [4] _____. Sabina hoped this was not an [5] _____
sign that the trip was going to end badly. As she used a stick to pry out the compass,
she noticed a [6] _____ assortment of bugs. These secret mountain
[7] _____ included spiders, ants, and a beetle. Sabina was amazed to
find this tiny but [8] _____ world of lively activity.

Exercise B *Revise each sentence so that the underlined vocabulary word is used in a logical way. Be sure to keep the vocabulary word in your revision.*

Example: He was a <u>worldwide</u> traveler, so he had never heard of Africa.
He was a <u>worldwide</u> traveler, so he had seen many parts of Africa.

1. The watch was so <u>intricate</u> that even a child could fix it easily.
   _____

2. During the flood, the water <u>receded</u> and soon covered the entire street.
   _____

3. It is <u>conceivable</u> that a patient trainer could teach a cat to talk.
   _____

4. An art museum could exhibit this <u>exquisite</u> frame because it is so plain and dull.
   _____

5. The puddle got bigger and bigger due to <u>evaporation</u>.
   _____

6. My sister's announcement was a <u>revelation</u> to us all, so we ignored it.
   _____

7. The <u>inorganic</u> parts of this garden include vegetables and flowers.
   _____

"The Marginal World" by Rachel Carson
Reading Warm-up A

Read the following passage. Pay special attention to the underlined words. Then, read it again, and complete the activities. Use a separate sheet of paper for your written answers.

When you are at the beach, notice the position of the shoreline. Look again five hours later, and the shoreline will probably have <u>visibly</u> changed. Sometimes, it can be an eerie <u>sensation</u> to feel bare land under your feet where just a few hours ago there was water. However, this change is one of Earth's natural cycles.

Every day on Earth, there are two high tides and two low tides. At any given time, Earth's water bulges in two directions. It bulges away from the moon and toward the moon. High tides occur in the areas near these bulges. As the moon orbits Earth, these bulges revolve around the planet.

Ocean <u>dwellers</u>, such as fish, crabs, and clams, must adapt to tides if they live near shores. Some animals use a tidal habitat only during high or low tide. For example, a beach might appear to be empty and dead at high tide. However, the area's <u>vital</u> energy is clear at low tide. Suddenly, birds and crabs come there to feed.

Tides push and pull many bodies of water on Earth, not just oceans. The effects of tides are <u>varied</u>, depending on the water's location. On a beach, tides cause water to move back and forth along the shore. In a river or lake, tides can cause water to rise and fall.

A tide pool is a body of water that fills with seawater during high tide. Water fills the <u>crevices</u> in boulders and the gaps in rock beds, creating a pool or lake. Some shallow tide pools dry out completely during low tides. Animals that live in tide pools must be able to live in both wet and dry conditions. Most of these animals are strong and highly adaptable, because if they were <u>fragile</u>, they could not survive these dramatic changes.

A tidal wave actually has nothing to do with Earth's tides, so many scientist's prefer the term *tsunami*. When a tsunami happens, the water may rapidly rush away from the beach. This <u>ominous</u> sign looks somewhat like a low tide, but it happens because a huge wave is coming. Most tsunamis are caused by underwater earthquakes.

1. Circle the word that describes something that will have <u>visibly</u> changed after five hours. Then, describe what someone who is *visibly* angry looks like.

2. Underline the words that specify what might cause an eerie <u>sensation</u>. Then, describe a *sensation* you might feel at midnight.

3. Circle three examples of ocean <u>dwellers</u>. Then, name three rain forest *dwellers*.

4. Underline a sentence that describes a scene's <u>vital</u> energy. Then, tell what *vital* means.

5. Underline the words that tell why the effects of tides are <u>varied</u>. Then, describe why people's reactions to a news report might be *varied*.

6. Circle the words that name something similar to <u>crevices</u> in boulders. Then, tell what *crevices* are.

7. Underline the words that tell what could happen to <u>fragile</u> animals. Then, describe something in your home that is *fragile*.

8. Underline the words that describe something that looks <u>ominous</u>. Then, describe an *ominous* sight you have seen.

"The Marginal World" by Rachel Carson
Reading Warm-up B

Read the following passage. Pay special attention to the underlined words. Then, read it again, and complete the activities. Use a separate sheet of paper for your written answers.

In all of my <u>worldwide</u> travels, from Jamaica to Peru, no place has ever surprised me as much as my favorite beach in the winter. When I go to Bolton Beach in the summer, every inch of sand buzzes with activity, from children building sand castles to teens playing volleyball or collectors looking for shells. The water is crowded with strong swimmers and splashing kids. So it was a <u>revelation</u> when I decided to visit Bolton Beach in early February. There was not a single person there.

First, I noticed the shape of the beach itself. I had always assumed that the beach followed a simple straight line. Now, without the crowds to block it, I saw that the shore actually followed an <u>intricate</u> pattern of curves, like the delicate edge of a lace napkin.

Next, I noticed the colors. When I think of the beach, I see the bright colors of <u>inorganic</u> objects, like the neon blue of a beach ball or the hot pink of a swimsuit. Today, the colors were all natural browns, grays, and tans.

As the waves created a steady rhythm, I felt as if the beach was my own secret, empty world. It did not seem <u>conceivable</u> that this was the same place that was so crowded and hectic during the summer. I happened to arrive during low tide, so the water had <u>receded</u> even farther from the shore, leaving a long stretch of wet sand exposed to the sun. In the summer, I knew, the hot sun would quickly cause the <u>evaporation</u> of all the water from this exposed sand, but today it stayed wet and dark. My footprints remained, following behind me like a long trail. At first, they seemed to be the only sign of life on the beach. Soon I realized that I was hardly alone. What I first saw as little red dots turned out to be tiny crabs with shells as bright red as an <u>exquisite</u> sunset. The crabs hurried into hidden sand holes when I walked near, but scurried back and forth on the sand when I stood still. These crabs were the true winter beach crowd.

1. Circle two places that this <u>worldwide</u> traveler has visited. Then, name three places *worldwide* that you would like to visit.

2. Underline the words that say when the <u>revelation</u> occurred. Then, tell what a *revelation* is.

3. Underline the words that describe an <u>intricate</u> pattern. Then, describe an object you have seen that is very *intricate*.

4. Circle the words that name two <u>inorganic</u> objects. Then, tell what *inorganic* means.

5. Underline the words that name something that does not seem <u>conceivable</u>. Then, tell about something you have experienced that did not seem *conceivable* but was true.

6. Underline the words that describe what happened because the water <u>receded</u>. Then, tell what *receded* means.

7. Circle the words that name one cause of <u>evaporation</u>. Then, describe a place you might see *evaporation* take place.

8. Circle the words that describe the color of the <u>exquisite</u> sunset. Then, describe one of the most *exquisite* things you have ever seen.

"The Marginal World" by Rachel Carson
Writing About the Big Question

Is there a difference between reality and truth?

Big Question Vocabulary

comprehend	concrete	confirm	context	differentiate
discern	evaluate	evidence	improbable	objective
perception	reality	subjective	uncertainty	verify

A. *Use one or more words from the list above to complete each sentence.*

1. Rachel Carson's observations were often _____ and personal, help-ing her see truth in a nonscientific way.

2. Scientists have to _____ their findings to make sure they are true.

3. The _____ of life for creatures in the ocean is very different from the experience of life on land.

4. Scientists try to _____, or understand, how sea creatures survive in difficult conditions.

B. *Follow the directions in responding to each of the items below.*

1. In several sentences, describe a time when what appeared to be the reality of a situa-tion was not really the truth. Use one or two of the Big Question vocabulary words.

_____

_____

2. Write one or two sentences explaining how you and others reacted to the situation you describe in the preceding item. Use one or two Big Question vocabulary words.

_____

_____

C. *Complete the sentence below. Then, write a short paragraph in which you connect this experience to the Big Question.*

Reality is sometimes best discovered by _____

_____

_____

_____

_____

Name _____ Date _____

"The Marginal World" by Rachel Carson
Literary Analysis: Author's Purpose

An **author's purpose** is his or her main reason for writing. An author may seek to inform, explain, persuade, describe, or entertain, or he or she may combine a variety of these purposes in a single work. To convey his or her purpose, an author may include specific details—a moving description or persuasive passages, for example. Recognizing the importance of certain details will help you to understand an author's purpose.

If the author's primary purpose is to inform or persuade, he or she presents a **thesis**—the main point the writer wants to make about the subject. To explain and prove the thesis, the author supplies support in the form of evidence, facts, and other details confirming the thesis.

A. DIRECTIONS: *Identify Carson's purpose for including the details in the following sentences from "The Marginal World."*

1. In this difficult world of the shore, life displays its enormous toughness and vitality by occupying almost every conceivable niche. _____

   _____

   _____

2. The shore is an ancient world, for as long as there has been an earth and sea there has been this place of the meeting of land and water. _____

   _____

   _____

3. I have seen hundreds of ghost crabs in other settings, but suddenly I was filled with the odd sensation that for the first time I knew the creature in its own world—that I understood, as never before, the essence of its being. _____

   _____

   _____

4. Here were creatures so exquisitely fashioned that they seemed unreal, their beauty too fragile to exist in a world of crushing force. Yet every detail was functionally useful, every stalk and hydranth and petal-like tentacle fashioned for dealing with the realities of existence. _____

   _____

   _____

B. DIRECTIONS: *Identify Carson's thesis and then explain how the following sentence supports her thesis.*

I have seen hundreds of ghost crabs in other settings, but suddenly I was filled with the odd sensation that for the first time I knew the creature in its own world—that I understood, as never before, the essence of its being.

_____

_____

_____

Name _____ Date _____

"**The Marginal World**" by Rachel Carson
Reading: Reread Passages to Analyze Cause and Effect

A **cause** is an event, an action, or a situation that produces a result. An **effect** is the result produced. To better follow a story, **analyze causes and effects** as you read, determining which earlier events cause which later events.

To analyze causes and effects, **reread** passages to determine whether they involve sequences of events or changing situations. Ask yourself whether the writer indicates any causes and effects in these sequences. Look for terms that signal cause or effect—*because, as a result, for that reason,* and so on.

In "The Marginal World," Carson often implies cause-and-effect connections by describing sequences of events that clearly lead from one to another.

Example of a cause-and-effect sequence from "The Marginal World":

One of them [a willet] stood at the edge of the water and gave its loud, urgent cry; an answer came from far up the beach and the two birds flew to join each other.

In this sentence, Carson implies the cause-and-effect relationships between the birds' actions. One willet cried out, which caused another willet to answer. This in turn caused the two willets to join each other (the effect).

DIRECTIONS: *Reread the following sentences from "The Marginal World." On the lines following each sentence, explain the cause-and-effect relationships you see.*

1. "I knew that if the wind held from the northwest and no interfering swell ran in from a distant storm the level of the sea should drop below the entrance to the pool." _____

_____

_____

2. "They were horn shells, and when I saw them I had a nostalgic moment when I wished I might see what Audubon saw, a century and more ago." _____

_____

_____

3. "Soon I found the tracks of a shore bird, probably a sanderling, and followed them a little; then they turned toward the water and were lost, for the tide had erased them and made them as though they had never been." _____

_____

_____

"The Marginal World" by Rachel Carson
Vocabulary Builder

Word List

elusive   ephemeral   manifestations   marginal   mutable   subjectively

A. DIRECTIONS: *In each of the following items, think about the meaning of the italicized word. Then, on the lines provided, write a new sentence in which you use the italicized word correctly in a new context.*

1. The weather in this area is *mutable,* so what starts out as a sunny day may end up in a hailstorm.

   _____

2. The joy we felt after our team's victory was *ephemeral,* for we lost the very next game.

   _____

3. Due to my home's *marginal* location, I do not know which school I should attend.

   _____

4. Two foggy circles on the cold glass were the *manifestations* of our anxious breathing as we waited for our father to pull into the driveway.

   _____

5. He decides *subjectively* about the quality of the art, rather than using any particular rules.

   _____

6. Sand crabs are *elusive* creatures that can be difficult to capture.

   _____

B. WORD STUDY: The Latin prefix *inter-* means "between" or "among," as in the word *intertidal.* Fill in each blank in the following sentences with the correct word from the list.

intermission   international   interscholastic   interrupt

1. Jan was named captain of the school's _____ basketball team.
2. The _____ flight made stops in three different countries.
3. It is rude to _____ when someone else is speaking.
4. The play stopped for an _____ after the second act.

"The Marginal World" by Rachel Carson
Enrichment: Connecting to Science

Rachel Carson writes, "Underlying the beauty of the spectacle there is meaning and significance. It is the elusiveness of that meaning that haunts us, that sends us again and again into the natural world where the key to the riddle is hidden." As a marine biologist, Carson drew her inspiration from the sea's beauty and from the strength and adaptability of marine life. Identifying marine organisms and learning more about where they can be found and how they are affected by their environment is the foundation of marine biology. Due to the growth of human population, however, marine biologists today are also called on to find new ways in which the ocean can meet increasing human demands for food, raw materials, and energy.

To meet demands for food, marine biologists study ways of harvesting more fish without harming existing marine life. They also study the use of the many species of fish in the ocean that people have not typically eaten. Other marine biologists explore the use of plankton—microscopic animal and plant life found floating on the ocean's surface—as an inexpensive source of protein, and they explore the more frequent use of seaweed as a food source. In addition to food sources, marine biologists study types of sponges that produce antibiotics and substances that might someday help in treating forms of cancer, possible oil deposits in the ocean floor, and the processes by which types of plankton capture and store the sun's energy.

DIRECTIONS: *Answer each of the following questions.*

1. When Rachel Carson visits the sea, she "senses that intricate fabric of life by which one creature is linked with another." In what ways are humans part of this intricate fabric of life, linked with the creatures of the sea? How is modern marine biology working to make this link even stronger?

   _____

   _____

   _____

2. Why does increased use of the ocean for food and other resources require such careful study? Why do you think it is necessary for marine biologists to understand how changes such as the harvesting of new fish will affect other marine life? In what way does this care relate to Carson's observations about the balance of life in the sea?

   _____

   _____

   _____

3. How is Rachel Carson's attitude toward the sea probably different from the attitude of modern marine biologists in search of resources? Why might a balance between the two perspectives be necessary in today's world?

   _____

   _____

   _____

"**The Marginal World**" by Rachel Carson
Open-Book Test

Short Answer *Write your responses to the questions in this section on the lines provided.*

1. Near the start of "The Marginal World," Rachel Carson says that the shore has a "dual nature." What does she mean by this phrase? Cite evidence from the essay to support your answer.

   _____

   _____

   _____

   _____

2. According to the first and fifth paragraphs of "The Marginal World," what causes the sea level to rise or to fall? List six causes in the appropriate columns in the chart. Then, on the line below, describe the sea level in a general statement.

Sea Level Rises	Sea Level Falls

   _____

3. What does Carson most admire about the life forms that inhabit the intertidal zone? Cite a detail from "The Marginal World" to support your response.

   _____

   _____

4. In "The Marginal World," Carson describes a tidal pool accessible only at very low tide. What does she suggest about the tidal pool by calling it a "fairy pool"? What does the word *fairy* make you think about?

   _____

5. According to Carson's description of the Florida coast toward the end of "The Marginal World," what has caused the mud flats to be covered with the shells of sea creatures? How have land creatures also affected the mud flats?

_____

_____

6. *Marginal* means "on the edge of something physically," but it also means "on the edge of existence; barely able to survive." Explain how both meanings apply to the world Carson describes in her essay "The Marginal World."

_____

_____

7. In "The Marginal World," Carson describes life forms in a hidden tidal pool as *ephemeral*. What would these life forms be like if they were the opposite of *ephemeral*?

_____

8. Think about Carson's many observations about nature in "The Marginal World." In one sentence, state the author's thesis about shore areas.

_____

_____

_____

9. As part of Carson's purpose in writing "The Marginal World," what attitude toward nature does she want to convince her readers to share? Cite two details to support your response.

_____

_____

_____

_____

10. How does Carson's description of the ghost crab help her achieve her purpose in writing "The Marginal World"?

_____

_____

_____

Essay

Write an extended response to the question of your choice or to the question or questions your teacher assigns you.

11. At the start of "The Marginal World," Carson states, "The edge of the sea is a strange and beautiful place." In a brief essay, show how the rest of the essay effectively demonstrates this sentence. Find parts of the selection where Carson talks about strange and beautiful creatures.

12. Choose one of the creatures that Carson describes and write a brief essay exploring why she chose to highlight this creature. In your essay, explain how Carson's description of the creature supports key points that she is trying to make in "The Marginal World."

13. What can you conclude about the role Carson believes nature plays in human lives? In what ways does she think human beings benefit from studying nature? Address these questions in an essay. Cite evidence from "The Marginal World" to support your points.

14. **Thinking About the Big Question: What is the difference between reality and truth?** Carson describes three main settings in "The Marginal World": a tidal pool, the mud flats of the Georgia coast, and the mangrove-lined coast of southwestern Florida. Choose one of these settings. In an essay, discuss the hidden truths behind the everyday reality that the average observer would see in this setting.

Oral Response

15. Go back to question 3, 5, or 6 or to the question your teacher assigns you. Take a few minutes to expand your answer and prepare an oral response. Find additional details in "The Marginal World" that support your points. If necessary, make notes to guide your response.

"The Marginal World" by Rachel Carson
Selection Test A

Critical Reading *Identify the letter of the choice that best answers the question.*

____ 1. What is Carson's main reason for writing about nature in "The Marginal World"?
   A. to share the meaning and significance she sees in life
   B. to inform her readers about the theory of evolution
   C. to entertain her readers with stories about funny animals
   D. to convince people to become nature conservationists

____ 2. Which of the following is an effect of night falling on a Georgia beach as described in "The Marginal World"?
   A. Herons and sanderlings are shore birds.
   B. Everything becomes totally silent and still.
   C. The shore becomes a different and mysterious world.
   D. Periwinkle snails climb out of the water to feed on the mangrove trees.

____ 3. Carson states that the shore has a dual nature. What does she mean?
   A. The shore is harsh, but beautiful.
   D. The shore is both ancient and frightening.
   C. The shore belongs to both the land and the sea.
   D. The shore at night is very different from the shore during the day.

____ 4. Which of the following is NOT a detail Carson uses to describe the pool in the cave at low tide?
   A. A starfish hangs from the ceiling and is reflected in the water below.
   B. Hundreds of periwinkles browse the branches and roots of the trees.
   C. The water is clear as glass and the bottom is carpeted with green sponge.
   D. Pale pink hydroid Tubularia look like flowers hanging from the ceiling.

____ 5. Which of the following words or phrases would Carson be LEAST likely to use to describe the life forms of the shore?
   A. tough
   B. adaptable
   C. sparse
   D. beautiful

_____ 6. Carson describes a scene in which she sees a ghost crab on the beach at night. What does she say surprises her about seeing the crab?
   A. Ghost crabs do not usually come out at night.
   B. The crab seems to be able to see in total darkness.
   C. There is only one crab where there are usually hundreds.
   D. She believes she understands the creature in its own world for the first time.

_____ 7. Carson describes a scene in which she sees horn shell snails winding through the sand. She thinks of the flamingos that once fed on the snails. What effect does this memory have on Carson?
   A. She is glad the snails are safe from the flamingos.
   B. She considers bringing a flock of flamingos back to the area.
   C. She feels anger toward humans who caused the flamingos to leave the area.
   D. She wishes she could have seen the flamingos as Audubon did.

_____ 8. Which of the following is NOT one of the three places that Carson describes in "The Marginal World"?
   A. a tidal pool in a cave
   B. a rocky Pacific intertidal zone
   C. a Georgia beach at night
   D. mangrove mud flats on the Florida coast

_____ 9. Which of the following best states the author's thesis in "The Marginal World"?
   A. The beauty of nature makes people want to explore its mysteries.
   B. The shore at night shows the realities of the world where land meets sea.
   C. The mangrove islands are crowded with infinite varieties of life.
   D. The pool in the cave is a magical and beautiful place.

_____ 10. Which of the following details best supports the author's purpose in "The Marginal World"?
   A. The ghost crab is a symbol of life because it is small and delicate, but it survives.
   B. The hydroid Tubularia looks like a flower, but it is in fact an animal, not a plant.
   C. Some forms of life on the shore are difficult for the casual observer to see.
   D. Two willets call out to each other and sanderlings scurry across the beach.

_____ 11. In "The Marginal World," why does Carson believe the shore is a particularly appropriate place to observe the forces of evolution at work?
   A. Time passes much more slowly at the shore.
   B. She believes that life began at the edge of the sea.
   C. There is more variety of life at the shore than anywhere else.
   D. Other creatures do not evolve as quickly as shore creatures do.

Vocabulary and Grammar

____ **12.** A street that runs between two neighborhoods is an example of something that is marginal. What is another example of something that is marginal?

    A. a river that forms the boundary between two countries

    B. the constantly changing trends in teen fashions

    C. an important event in one's life

    D. a star in its solar system

____ **13.** Carson describes the life forms in the hidden tidal pool as _____ because they exist only until the sea returns to fill the little cave.

    A. primeval   **C.** mutable

    B. marginal   **D.** ephemeral

____ **14.** Identify the relative pronoun in the following sentence from "The Marginal World."

    The little crab alone with the sea became a symbol that stood for life itself. . . .

    A. alone   **C.** that

    B. with   **D.** itself

Essay

15. Choose one of the creatures that Carson described in detail in "The Marginal World," such as the hydroid Tubularia, the ghost crab, or the mangrove periwinkle snail. Write an essay in which you explain Carson's purpose for describing this creature in detail. Explain how her description of the creature supports one or more of the points she is trying to make in "The Marginal World."

16. Think of a place in nature that you have visited. In an essay, describe one interesting plant or animal you saw there and explain what you thought about it. Use Carson's writing style to describe a scene in some detail and then explain the importance of what you observed.

17. **Thinking About the Big Question: Is there a difference between reality and truth?** In "The Marginal World," Carson describes three main places: a tidal pool, the mud flats of the Georgia coast, and the coast of southwestern Florida. Each of these places has more to it than you might see at first. Choose one of the three places. In an essay, describe the hidden secrets that an average observer might miss in this place. Support your response with examples from the selection.

"**The Marginal World**" by Rachel Carson
Selection Test B

Critical Reading *Identify the letter of the choice that best completes the statement or answers the question.*

_____ 1. What is the central idea of "The Marginal World"?
   A. The most beautiful forms of plant and animal life can be easily found in shore areas.
   B. The shore is an especially good place to examine the variability and adaptability of plant and animal life.
   C. The first forms of life on this planet developed in shore areas and evolved over a period of thousands of years.
   D. Shore areas provide important clues about problems that humans are likely to face in the future.

_____ 2. What was Carson's main purpose for writing "The Marginal World"?
   A. to convince her readers that one can find meaning and significance in observing nature
   B. to persuade her readers to work to protect endangered species that live on the shore
   C. to entertain her readers with amusing anecdotes about creatures that behave strangely
   D. to inform readers about how the process of evolution has changed many creatures of the shore

_____ 3. What does Carson mean when she says that the shore has a dual nature?
   A. The shore has two primary functions.
   B. The shore is an unstable environment.
   C. The shore at night is very different from the shore during the day.
   D. The shore belongs to both the land and sea.

_____ 4. Why does Carson admire the life forms that inhabit the intertidal zone?
   A. They are difficult to see, and casual observers might not believe they are there.
   B. They are ancient creatures that have not changed significantly for thousands of years.
   C. They are completely different at night, existing in a primeval world frozen in time.
   D. They are tough and adaptable creatures that can survive in very changeable conditions.

_____ 5. Which of the following is an effect of the low tide described in this essay?
   A. Herons are a popular shore bird.
   B. The author reveals how the past shapes the present.
   C. Delicate flower-like creatures are visible on a cave's roof.
   D. The author evaluates the relationship between land and sea life.

_____ 6. Why is the pool in the cave so special to the author?
   A. It contains species of plants and animals that exist nowhere else on Earth.
   B. It is the first place the author visited after becoming a naturalist.
   C. It can be visited only briefly during the lowest of the year's low tides.
   D. She goes there often to relax and swim in its cool waters.

____ 7. What do you think the hydroid Tubularia, "the most delicately beautiful of the shore's inhabitants," symbolizes for Carson?
   A. the fragility of tidal pool life
   B. the unreal nature of marine life
   C. the strangeness and adaptability of marine life
   D. the beauty, tenacity, and functionality of tidal pool life

____ 8. Which of the following is NOT a detail Carson uses to describe the pool in the cave at low tide?
   A. A starfish hangs from the ceiling and is reflected in the water below.
   B. Hundreds of periwinkles browse the branches and roots of the trees.
   C. The water is clear as glass and the bottom is carpeted with green sponge.
   D. Pale pink hydroid Tubularia look like flowers hanging from the ceiling.

____ 9. How does Carson describe the mud flats at night?
   A. as very similar to the way they are during the day
   B. as a different world that is mysterious and primeval
   C. as frightening and dangerous to humans
   D. as enchanting and magical in their ephemeral beauty

____ 10. Carson describes a scene in which she sees a ghost crab alone at night, facing the sea in complete darkness. What effect does this scene have on Carson?
   A. She feels sorry for the crab because it seems lonely.
   B. She laughs in amusement at how silly the crab looks to her.
   C. She feels she knows the creature in its own world for the first time.
   D. She is frightened by the darkness and the sounds of wind and waves.

____ 11. In "The Marginal World," Carson describes how she believes that, over the course of thousands of years, mangrove periwinkle snails broke their ties to salt water. What does she say is the effect of this development?
   A. The snails cause great damage to the mangrove trees.
   B. The snails do not survive as long as their ancestors did.
   C. The snails live far from the sea and have no need for salt water.
   D. The snails live many feet above the water and return to it only rarely.

____ 12. Which of the following is the best statement of the author's thesis in "The Marginal World"?
   A. The pool in the cave is a magical and beautiful place visible only for a brief period of time at low tide.
   B. The shore at night is a different world that brings into sharp focus the elemental realities of the ancient world where land meets sea.
   C. The beauty of the natural world makes people want to explore its mysteries and find answers about the meaning of life.
   D. The shore is a place crowded with infinite varieties of life that are among the most adaptable and hardy creatures on the planet.

___ 13. Which of the following alternative titles best represents the author's purpose in "The Marginal World"?
A. "Appreciating the Spectacle of Life"
B. "Exploring the Ancient Shore"
C. "Ghost Crabs and Periwinkles"
D. "The Dual Nature of the Shore"

Vocabulary and Grammar

___ 14. Which of the following is an example of something that is marginal?
A. a river that forms the boundary between two countries
B. the constantly changing trends in teen fashions
C. an important event in one's life
D. a star in its solar system

___ 15. What is an example of something Carson described in "The Marginal World" that is NOT mutable?
A. the pool in the cave
B. the shape of the shoreline
C. snails in the mangrove trees
D. the existence of the shore

___ 16. Identify the relative pronoun in the following sentence from "The Marginal World."
I have seen hundreds of ghost crabs in other settings, but suddenly I was filled with the odd sensation that for the first time I knew the creature in its own world. . . .
A. other
B. but
C. that
D. its

___ 17. How many relative pronouns appear in the following sentence from "The Marginal World"?
The floor of the cave was only a few inches below the roof, and a mirror had been created in which all that grew on the ceiling was reflected in the still water below.
A. 0
B. 1
C. 2
D. 3

Essay

18. Write an essay in which you explain Carson's purpose for describing the hydroid Tubularia, the ghost crab, and the mangrove periwinkles in such detail. Explain how her description of these creature supports the points she is trying to make in "The Marginal World."

19. Think of a place in nature that you have visited. In an essay, describe one interesting plant or animal you saw there and explain what you thought about it. Use Carson's writing style to describe a scene in some detail and then explain the importance of what you observed.

20. **Thinking About the Big Question: Is there a difference between reality and truth?**
Carson describes three main settings in "The Marginal World": a tidal pool, the mud flats of the Georgia coast, and the mangrove-lined coast of southwestern Florida. Choose one of these settings. In an essay, discuss the hidden truths behind the everyday reality that the average observer would see in this setting.

Vocabulary Warm-up Word Lists

Study these words from "Making History With Vitamin C." Then, complete the activities that follow.

Word List A

compelling [kuhm PEL ing] *adj.* attracting interest; persuasive
His argument was so <u>compelling</u> that his listeners were soon convinced.

consuming [kuhn SOO ming] *v.* eating; destroying
We watched the snake <u>consuming</u> a field mouse.

desirable [di ZY ruh buhl] *adv.* worth having; pleasurable
A sunny beach would be a <u>desirable</u> location for our family trip.

development [di VEL uhp muhnt] *n.* something that is newly formed
The new clue led to a surprising <u>development</u> in the murder case.

effective [uh FEK tiv] *adj.* producing the desired result
I took a course that teaches <u>effective</u> study methods.

objectives [uhb JEK tivz] *n.* goals; aims
Our <u>objectives</u> for the trip are to have fun and collect fossils.

resulting [ri ZUL ting] *adj.* following as a consequence
She worked in the yard for weeks and the <u>resulting</u> garden was a delight.

symptom [SIMP tuhm] *n.* a sign or indication of a disease or condition
Tell a doctor if you feel an unusual <u>symptom</u>, such as dizziness or itching.

Word List B

accomplishments [uh KAHM plish muhnts] *n.* things done successfully
Her many <u>accomplishments</u> include winning the race and learning to type.

decades [DEK aydz] *n.* periods of ten years
The conflict lasted for three <u>decades</u> before it was finally resolved.

demonstration [dem uhn STRAY shuhn] *n.* evidence or proof of something
The army's <u>demonstration</u> of force caused the enemy to retreat.

derived [di RYVD] *v.* to come from a source
We <u>derived</u> a lot of pleasure from my cousin's singing.

exotic [eg ZAH tik] *adj.* very unusual; from a foreign place or culture
My goal is to someday travel to <u>exotic</u> places in the Southern Hemisphere.

infectious [in FEK shuhs] *adj.* able to be passed from one person to another
I know the sore throat was <u>infectious</u> because I caught it from my sister.

initially [i NISH uhl lee] *adv.* at first
<u>Initially</u> my dog was afraid of water, but now she loves to swim.

scenario [suh NER ee oh] *n.* imagined series of events
He dreamed of a <u>scenario</u> that ended with winning an Olympic medal.

"Making History With Vitamin C" by Penny Le Couteur and Jay Burreson
Vocabulary Warm-up Exercises

Exercise A *Fill in each blank in the paragraph below with an appropriate word from Word List A. Use each word only once.*

My science fair project is going to be a terrific success. I have studied the
[1] _____ of mold on a piece of fruit. I discovered by accident that
leaving a peach in a bag is an [2] _____ way to grow mold. After just three
weeks, the [3] _____ mold is an amazing sight. At the start, the peach
looked quite tasty and [4] _____. Now, it is covered with mold that looks
like black fur, so I do not think anyone will be [5] _____ it any time soon.
My project presents a very [6] _____ argument for storing fruit properly.
The [7] _____ of my project include showing how mold grows; I also show
that mold is a [8] _____ that can be reduced by refrigerating the peach.

Exercise B *Answer the questions with complete explanations.*

Example: What is one <u>scenario</u> for next year that you would enjoy?
A <u>scenario</u> I would enjoy for next year would be extra gym classes and no physics.

1. How might a child respond <u>initially</u> when seeing fire for the first time?
   _____

2. What is one way that an answer to a mystery can be <u>derived</u>?
   _____

3. Why might someone choose an <u>exotic</u> location as the setting for a movie?
   _____

4. What are two of your proudest <u>accomplishments</u>?
   _____

5. Where might you go to see a <u>demonstration</u> of how to paint a picture?
   _____

6. What are two ways you can protect yourself against <u>infectious</u> diseases?
   _____

7. How many <u>decades</u> are there in two centuries?
   _____

Name _____ Date _____

"Making History With Vitamin C" by Penny Le Couteur and Jay Burreson
Reading Warm-up A

Read the following passage. Pay special attention to the underlined words. Then, read it again, and complete the activities. Use a separate sheet of paper for your written answers.

You cannot see vitamins. They have no taste. Yet vitamins are an important part of your diet. Your body needs vitamins to stay healthy, but it cannot produce these chemicals. Therefore, you need to get these nutrients by <u>consuming</u> them as part of your regular diet.

Long ago, people understood the value of eating certain foods. For example, if someone in ancient Egypt experienced night blindness, a doctor would have the patient eat liver. Scientists now know that this treatment was <u>effective</u> because liver is rich in vitamin A. Night blindness is one <u>symptom</u> of not getting enough vitamin A.

Scientists found out that these health problems are caused by not getting enough of a single vitamin. For example, sailors on long sea voyages often got a disease called scurvy. James Lind discovered that eating citrus fruits could prevent this disease. Sailors' diets included no fruits, which caused a <u>resulting</u> lack of vitamin C. Once ships began to carry citrus fruits such as limes, sailors avoided scurvy by eating these fruits. They also got a new nickname: *limeys*.

William Fletcher made a similar discovery in 1905. He studied diets in Asia. The <u>development</u> of a disease called beriberi was common in this area. He discovered that people with beriberi usually ate rice that had been polished. This process removes the outer layer of the rice. Fletcher learned that polishing rice also removes an essential vitamin—B1—from the rice. His research provided a <u>compelling</u> reason to eat unpolished rice.

The discovery of vitamins has helped prevent diseases caused by incomplete diets. Researchers have identified the vitamins that humans need. These nutrients are more than <u>desirable</u>. They are necessary parts of a healthy diet. One of the United States Department of Agriculture's most important <u>objectives</u> is providing Recommended Daily Allowances (RDAs) of vitamins. These statistics help you plan your diet.

1. Circle the word that names something you should be <u>consuming</u> as part of your regular diet. Then, tell what *consuming* means.

2. Underline the words that tell why eating liver was an <u>effective</u> cure. Then, describe something that can be an *effective* cure for a bad mood.

3. Circle the words that name a <u>symptom</u>. Then, describe one *symptom* of the common cold.

4. Underline the words that name the <u>resulting</u> effect of a diet with no fruit. Then, tell what *resulting* means.

5. Underline the words that name the <u>development</u> studied by Fletcher. Describe a recent *development* in your community.

6. Underline the words that state the <u>compelling</u> reason to eat unpolished rice. Then, write about a *compelling* ad that you have seen.

7. Circle a word that is similar in meaning to <u>desirable</u>, but stronger. Then, tell what *desirable* means.

8. Underline the words that tell about one of the department's <u>objectives</u>. Then, name two of your *objectives* for this school year.

Name _____ Date _____

"Making History With Vitamin C" by Penny Le Couteur and Jay Burreson
Reading Warm-up B

Read the following passage. Pay special attention to the underlined words. Then, read it again, and complete the activities. Use a separate sheet of paper for your written answers.

The sea voyages of James Cook (1728–1779) took him across the world, touching all seven continents, crossing the Pacific Ocean three times, and visiting <u>exotic</u> lands that most people only read about in books. As a teenager, he became fascinated by the sea and was determined to see more of it. <u>Initially</u>, he was an apprentice on coal ships, but soon he joined the Royal Navy. During this time, he showed a talent for mapmaking. His careful maps of the coast of Newfoundland in Canada were an excellent <u>demonstration</u> of these skills. As a result, the Royal Society hired Cook in 1768 to lead a voyage to the Pacific Ocean. The first four <u>decades</u> of his life had prepared him well for this new challenge.

One of the goals of the trip was to find the continent of Terra Australis. This continent appeared on many maps, but its existence was <u>derived</u> from stories and legends, not from actual evidence. Cook and his men reached New Zealand and Australia. They discovered the Great Barrier Reef and then sailed to New Guinea. Later in the journey, many sailors caught malaria. This <u>infectious</u> disease spread from person to person, killing many men in his crew before they returned home in 1771.

One year later, the Royal Society asked Cook to begin another voyage in search of Terra Australis. On this journey, Cook and his crew became the first Europeans to cross the Antarctic Circle. This expedition led to one of Cook's major <u>accomplishments</u>: showing that Terra Australis did not exist. By crossing the globe at a high southern latitude, Cook proved that this continent had to be imaginary.

Cook's third sea voyage began in 1776, at the island of Tahiti. From there they traveled to Hawaii and then north to Alaska. Cook imagined a <u>scenario</u> in which they would sail through the Bering Strait, but this was impossible. They returned to Hawaii, where Cook was killed during a fight.

1. Underline the words that describe most people's experience with <u>exotic</u> lands. Name an *exotic* place you would like to visit.

2. Underline the words that tell what Cook <u>initially</u> did at sea. Explain what *initially* means.

3. Underline the words that name something that was a <u>demonstration</u> of Cook's skills. Tell how you might give a *demonstration* of one of your talents.

4. Circle the word that tells how many <u>decades</u> there are between 1728 and 1768. Then, predict what you will be doing two *decades* from now.

5. Circle the words that tell how the existence of Terra Australis was <u>derived</u>. Tell what *derived* means.

6. Underline the words that tell how <u>infectious</u> diseases travel. Write a sentence about one *infectious* disease.

7. Underline the words that name one of Cook's major <u>accomplishments</u>. Describe two *accomplishments* of someone you admire.

8. Underline the words that describe the <u>scenario</u> Cook imagined. Then, tell what a *scenario* is.

Name _____ Date _____

"Making History With Vitamin C" by Penny Le Couteur and Jay Burreson
Writing About the Big Question

? **Is there a difference between reality and truth?**

Big Question Vocabulary

comprehend	concrete	confirm	context	differentiate
discern	evaluate	evidence	improbable	objective
perception	reality	subjective	uncertainty	verify

A. *Explain why the underlined word in each sentence is used correctly or incorrectly.*

1. Ships' captains had to <u>evaluate</u> whether the claim for citrus juice as a cure for scurvy was the truth or a coincidence.

    _____

2. Doctors in the past experienced <u>uncertainty</u> about the real causes of scurvy.

    _____

3. A solution as simple as citrus juice seemed <u>improbable</u> as a cure for the ugly reality of the disease scurvy.

    _____

4. His ideas about disease were <u>concrete</u>, and everyone seemed to think he was talking about something that lacked reality.

    _____

B. *Follow the directions in responding to each of the items below.*

1. Think about some of the diseases you have learned about from history. Write one or two sentences explaining what people of the time thought about the reality of the disease.

    _____

    _____

2. Write one or two sentences explaining what truth about the disease you discussed above was later discovered.

    _____

    _____

C. *Complete the sentence below. Then, write a short paragraph in which you connect this situation to the Big Question.*

Ship's captains treated scurvy as _____

_____

_____

Name _____ Date _____

"Making History with Vitamin C" by Penny Le Couteur and Jay Burreson
Literary Analysis: Author's Purpose

An **author's purpose** is his or her main reason for writing. An author may seek to inform, explain, persuade, describe, or entertain, or he or she may combine a variety of these purposes in a single work. To convey his or her purpose, an author may include specific details—a moving description or persuasive passages, for example. Recognizing the importance of certain details will help you to understand an author's purpose.

If the author's primary purpose is to inform or persuade, he or she, presents a **thesis**—the main point the writer wants to make about the subject. To explain and prove the thesis, the author supplies support in the form of evidence, facts, and other details confirming the thesis.

A. DIRECTIONS: *Identify the authors' purpose for including the details in the following sentences from "Making History with Vitamin C."*

1. Changes in bone structure in Neolithic remains are thought to be compatible with scurvy, and hieroglyphs from ancient Egypt have been interpreted as referring to it. _____
   _____
   _____

2. It is estimated that for centuries scurvy was responsible for more death at sea than all other causes; more than the combined total of naval battles, piracy, shipwrecks, and other illnesses. _____
   _____
   _____

3. Astonishingly, preventives and remedies for scurvy during these years were known—but largely ignored. _____
   _____

4. Thanks to vitamin C, the ascorbic acid molecule, Cook was able to compile an impressive list of accomplishments: the discovery of the Hawaiian Islands and the Great Barrier Reef, the first circumnavigation of New Zealand, the first charting of the coast of the Pacific Northwest, and the first crossing of the Antarctic Circle. _____
   _____
   _____

B. DIRECTIONS: *Identify the authors' thesis and then explain how the following sentence supports this thesis.*

Thanks to vitamin C, the ascorbic acid molecule, Cook was able to compile an impressive list of accomplishments: the discovery of the Hawaiian Islands and the Great Barrier Reef, the first circum-navigation of New Zealand, the first charting of the coast of the Pacific Northwest, and the first crossing of the Antarctic Circle.

_____
_____
_____

Name _____ Date _____

"Making History with Vitamin C" by Penny Le Couteur and Jay Burreson
Reading: Reread Passages to Analyze Cause and Effect

A **cause** is an event, an action, or a situation that produces a result. An **effect** is the result produced. To better follow a story, **analyze causes and effects** as you read, determining which earlier events cause which later events.

To analyze causes and effects, **reread** passages to determine whether they involve sequences of events or changing situations. Ask yourself whether the writer indicates any causes and effects in these sequences. Look for terms that signal cause or effect—*because, as a result, for that reason,* and so on.

In "Making History with Vitamin C," Le Couteur and Burreson often imply cause-and-effect connections by describing sequences of events that clearly lead from one to another.

Example of a cause-and-effect sequence from "Making History with Vitamin C":

In the fourteenth and fifteenth centuries, as longer voyages were made possible by the development of more efficient sets of sails and fully rigged ships, scurvy became commonplace at sea.

In this sentence, the authors explain how more efficient ships caused longer voyages to become possible. The effect of longer voyages was an increase in the number of cases of scurvy.

DIRECTIONS: *Reread the following passages from "Making History with Vitamin C." On the lines that follow each passage, explain the cause-and-effect relationships you see.*

1. Anyone who showed signs of scurvy was dosed with three teaspoons of lemon juice every morning. On arrival at the Cape of Good Hope, none of the men on board the Dragon was suffering from scurvy, but the toll on the other three ships was significant. _____

   _____

   _____

2. A healthy, well-functioning crew was essential for Cook to accomplish what he did on his voyages. This fact was recognized by the Royal Society when it awarded him its highest honor, the Copley gold medal, not for his navigational feats but for his demonstration that scurvy was not an inevitable companion on long ocean voyages. _____

   _____

   _____

3. He records that a 'Sour Kroutt' prepared from local plants was initially made available only to the officers; within a week the lower ranks were clamoring for their share. _____

   _____

   _____

Name _____ Date _____

"Making History with Vitamin C" by Penny Le Couteur and Jay Burreson
Vocabulary Builder

Word List

alleviate   compulsory   deficiency   incessant   obscured   replenished

A. DIRECTIONS: *In each of the following items, think about the meaning of the italicized word. Then, on the lines provided, write a new sentence in which you use the italicized word correctly.*

1. A *deficiency* of water causes dehydration.

   _____

2. I took a part-time job and *replenished* my bank account after buying new school clothes.

   _____

3. My sister's *incessant* interruptions last night made it difficult for me to finish my homework.

   _____

4. The thick curtains *obscured* the bright sun and kept the room cool and dark.

   _____

5. Since attendance at the meeting was *compulsory*, we had to go.

   _____

6. This ointment will *alleviate* the pain of the scratch.

   _____

B. WORD STUDY: *The Latin prefix ob- means "against or inverse." Fill in the blanks in the following sentences with the correct word from the list.*

object   obsolete   obliterate

1. Your teammates will _____ if you decide to quit the team.
2. The authorities are going to use explosives to _____ the old building.
3. The technology from the 1990s is _____ .

Name _____ Date _____

Enrichment: Connecting to Social Studies

Choose one of the explorers mentioned in the essay (Magellan, da Gama, Lancaster, Cook, Cartier) or any other explorer you have studied. On the following lines, write about how the course of history might have changed if this explorer had known about vitamin C and therefore had not been affected by scurvy on his expedition(s).

_____

_____

_____

_____

_____

_____

_____

_____

_____

_____

_____

_____

_____

_____

_____

_____

_____

_____

_____

_____

_____

_____

_____

_____

_____

_____

_____

_____

"Making History with Vitamin C" by Penny Le Couteur and Jay Burreson
"The Marginal World" by Rachel Carson

Integrated Language Skills: Grammar

Relative Pronouns

Pronouns are words that are used in place of or refer to nouns or other pronouns. A relative pronoun is a pronoun that connects one part of a sentence, called a subordinate clause, to the noun or pronoun that the clause tells more about.

RELATIVE PRONOUNS
that   which   who   whom   whose

Examples: In the following sentences, relative pronouns (boldfaced) connect a subordinate clause (underlined) to a word (in italics).

Rachel Carson, **whose** <u>life's work was studying and writing about nature</u>, felt that the shore was a particularly magical place.

The *creatures* **that** <u>live at the edge of the sea</u> are hardy and adaptable.

PRACTICE: *The following sentences are based on "The Marginal World" or "Making History with Vitamin C." Circle each relative pronoun, underline each subordinate clause, and draw an arrow from the relative pronoun to the noun to which it refers.*

1. The hidden cave, which is visible only at the lowest of the year's low tides, is a place of special beauty.

2. The little crab that Carson saw on the beach one night became a symbol for life itself.

3. For decades, sailors ignored proven remedies that could prevent or cure scurvy.

4. Sailors who were used to hardtack and salted meat did not want to eat fresh fruits and vegetables.

5. Captain Cook, who insisted on cleanliness and a good diet on his ships, lost very few men to disease.

"The Marginal World" by Rachel Carson
"Making History With Vitamin C" by Penny Le Couteur and Jay Burreson

Integrated Language Skills: Support for Writing a Proposal for a Documentary

For your documentary proposal, use the following graphic organizer to help you come up with a thesis, supporting scenes, and topics for discussion or commentary. Your thesis should be the point you are trying to make in your documentary. It should be similar to the authors' thesis in "The Marginal World" or "Making History With Vitamin C" since your documentary will be based on one of the essays. Choose visuals, action, and comments that clearly support your thesis.

Thesis:
Scenes or items to film:
Topics to be covered or commented upon:

Now, use your notes to write your proposal for a documentary on life at the edge of the sea or on Cook's efforts to solve the problem of scurvy.

Name _____ Date _____

"The Marginal World" by Rachel Carson
"Making History With Vitamin C" by Penny Le Couteur and Jay Burreson
Integrated Language Skills: Support for Extend Your Learning

Research and Technology: "The Marginal World"
Create a wildlife spreadsheet to record your observations of living things in your area. Note what you see each day in the space below.

Date	Time	Observation (Detailed Description)

Conclusion about your environment: _____

_____

Comparison to Carson's conclusion: _____

_____

Research and Technology: "Making History With Vitamin C"
Create a personal diet spreadsheet by keeping track of what you eat for one week. Record the foods you eat with each meal.

Date	Meal 1	Meal 2	Meal 3	Other

How your diet compares to the diet of a typical sailor in Cook's day:

_____

_____

"Making History With Vitamin C" by Penny Le Couteur and Jay Burreson
Open-Book Test

Short Answer *Write your responses to the questions in this section on the lines provided.*

1. Explain what the authors of "Making History With Vitamin C" mean when they say that scurvy is caused by a *deficiency* of vitamin C in the diet. How can scurvy be prevented?

   _____

   _____

   _____

2. What are the effects of scurvy? Using the information in "Making History With Vitamin C," write six effects in the circles on this diagram. Then, on the line below, describe how a person with scurvy must feel.

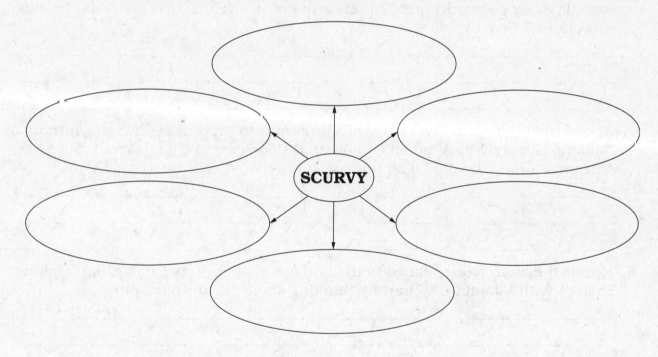

   _____

3. According to "Making History With Vitamin C," why was scurvy more of a problem for sailors in the Age of Discovery than for sailors in ancient Egypt, Greece, and Rome?

   _____

   _____

   _____

   _____

4. According to the authors of "Making History With Vitamin C," people knew how to prevent or to cure scurvy long before most ships put the remedy into practice. List two causes for this delay.

   _____

   _____

5. "Making History With Vitamin C" provides many details about James Cook, a captain in the British navy in the 1700s. Reread the passages about Cook. Then, summarize three of his main achievements.

   _____

   _____

   _____

6. As the authors of "Making History With Vitamin C" explain, Captain Cook sometimes gave sauerkraut to his crew to help prevent scurvy. Why did he choose sauerkraut? Give two reasons.

   _____

   _____

   _____

7. In describing Captain Cook's use of sauerkraut to prevent scurvy, the authors of "Making History With Vitamin C" note that Cook gave the sauerkraut only to his officers at first. Why did he do that?

   _____

   _____

   _____

8. How is the essay's title related to the authors' main purpose in writing "Making History With Vitamin C"? Start by thinking about the authors' purpose.

   _____

   _____

9. In one sentence, state the authors' thesis in "Making History With Vitamin C."

   _____

   _____

10. In "Making History With Vitamin C," the authors include extensive details about the voyages of Captain Cook. How does using Cook as an example help the authors achieve their purpose?

   _____

   _____

   _____

Essay

Write an extended response to the question of your choice or to the question or questions your teacher assigns you.

11. Write a short cause-and-effect essay about scurvy. Explain the disease's cause, its effects on the body, and how eating foods with vitamin C affects the disease. Use examples from "Making History With Vitamin C" to support your general statements about the disease.

12. Write a brief essay in which you explain the importance of vitamin C in history. Support your points with examples from "Making History With Vitamin C." Include examples involving Captain James Cook.

13. Based on the information in "Making History With Vitamin C," write an essay about sailors in the Age of Discovery. Begin with a thesis stating what the sailors' lives were like on sea voyages. Then elaborate on your thesis by supporting it with details from the selection. Be sure to distinguish between the lives of ship's officers and those of other sailors.

14. **Thinking About the Big Question: What is the difference between reality and truth?** Although many people knew how to prevent and to cure scurvy by the 1700s, few ships put these ideas into practice. Write an essay in which you compare the truth about scurvy with the reality that kept many sailors from trying the remedy. Use information from "Making History With Vitamin C" to support your points.

Oral Response

15. Go back to question 7, 8, or 9 or to the question your teacher assigns you. Take a few minutes to expand your answer and prepare an oral response. Find additional details in "Making History With Vitamin C" that support your points. If necessary, make notes to guide your response.

"Making History With Vitamin C" by Penny Le Couteur and Jay Burreson
Selection Test A

Critical Reading *Identify the letter of the choice that best answers the question.*

_____ 1. According to Le Couteur and Burreson, the lack of which molecules almost ended the Age of Discovery?
   A. ascorbic acid molecules
   B. sulphuric acid molecules
   C. scurvy molecules
   D. spice molecules

_____ 2. Early Greek, Roman, and Arab small sailing boats rarely had problems with scurvy. What caused these early sailors to suffer less scurvy than later sailors?
   A. Their boats were less crowded than later sailing ships would be.
   B. They relied heavily on preserved foods such as salted beef and hardtack.
   C. They were careful not to expose themselves to people who had the disease.
   D. They never went far from the coast, so they could resupply their fresh food often.

_____ 3. According to "Making History with Vitamin C," what cures scurvy?
   A. salted beef and hardtack
   B. sweetened gruel and mutton broth
   C. seawater and sulfuric acid
   D. lemon juice and sauerkraut

_____ 4. Le Couteur and Burreson state that sailors ate mostly preserved foods such as dried meat and hardtack. What do they say this caused?
   A. uncontrolled fires
   B. weevil infestations
   C. a rise in cases of scurvy
   D. the growth of mold and mildew

_____ 5. According to "Making History with Vitamin C," why did fewer ship's officers get scurvy than regular crew members?
   A. Officers would not share their medicines.
   B. Officers were vaccinated against scurvy.
   C. Officers ate better diets and different kinds of foods.
   D. Officers would not serve on ships that were not clean.

____ 6. James Cook was known for his insistence on maintaining high levels of diet and hygiene aboard his ships. What effect did this have on his voyages?

    A. His crewmen enjoyed better health and a lower death rate than other sailors.

    B. Cook's crew hated him for his strictness and the lack of meat, so they mutinied.

    C. He stayed near the coast since he had to have access to fresh fruits and vegetables.

    D. Cook never discovered any new lands because he was so focused on cleanliness.

____ 7. Le Couteur and Burreson tell a story about James Cook's ship, the *Endeavour*, hitting a coral reef. The ship got a hole in it that the crew had to work very hard to fix. They succeeded after many hours of effort. Why do the authors tell this story?

    A. to show readers how brave Cook and his crew were

    B. to show readers that a healthy crew had a better chance of surviving

    C. to make readers feel glad that sea travel is much less dangerous now

    D. to help readers see that scurvy did not keep sailors from doing their duty

____ 8. According to "Making History with Vitamin C," how did Cook persuade his men to want sauerkraut?

    A. He flogged them if they refused to eat it.

    B. He made it available only to the officers at first.

    C. He showed them what a man very sick with scurvy looked like.

    D. He tried new recipes every week until he found one they liked.

____ 9. What probably would have happened to James Cook's expeditions if he had not required cleanliness and a balanced diet for his crew?

    A. He probably would not have made many of the discoveries he did.

    B. He would have discovered even more wonderful new lands and peoples.

    C. His crew probably would have rebelled against him and taken over the ship.

    D. His officers would have demanded that he force the crew to maintain cleanliness.

___ 10. What is the authors' main point, or thesis, in "Making History with Vitamin C"?

    A. James Cook was the best sea captain in history.

    B. Scurvy killed many sailors during the Age of Discovery.

    C. Vikings stayed close to the coast and rarely suffered from scurvy.

    D. Many discoveries would not have been possible without vitamin C.

___ 11. What purpose did the authors have for writing "Making History with Vitamin C"?

    A. to notify readers about the benefits of vitamin C

    B. to persuade readers to take vitamin C every day

    C. to inform readers about the historical role of vitamin C

    D. to entertain readers with stories about scurvy

Vocabulary and Grammar

___ 12. If *incessant* means "constant," what word means the opposite of it?

    A. steady   C. occasional

    B. relentless   D. unfriendly

___ 13. What is the relative pronoun in the following sentence from "Making History with Vitamin C"?

    Within six days the men who received the citrus fruit were fit for duty.

    A. men   C. were

    B. who   D. for

Essay

14. In "Making History with Vitamin C," the authors write about how James Cook ran his ships. They describe how he required his crews to keep a clean ship and eat balanced, healthy meals. In an essay, explain the effects Cook's policies had on his crew and expeditions.

15. In "Making History with Vitamin C," the authors explain that effective treatments for scurvy were known and proven by the mid-1700s. However, very few seamen used them. In an essay, explain why known treatments were seldom used at this time. List and explain at least two reasons from the article.

16. **Thinking About the Big Question: Is there a difference between reality and truth?** Sometimes people miss out on the truth because they want to live in their own reality. By the 1700s, many people knew how to prevent scurvy, but few ships used this information. Most people chose to believe the wrong thing about the disease and how to treat it. In an essay, answer the following questions: What is the true way to prevent scurvy? What wrong information did people choose to believe? Why do you think they made this choice? Use information from "Making History With Vitamin C" to support your points.

"Making History with Vitamin C" by Penny Le Couteur and Jay Burreson
Selection Test B

Critical Reading *Identify the letter of the choice that best completes the statement or answers the question.*

_____ 1. Oar-propelled galleys of the Greeks and Romans and the small sailing boats of Arab traders stayed fairly close to the coast. What effect did this have on outbreaks of scurvy and why?
   A. There was very little scurvy because they were able to get fresh food easily.
   B. There was very little scurvy because they did not expose themselves to people with the disease.
   C. There was a great deal of scurvy because they were regularly exposed to people with the disease.
   D. There was a great deal of scurvy because they ate plants that made them sick.

_____ 2. In "Making History with Vitamin C," what development made scurvy more common-place at sea?
   A. The Vikings raided the Atlantic coast of Europe, bringing the disease with them.
   B. More efficient sets of sails and fully rigged ships made longer voyages possible.
   C. Sailors began eating salted meat and hardtack more than in the past.
   D. The use of pitch to seal wooden ships made fire a great danger.

_____ 3. According to Le Couteur and Burreson, why did a reliance on preserved food cause a rise in cases of scurvy on long sea voyages?
   A. Sea captains mistakenly believed that preserved foods would cure scurvy.
   B. Men who had scurvy could not chew dried meat and hardtack because their gums were sore.
   C. Preserved foods contained little or no vitamin C, which is easily destroyed by heat, light, and long storage.
   D. Preserved foods were more likely to contain the scurvy bacteria.

_____ 4. Why did Le Couteur and Burreson call it a "false economy" for ship owners to refuse to use precious cargo space for scurvy-preventing foods for the crew?
   A. because the cost was actually higher in the end to lose up to half of one's crew to the disease
   B. because ship owners frequently lied about their profits in order to recruit new crew members
   C. because fruit was considered too expensive to buy for lowly sailors, who usually did not want it anyway
   D. because the fruit would go bad too quickly and would be both wasted money and cargo space

_____ 5. Le Couteur and Burreson state that ship owners were hesitant to use "precious cargo space" for fresh fruits and vegetables for their crews. What does this imply about the ship owners' priorities?
   A. They valued their crews' health more than they valued their cargoes.
   B. They valued their cargo and profit more than they valued their crews' lives.
   C. They valued fruits and vegetables more than they valued their regular cargoes.
   D. They valued having large crews more than they valued having variety in their diets.

____ 6. According to "Making History with Vitamin C," why was scurvy less of a problem among a ship's officers than among regular crew members?
   A. Officers kept all the scurvy-preventing foods to themselves.
   B. Officers had access to doctors and medicines that regular crew members could not afford.
   C. Officers were from a higher social class and would eat fresh fruits and vegetables when in port.
   D. Officers ate mostly fresh meat, bread, cheese, butter, and beer.

____ 7. In "Making History with Vitamin C," who was the first ship's captain on record for ensuring that his crews remained scurvy free?
   A. Ferdinand Magellan
   B. Vasco da Gama
   C. Richard Hawkins
   D. James Cook

____ 8. James Cook was known for his insistence on maintaining high levels of diet and hygiene aboard his ships. What effect did this have on his voyages?
   A. His crewmen enjoyed better health and a lower death rate than other sailors.
   B. Cook's crew hated him for his strictness and the lack of meat, so they mutinied.
   C. He stayed near the coast since he had to have access to fresh fruits and vegetables.
   D. Cook never discovered any new lands because he was so focused on cleanliness.

____ 9. Le Couteur and Burreson tell a story about Cook's ship, the *Endeavour*, running aground on coral of the Great Barrier Reef. They explain how the crew had to work for twenty-three hours straight to save the ship. What was the authors' main purpose for telling this story?
   A. to show how Cook was a demanding but fair captain
   B. to emphasize how important a healthy crew was to survival
   C. to explain how dangerous coral reefs were to ships at that time
   D. to entertain readers with an interesting story about a near disaster

____ 10. What is the authors' thesis, or the main point they want to make, in "Making History with Vitamin C"?
   A. Scurvy is and always has been a deadly illness.
   B. James Cook was the best sea captain in history.
   C. Vitamin C is a very important substance because it keeps sailors healthy.
   D. Many historical discoveries would not have been possible without vitamin C.

____ 11. Which of the following details from "Making History with Vitamin C" best supports the authors' thesis?
   A. Scurvy is an ancient disease.
   B. The standard sailor's food did nothing to improve his health.
   C. Preventives and remedies for scurvy were known, but they were largely ignored.
   D. Thanks to vitamin C, Cook was able to compile an impressive list of accomplishments.

Vocabulary and Grammar

___ 12. In "Making History with Vitamin C," the authors describe how there was incessant dampness aboard wooden sailing ships during the fifteenth century. What else might they describe as incessant at that time?
  A. sailors' bad diet and poor health
  B. most captains' insistence on cleanliness
  C. the availability of fresh foods on long voyages
  D. ship owners' demands for crews to eat fresh fruit

___ 13. Which of the following words is the opposite of *replenished*?
  A. opened   C. filled
  B. blocked   D. emptied

___ 14. Which of the following sentences contains a relative pronoun?
  A. Many sailors did not want to eat fresh fruits and vegetables.
  B. Scurvy is a disease that struck many men on long sea voyages.
  C. Very few early sailors recognized or believed in remedies for scurvy.
  D. It was common for over half a ship's crew to die on a long voyage.

___ 15. Which of the following sentences contains an indefinite pronoun?
  A. Many showed signs of scurvy just six weeks out of port.
  B. Ships were found drifting with entire crews dead from scurvy.
  C. Scurvy-stricken sailors were too weak to do their jobs properly.
  D. Ship owners hired extra crew members to make up for expected losses.

Essay

16. In an essay, explain why most seamen during the Age of Discovery ignored the known preventives and remedies for scurvy. Use examples from "Making History with Vitamin C" to support your explanation.

17. In an essay, describe Captain James Cook and his accomplishments in your own words. Explain why the authors wrote about him and his expeditions in such detail in "Making History with Vitamin C."

18. **Thinking About the Big Question: Is there a difference between reality and truth?** Although many people knew how to prevent and to cure scurvy by the 1700s, few ships put these ideas into practice. Write an essay in which you compare the truth about scurvy with the reality that kept many sailors from trying the remedy. Use information from "Making History With Vitamin C" to support your points.

Vocabulary Warm-up Word Lists

Study these words from the selection. Then, complete the activities.

Word List A

assailed [uh SAYLD] *v.* attacked either physically or with words or noise
Long ago, poor actors were often <u>assailed</u> by tomatoes thrown from the audience.

culinary [KEW lin nair ee] *adj.* relating to cooking or kitchens
Although she was not known for her <u>culinary</u> skill, Jen could make delicious pancakes.

engulfed [en GULFT] *v.* swallowed up
The flames quickly <u>engulfed</u> the entire structure.

imminent [IM mi nent] *adj.* could happen at any moment
We heard the car in the driveway, so we knew John's arrival was <u>imminent</u>.

incessantly [in SES uhnt lee] *adv.* without stopping, constant
The children were reprimanded for whispering <u>incessantly</u> during the play.

medley [MED lee] *n.* a mixture; a series of different pieces of music
The stew was a <u>medley</u> of vegetables, rice, and fish.

prospects [PRAH spects] *n.* possibilities for the future
After she finished the test, Danielle knew her <u>prospects</u> for getting an A were good.

sullen [SUHL en] *adj.* in a bad mood, gloomy, sulking
When he doesn't get his way, Roger becomes cranky and <u>sullen</u>.

Word List B

consolation [kahn so LAY shun] *n.* the act of comforting someone or being comforted
Although he was not elected, Will felt some <u>consolation</u> in knowing he lost by only one vote.

duly [DOO lee] *adv.* properly; at the expected time
We were <u>duly</u> informed before entering the museum that we could not take pictures.

headlong [hed lawng] *adv.* or adj. head first; without thinking, hastily
Without knowing where she was going, Mira rushed <u>headlong</u> into the busy station.

inclinations [in clin NAY shuns] *n.* preferences, leanings
Those with mathematical <u>inclinations</u> also tend to do well in music.

sermonized [SER muh nyzd] *v.* gave a sermon or lecture; preached
When Ian misplaced his textbook, Mr. Tuttle <u>sermonized</u> on the importance of organization.

scarcity [SKAIR si tee] *n.* shortage, lack
Due to the <u>scarcity</u> of water in this region, few houses have lawns.

shirked [shurkd] *v.* avoided work or responsibility
It was surprising that Janna was late for work, since she had never <u>shirked</u> her duty.

stupefied [STOO pi fyd] *v.* stunned; astonished to the point of being speechless
After watching her brother break the plate, Laverne was <u>stupefied</u> by his denial.

"**Like the Sun**" by R.K. Narayan
"**The Open Window**" by Saki

Vocabulary Warm-up Exercises

Exercise A *Fill in the blanks, using each word from Word List A only once.*

When Antonio invited me for dinner, I knew my [1] _____ were good for enjoying

a delicious meal. Antonio had been developing his [2] _____ skills by watching

cooking shows on television. He was interested only in food. In fact, he talked almost

[3] _____ about recipes he wanted to try. As I approached his house, however, I

knew something was wrong. Antonio opened the door, and my nostrils were

[4] _____ by the smell of something burning. The [5] _____ expression

on Antonio's usually smiling face confirmed my fears. In the kitchen, I saw the smoking

remains of our dinner. Antonio explained. Knowing that my arrival was

[6] _____, he had turned the heat up to cook the sauce more quickly. Suddenly,

he saw that the pan was [7] _____ in flames. He had just extinguished them. It

didn't take long for Antonio to recover from the incident. Taking every box off the shelf,

he asked me how I'd like a [8] _____ of cold cereals for dinner.

Exercise B True or False? Decide whether each statement below is true or false. Explain
your answers.

1. A soldier who <u>shirked</u> her duty is likely to receive honors.
   _____

2. A person who jumps <u>headlong</u> into a project usually takes time to prepare.
   _____

3. Sending a caring letter can provide <u>consolation</u> to someone who is sad.
   _____

4. A <u>scarcity</u> of gasoline can lead to higher prices and long lines at service stations.
   _____

5. Winners of beauty pageants often look <u>stupefied</u> when their names are announced.
   _____

6. It might be boring to listen to someone who constantly <u>sermonized</u>.
   _____

7. An arresting officer must avoid <u>duly</u> notifying people of their rights.
   _____

8. People with artistic <u>inclinations</u> often dress creatively.
   _____

Name _____ Date _____

"**Like the Sun**" by R.K. Narayan
"**The Open Window**" by Saki
Reading Warm-up A

Read the following passage. Pay special attention to the underlined words. Then, read it again, and complete the activities. Use a separate sheet of paper for your written answers.

When you consider it, truth can be a slippery thing. A recent interaction with my Aunt Artesia will serve as an illustration. This esteemed relative calls, asking me whether I like the homemade cookies she sent me. Now, Aunt Artesia is not known for her <u>culinary</u> ability. On the contrary, one might say that for the good of humanity she should be prohibited from any kitchen. Her escapades are renowned. There was the infamous occasion on which the pages of her cookbook stuck together, causing her to combine the recipes for clam sauce and pecan pie. Then there was the Notorious Pantry Incident, when she was so concerned the foods in her cupboard would expire that she improvised a dish that was a <u>medley</u> of pinto beans, canned peaches, and sardines. That is not a memory I wish to dwell on <u>incessantly</u>.

So how do I respond to Aunt Artesia's inquiry? If I tell her that the cookies were delicious, which I know to be a lie, it improves my <u>prospects</u> for receiving more baked goods, a consequence I do not desire. And yet, I know that if I tell her the literal truth, I will be <u>engulfed</u> by feelings of guilt for hurting her feelings. After all, the gift of the cookies was meant as a thoughtful gesture, not a malevolent act with the goal of poisoning me and causing my <u>imminent</u> demise.

My indecision, which takes place in the space of a moment, makes me feel <u>sullen</u> and mean-spirited. I am <u>assailed</u> by feelings of uncertainty about my own worth as a human being, not an agreeable feeling. Who could imagine all of this anguish over an apparently simple "yes" or "no" to a straightforward question?

I expect that you can guess my response to my aunt, and I predict that yours would be the same. Is it the truth? Who knows? As I said, the truth can be very slippery indeed.

1. Circle words that are clues to <u>culinary</u>. Give a synonym that could replace *culinary* in the sentence.

2. Underline the phrases that tell what is in the <u>medley</u>. Use the word *medley* in a sentence.

3. Circle the words that give a clue to <u>incessantly</u>. Give a word or phrase that means the opposite of *incessantly*.

4. What <u>prospects</u> were improved for the narrator? Give a synonym for *prospects*.

5. Underline the phrase that tells what feelings the narrator will be <u>engulfed</u> by. Why will the narrator be *engulfed* by these feelings?

6. Use the word <u>imminent</u> in a sentence. Explain the difference between *imminent* and *possible*.

7. Circle the word that gives a clue to the meaning of <u>sullen</u>. Give an antonym for *sullen*.

8. Underline the phrase that tells what <u>assailed</u> the narrator. Give another word that means the same as *assailed*.

"Like the Sun" by R.K. Narayan
"The Open Window" by Saki
Reading Warm-up B

Read the following passage. Pay special attention to the underlined words. Then, read it again, and complete the activities. Use a separate sheet of paper for your written answers.

There is a fine line between telling an actual lie and simply exaggerating. The American literary tradition of the "tall tale" is based on this distinction, and one of the masters of this form of fiction was the beloved writer Mark Twain. Many of his works feature at least one character who bends the truth to improve a story.

Mark Twain was the pen name of Samuel Clemens, who was born in Missouri in 1835. His father died when Samuel was 11 years old, leaving the family with a <u>scarcity</u> of financial resources. Samuel left school and went to work for a newspaper, showing his <u>inclinations</u> towards writing at a young age. In his early twenties, after living in New York and Philadelphia, he moved to St. Louis, where he earned a steamboat pilot's license and traveled up and down the Mississippi. The name "Mark Twain" comes from a term used on riverboats to determine the depth of the water.

Mark Twain was a keen observer of hypocrisy in American life, and he never <u>shirked</u> the task of writing about it. He rarely, if ever, preached or <u>sermonized</u>, however. Instead, he used biting humor and satire to get the point across.

Tom Sawyer and Huck Finn are two of Twain's most enduring creations. Of the two, Tom Sawyer is the one best known for stretching the truth. When caught in a lie, Tom is always <u>duly</u> reprimanded by his guardian, Aunt Polly, yet this never stops him from plunging <u>headlong</u> into his next scheme or adventure in which fibbing plays a part.

Although he was friendly with presidents, politicians were often targets for Twain's wit. He claimed to have been <u>stupefied</u> by their irresponsible behavior, and is said to have written, "No one's life, liberty, or property is safe while the legislature is in session." Those who see politicians the same way today might feel some <u>consolation</u> and relief in knowing that a sharp social critic like Mark Twain shared their views.

1. Circle the phrase that tells what there is a <u>scarcity</u> of. Use the word *scarcity* in a sentence.

2. Underline the word that describes Twain's <u>inclinations</u>. What synonym for *inclinations* would also work in the sentence?

3. What was it that Twain never <u>shirked</u>? Give a word that means the same thing as *shirked*.

4. Circle the word that gives a clue to <u>sermonized</u>. If Twain never *sermonized*, explain how he expressed his views.

5. Who <u>duly</u> reprimands Tom Sawyer? For what is he *duly* reprimanded?

6. Circle the verb that gives a clue to <u>headlong</u>. Give a word or phrase that is an antonym for *headlong*.

7. Underline the phrase that tells what <u>stupefied</u> Twain. How did he use his being *stupefied* in his writing?

8. Circle the word that gives a clue to <u>consolation</u>. Give a synonym for *consolation*.

"**Like the Sun**" by R.K. Narayan

"**The Open Window**" by Saki

Writing About the Big Question

Is there a difference between reality and truth?

Big Question Vocabulary

comprehend	concrete	confirm	context	differentiate
discern	evaluate	evidence	improbable	objective
perception	reality	subjective	uncertainty	verify

A. *Write the word from the list above that is a* synonym *for the underlined phrase or word in each sentence.*

1. Noah's <u>way of seeing</u> things sometimes led him to make mistakes about other people's intentions. _____

2. Some people are unable to <u>tell the difference</u> between truth and lies. _____

3. Framton did not <u>verify</u> that Vera was telling the truth. _____

4. Jessica tries to remain <u>unprejudiced</u> about a situation even when she is angry. _____

5. The <u>details that furnish proof</u> of a crime can sometimes be misleading. _____

B. *Follow the directions in responding to each of the items below.*

1. In a short paragraph, describe a time when your perception of reality about a situation was affected by your belief about that situation.

_____

_____

2. In one or two sentences, explain how you learned the truth about the situation, which was different from your first perception.

_____

_____

C. *Complete the sentence below. Then, write a short paragraph in which you connect this experience to the Big Question.*

When things do not turn out as you plan, _____

_____

_____

_____

_____

"Like the Sun" by R.K. Narayan
"The Open Window" by Saki

Literary Analysis: Irony and Paradox

Irony is the effect created when a writer makes a forceful contrast between words or expectations and reality.

- In **situational irony,** something happens that directly contradicts strong expectations. For example, if you go through a door expecting a surprise party and instead find an empty room, you actually *will* be surprised.
- In **verbal irony,** words are used to "say" the opposite. If it starts to rain, and you say, "Oh, this is *great*" to mean "Oh, this is *awful*," you are using verbal irony.
- In **dramatic irony,** the reader or audience knows something that a character or speaker does not. In "Like the Sun," for example, the reader knows about Sekhar's experiment, but the headmaster does not.

Another kind of contrast writers use is **paradox.** A paradox expresses two contradictory ideas and yet also reveals a truth. "You must sometimes be cruel to be kind" is one example of a paradox.

A. DIRECTIONS: *Explain what is ironic in each of the following passages from "Like the Sun" and "The Open Window." Then identify the type of irony in each passage.*

"Like the Sun"

1. "No. I want it immediately—your frank opinion. Was it good?" "No, sir. . ." Sekhar replied.

_____

_____

Type of irony: _____

"The Open Window"

2. "My aunt will be down presently, Mr. Nuttel," said a very self-possessed young lady of fifteen; "in the meantime you must try and put up with me."

_____

_____

Type of Irony: _____

B. DIRECTIONS: *Explain how each paradox is illustrated in "Like the Sun" or "The Open Window."*

"Like the Sun"

1. "You have to be cruel to be kind." _____

_____

"The Open Window"

2. "One would think he had seen a ghost." _____

_____

"Like the Sun" by R.K. Narayan

"The Open Window" by Saki

Vocabulary Builder

Word List

delusion   endeavored   falteringly   ingratiating   scrutinized   tempering

A. DIRECTIONS: *Write a complete sentence to answer each question. For each item, use a word from the Word List in place of the underlined word(s) with a similar meaning.*

Example: Why might belief in Martian invaders be considered a <u>false belief</u>?

Answer: Belief in Martian invaders might be considered a <u>delusion</u> since there is no evidence for them.

1. When can <u>softening</u> your tone come in handy?

_____

2. Why might a person's signature be <u>closely examined</u>?

_____

3. Why do many people find behavior <u>intended to win someone's favor</u> annoying?

_____

4. How would you feel if someone <u>tried to</u> harm you?

_____

5. Why might a person speak with <u>a wavering voice</u>?

_____

B. DIRECTIONS: *On the line, write the letter of the word that is most nearly* opposite *in meaning to the word in CAPITAL LETTERS.*

____ 1. SCRUTINIZED:
   A. punished   B. celebrated   C. purchased   D. ignored

____ 2. TEMPERING:
   A. moderating   B. increasing   C. reducing   D. frightening

____ 3. FALTERINGLY:
   A. angrily   B. strongly   C. plainly   D. weakly

____ 4. INGRATIATING:
   A. civilized   B. thankful   C. disrespectful   D. soothing

Name _____ Date _____

"**Like the Sun**" by R.K. Narayan
"**The Open Window**" by Saki

Integrated Language Skills: Support for Writing to Compare Literary Works

Before you draft your essay comparing and contrasting the ideas of honesty and deception in these two stories, complete the graphic organizer below.

	"Like the Sun"	"The Open Window"
Examples of a character's honesty or deception		
How a character's attitude toward honesty or deception changes		
Resulting ironies or paradoxes		
Important idea(s) the author wants to convey		

Now, use your notes to write an essay comparing and contrasting the authors' ideas about honesty and deception. In your essay, examine how each author uses irony or paradox to express these ideas.

Name _____   Date _____

"Like the Sun" by R. K. Narayan
"The Open Window" by Saki
Open-Book Test

Short Answer *Write your responses to the questions in this section on the lines provided.*

1. In R. K. Narayan's short story "Like the Sun," Sekhar responds to his wife's cooking. What is unexpected and ironic about this situation? Think about what Sekhar's wife expects.

   _____

   _____

2. In "Like the Sun," what is ironic about the headmaster's response to Sekhar the day after Sekhar visits the headmaster's home?

   _____

   _____

   _____

3. At the end of "Like the Sun," what does Sekhar seem to mean by the paradoxical statement that telling the truth is like a luxury?

   _____

   _____

   _____

4. Near the beginning of Saki's short story, "The Open Window," Vera says to Framton Nuttel, "Then you know practically nothing about my aunt?" What does this question lead Vera to do?

   _____

   _____

   _____

   _____

5. The name Vera comes from the Latin word for "true." Why is this word derivation ironic in the context of "The Open Window"?

   _____

   _____

   _____

6. Use the Venn diagram to compare and contrast the main characters of Sekhar in "Like the Sun" and Vera in "The Open Window." Then, answer the question that follows the diagram.

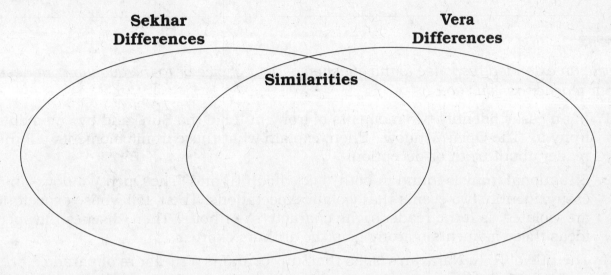

Sekhar Differences

Vera Differences

Similarities

Why do you think one character is more believable than the other?

_____

_____

7. Briefly explain the difference between Sekhar's attitude toward truth in "Like the Sun" and Vera's attitude toward truth in "The Open Window."

_____

_____

_____

_____

8. Why are the endings of "Like the Sun" and "The Open Window" both a humorous surprise?

_____

_____

_____

9. Authors' attitudes toward their subject matter, characters, or audience can vary widely. Are the authors' attitudes in "Like the Sun" and "The Open Window" alike or different? Explain your answer.

_____

_____

_____

10. If you *scrutinized* a document, what would you be doing? Base your answer on the meaning of *scrutinized*.

_____

_____

Essay

Write an extended response to the question of your choice or to the question or questions your teacher assigns you.

11. In an essay, identify two moments of irony in "Like the Sun" and two moments of irony in "The Open Window." Then, explain what these ironic moments tell the reader about truth or deception.

12. Situational irony is found in both "Like the Sun" and "The Open Window." In an essay, identify two events that violate expectations. Then, tell whose expectations are violated. Is it the reader's, the characters', or both? Then, discuss the specific ideas these moments of irony help the authors express.

13. The title of R. K. Narayan's "Like the Sun" contains a measure of paradox, or contradiction. In an essay, explain how this is so. As you consider the title, think about Sekhar's comment that "truth is like the sun." In what ways is truth like the sun? In what ways is it not like the sun? Discuss these issues in an essay, supporting your main ideas with details from the story.

14. **Thinking About the Big Question: What is the difference between reality and truth?** In a brief essay, discuss the issues of reality and truth as they relate to the main characters of Sekhar in "Like the Sun" and Vera in "The Open Window." How does each character perceive truth? How does each perception relate to the reality of the world around the character?

Oral Response

15. Go back to question 3, 6, or 8 or to the question your teacher assigns you. Take a few minutes to expand your answer and prepare an oral response. Find additional details in the selections that support your points. If necessary, make an outline to guide your oral response.

"**Like the Sun**" by R. K. Narayan
"**The Open Window**" by Saki
Selection Test A

Critical Reading *Identify the letter of the choice that best answers the question.*

___ 1. In "Like the Sun," what experiment does Sekhar conduct?
    A. observing how anger affects different people
    B. keeping the ungraded papers a secret for ten days
    C. studying the effects of sunlight
    D. telling the truth for one day

___ 2. In "Like the Sun," Sekhar makes a comment about breakfast to his wife. What is the result of this comment?
    A. He has a bad day at work.
    B. She prepares another meal.
    C. Her feelings are hurt.
    D. He gets another helping.

___ 3. In "Like the Sun," how does Sekhar feel when he is asked to critique the headmaster's singing?
    A. excited
    B. uneasy
    C. angry
    D. pleased

___ 4. In "Like the Sun," Sekhar fears that because of his actions, he may lose his friends and his job. Why does he fear these things?
    A. because he is wasting time on his experiment
    B. because people do not want Sekhar to improve himself
    C. because people are generally against change
    D. because hearing the truth can be painful for people

___ 5. Which is an ironic event in "Like the Sun"?
    A. Sekhar has an idea for an experiment.
    B. Sekhar goes to the headmaster's house for dinner.
    C. The headmaster sings traditional Indian songs.
    D. The headmaster thanks Sekhar for his opinion.

_____ 6. Why is Framton Nuttel visiting the Sappletons in the country?

   A. He hopes to go on a hunting expedition.

   B. He hopes to rest and relax his nerves.

   C. He is attending a family reunion.

   D. He is delivering a message from his sister.

_____ 7. Why does Vera confirm the fact that Framton Nuttel does not know her aunt well at all?

   A. She wants to prepare him for her aunt's strange behavior if he does not know her.

   B. She believes she has seen him at the house before.

   C. She must confirm the fact he does not know her aunt before she decides that she does not like him.

   D. She must confirm the fact that he does not know her aunt before she creates her fictional tale about her aunt and the open window.

_____ 8. Until Mr. Sappleton returns, Framton believes that Mrs. Sappleton is

   A. sadly deranged.

   B. rather cold-hearted.

   C. exceptionally boring.

   D. perfectly normal.

_____ 9. In what does Framton seem to be mainly interested?

   A. Vera's coquettish behavior

   B. the masculine atmosphere

   C. Mrs. Sappleton's mood

   D. his own problems.

_____ 10. Which idea is explored in both "Like the Sun" and "The Open Window"?

   A. death

   B. greed

   C. truthfulness

   D. affection

_____ 11. How are Sekhar in "Like the Sun" and Vera in "The Open Window" alike?

   A. They both have a plan.

   B. They are both musicians.

   C. They both lose their jobs.

   D. They are both kind to others.

___ 12. What is a paradox?

    A. a statement that expresses contradictory ideas, but is true

    B. a clue to the outcome of the story

    C. a person, place, or thing that stands for something other than itself

    D. a conflict between a character and his or her surroundings

___ 13. What is the irony in the effects on Sekhar and Vera in handling the truth?

    A. Neither care that others have been hurt.

    B. Both have succeeded in manipulating others' behaviors.

    C. Both characters succeed in achieving their goal, one by lying and one by telling the truth.

    D. Sekhar suffers for telling the truth; Vera is not punished for lying.

Vocabulary

___ 14. What might an *ingratiating* person do?

    A. forgive a friend   C. flatter others

    B. welcome a stranger   D. watch too much

___ 15. Which is the most likely to be *scrutinized*?

    A. dirty dishes   C. a nursery rhyme

    B. a crime scene   D. a cold drink

Essay

16. Both Vera in "The Open Window" and Sekhar in "Like the Sun" have a mission. In a brief essay, identify each character's mission. Does it succeed or does it fail? Why? Be sure to include examples from the stories to support what you say.

17. In an essay, identify two moments of irony in "Like the Sun" and two moments of irony in "The Open Window." Then explain how these ironic moments help the author express a certain message about truth or deception.

18. **Thinking about the Big Question: Is there a difference between reality and truth?** Sometimes people miss the whole truth because they create their own version of reality. Vera, the main character in "The Open Window," makes up stories. How do her stories change the way she sees the truth about the world around her? Answer this question in a brief essay. Provide at least two examples from the story to support your response.

"Like the Sun" by R. K. Narayan
"The Open Window" by Saki
Selection Test B

Critical Reading *Identify the letter of the choice that best completes the statement or answers the question.*

_____ 1. In "Like the Sun," what reason does Sekhar give for his experiment?
   A. It will be amusing to see people's reactions.
   B. Without truth, life is meaningless.
   C. Pleasing people has become tedious.
   D. The sun shines, but not forever.

_____ 2. In "Like the Sun," how is Sekhar's response to his wife's cooking ironic?
   A. She spent hours preparing a special meal.
   B. He usually enjoys breakfast.
   C. She knew he would not like the meal.
   D. She did not expect him to be so honest.

_____ 3. In "Like the Sun," what becomes the most difficult test of Sekhar's vow?
   A. being honest with his co-workers
   B. telling the truth about the headmaster's singing
   C. listening to music he does not typically enjoy
   D. grading one hundred test papers in a single night

_____ 4. In "Like the Sun," what is ironic about the headmaster's response to Sekhar the day after Sekhar visits his home?
   A. The headmaster is openly angry with Sekhar.
   B. The headmaster refuses to speak to Sekhar.
   C. The headmaster has accepted Sekhar's opinion.
   D. The headmaster rewards Sekhar for telling the truth.

_____ 5. In "Like the Sun," what does Sekhar's firm commitment to his experiment say about his character?
   A. He wants to become an honest person.
   B. He does not truly value his friends and loved ones.
   C. He wants to be considerate at all costs.
   D. He enjoys hurting people's feelings.

_____ 6. In "Like the Sun," what does Sekhar mean when he says telling the truth is a "luxury"?
   A. Being honest at all times is a challenge.
   B. The experiment has proved to be a waste of time.
   C. Only people who do not need to succeed or be liked can practice total honesty.
   D. It is expensive to be honest and so should only be practiced by the very wealthy.

_____ 7. Which of the following events occurs first in "The Open Window"?
   A. Vera makes up a story about Framton's fear of dogs.
   B. Framton grabs his belongings and runs frantically from the house.
   C. Framton goes into detail about his ailments and infirmities.
   D. Mrs. Sappleton announces that her husband and brothers will soon return from shooting.

____ 8. Why is Vera able to fool Framton so easily?

  A. Framton was planning to leave early anyway.

  B. Framton seems tired and lacking in good judgment.

  C. Vera is shrewd and manipulative, while Framton is self-absorbed and conventional.

  D. Vera has tricked other house guests into leaving.

____ 9. Based on details in "The Open Window," what caused Vera to tell Framton the story of her aunt's "great tragedy"?

  A. She wanted him to understand her aunt's present state of mind.

  B. She was upset and felt that Framton was someone she could talk to.

  C. She had no self-control and blathered on about private family matters.

  D. She found Framton's company insufferable and wanted to get rid of him.

____ 10. What is ironic about Mrs. Sappleton's remark, "One would think he had seen a ghost"?

  A. She does not realize that Framton believes he has seen a ghost.

  B. Framton definitely has seen a ghost.

  C. Mrs. Sappleton does not understand why Framton leaves.

  D. Mrs. Sappleton seems annoyed with Framton.

____ 11. "The Open Window" by Saki is mostly about

  A. how to behave around particularly boring visitors.

  B. how misinformation affects our perceptions.

  C. the unexpected effects of playing tricks.

  D. the possibility that ghosts really exist.

____ 12. Which of the following is a central idea of "The Open Window"?

  A. It is impossible to please everyone.

  B. Young people care only about themselves.

  C. Self-centered people tend to be gullible.

  D. Dealing with strangers can be risky.

____ 13. Both "Like the Sun" and "The Open Window" explore themes related to

  A. betrayal and death.

  B. greed and power.

  C. honesty and deception.

  D. knowledge and ignorance.

____ 14. How are Sekhar in "Like the Sun" and Vera in "The Open Window" alike?

  A. Both have a "noble mission."

  B. Both experiment with the truth.

  C. Both lose their jobs.

  D. Both betray themselves.

____ 15. Which occurs when the reader knows something that a character or speaker does not?

  A. situational irony

  B. verbal irony

  C. dramatic irony

  D. paradox

____ **16.** Which quality is shared by Sekhar in "Like the Sun" and Vera in "The Open Window"?
   A. insensitivity   **C.** ambition
   B. sensitivity   **D.** self-deception

____ **17.** What do the headmaster in "Like the Sun" and Mr. Framton in "The Open Window" have in common?
   A. Both are gullible.
   B. Both manipulate others.
   C. Both insist on the absolute truth.
   D. Both have their expectations violated.

Vocabulary

____ **18.** In "The Open Window," Vera claims that Mrs. Sappleton suffers under a *delusion* that
   A. her dead husband and brothers will return.
   B. her husband is dead.
   C. she is being haunted by ghosts.
   D. Vera is her daughter.

____ **19.** When the headmaster tells Sekhar the students' papers need to be *scrutinized* in "Like the Sun," what does he want Sekhar to do?
   A. throw the papers away   **C.** give the papers to him
   B. examine the papers closely   **D.** glance at the papers

____ **20.** Which of these might be considered *ingratiating*?
   A. a shriek   **C.** flattery
   B. a critical comment   **D.** an unusual request

Essay

21. Both "Like the Sun" and "The Open Window" make use of situational irony. In an essay, explain how. For each story, identify at least two events that violate the expectations either of the reader or of characters in the story. What specific ideas do these moments of irony help each author express?

22. The main characters in both "Like the Sun" and "The Open Window" challenge an accepted way of doing things. In an essay, identify what each character challenges; how he does so; and what his reasons are. In your opinion, is either character successful? Why?

23. The title of each of these selections—"Like the Sun" and "The Open Window"—contains a measure of paradox, or contradiction. In an essay, explain how this is so. As you consider the title "Like the Sun," think about Sekhar's comment that "Truth is like the sun." In what ways *is* it like the sun? In what ways is it *not*? As you consider the title "The Open Window," ask yourself why the window is open.

24. **Thinking about the Big Question: Is there a difference between reality and truth?** In a brief essay, discuss the issues of reality and truth as they relate to the main characters of Sekhar in "Like the Sun" and Vera in "The Open Window." How does each character perceive truth? How does each perception relate to the reality of the word around the character?

Name _____ Date _____

Exposition: Cause-and-Effect Essay

Prewriting: Gathering Details

Organize your ideas and details in one of the following cause-and-effect charts to help you form a clear picture of the relationship you will write about.

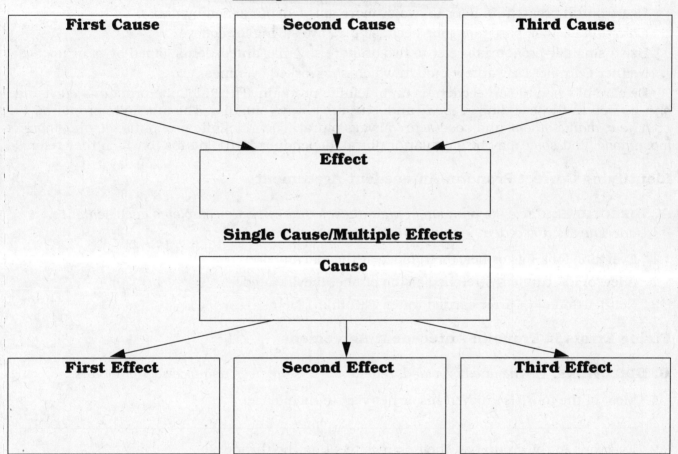

Multiple Causes/One Effect

| First Cause | Second Cause | Third Cause |

Effect

Single Cause/Multiple Effects

Cause

| First Effect | Second Effect | Third Effect |

Drafting: Choosing a Logical Organization

Use the following graphic organizer to organize your ideas in either chronological order or order of importance.

First Event	Second Event	Third Event	Fourth Event
Least Important	Next Important	Next Important	Most Important

Writing Workshop
Cause-and-Effect Essay: Integrating Grammar Skills

Revising Pronoun-Antecedent Agreement

A pronoun should agree with its antecedent in person, number, and gender. The **antecedent** is the word or words to which a pronoun refers. In the following example, the pronoun *she* and its antecedent *Cara* are both third-person, singular, and female.

> *Cara* took a part-time job because *she* is saving for college.

Use a plural pronoun to refer to two or more antecedents joined by *and*.

> *Cara and Liz* took part-time jobs because *they* are saving for college.

Use a singular pronoun to refer to two or more singular antecedents joined by *or* or *nor*.

> Neither *Cara nor Liz* wanted a job in which *she* worked evenings.

Be careful when the antecedent is an indefinite pronoun. The indefinite pronouns *each* and *one*, as well as those ending in *-body* and *-one*, are always singular. The indefinite pronouns *both, few, many, others*, and *several* are always plural. The indefinite pronouns *all, any, more, most, none*, and *some* may be singular or plural, depending on the nouns to which they refer.

Identifying Correct Pronoun-Antecedent Agreement

A. DIRECTIONS: *Circle the pronoun in parentheses that correctly completes each sentence. Underline the antecedent with which the pronoun agrees.*

1. Everyone took (his or her, their) place at the starting line.

2. A few of the runners stretched as (he or she, they) waited.

3. Neither Bob nor Carter carried water with (him, them).

Fixing Errors in Pronoun-Antecedent Agreement

B. DIRECTIONS: *On the lines provided, rewrite these sentences using correct pronouns.*

1. Most of the tourists enjoyed his or her visit to the palace.

   _____

2. Everyone in the group had their chance to sit on the throne.

   _____

3. Either Eric or Todd had their picture taken with a palace guard.

   _____

Unit 1 Vocabulary Workshop—1
Using a Dictionary and Thesaurus

A **dictionary** is an alphabetical listing of words. It gives definitions, pronunciation guides, parts of speech, etymology, and more. A **thesaurus** is a dictionary that lists synonyms, or words with similar meanings.

A. DIRECTIONS: *Use the dictionary entry below to complete the activities that follow.*

> **perspective** (per spek′ tiv) *n.* [Middle English *perspectyf*, from Medieval Latin *perspectivum*, from neuter of *perspectivus* of optics, from Latin *perspectus*, past participle of *perspicere* to look through, see clearly, from *per-* through + *specere* to look] **1** the drawing or painting of parallel lines as converging in order to give the appearance of distance or depth **2** the view of things in their true relations or relative importance <maintain your *perspective*> **3** a mental view, outlook, or prospect <gaining a broader *perspective*> —**perspectival** (per spek′ ti vel) *adj.*[1]

1. Circle the part of speech in the dictionary entry above. What is the part of speech?

    _____

2. Underline the word's etymology. What does "etymology" mean?

    _____

3. From what languages does the word *perspective* come?

    _____

4. Write the number of the definition that would best help you understand what an *author's perspective* is.

    _____

B. DIRECTIONS: Use the thesaurus entry below to complete the activities that follow.

> **insight**
> SYNONYMS acumen, awareness, comprehension, discernment, divination, intuition, judgment, observation, perception, perspicacity, sagacity, savvy, shrewdness, understanding, vision, wisdom
> ANTONYMS denseness, dullness, ignorance, ineptness, naivete, stupidity[2]

1. Based on the synonyms listed in this thesaurus entry, write a definition for *insight* in your own words.

    _____

2. What is a word that means the opposite of *insight*?

    _____

Unit 1 Resources: Fiction and Nonfiction
231

Unit 1 Vocabulary Workshop—2
Using a Dictionary and Thesaurus

A **dictionary** is an alphabetical listing of words. It gives definitions, pronunciation guides, parts of speech, etymology, and more. A **thesaurus** is a dictionary that lists synonyms, or words with similar meanings.

A. DIRECTIONS: *Use a dictionary to look up a word of your choice. On the lines below, copy the entire dictionary entry. Then, complete the activities that follow.*

_____

_____

_____

_____

_____

1. Circle the part of speech in the dictionary entry above.
2. Underline the word's etymology.

B. DIRECTIONS: *Use a thesaurus to look up a word of your choice. On the lines below, copy the thesaurus entry. Then, complete the activities that follow.*

_____

_____

_____

_____

_____

1. Write a sentence using the word you looked up.

_____

2. Can you directly substitute a synonym for the word you looked up in the sentence you wrote? Does it change the meaning of the sentence at all?

_____

_____

_____

_____

_____

_____

Name _____ Date _____

Communications Workshop
Analyzing Media Presentations

Analyze a television newscast or advertisement. Use the following chart to help you with your analysis.

Topic and Type of Media Presentation: _____

What was the main purpose of the media presentation?
How well did the presentation use facts to support its purpose?
How effectively did the presentation use opinions to support its purpose?
What aspects of the presentation were handled well or poorly?
How, if at all, did the presentation use charged language, images, or stereotypes?
Assess the reliability and objectivity of the presentation.

Unit 1: Fiction and Nonfiction
Benchmark Test 2

MULTIPLE CHOICE

Literary Analysis: Conflict and Resolution

Read the passage from a short story. Then, answer the questions that follow.

Ollie heard someone tapping on his bedroom window. He climbed out of bed and went to the window. His friends Lane and Andy stood in the moonlight outside, looking anxious. "It's about time!" Andy said with exasperation. "You've got to help us, or else we're in big trouble. We sneaked my dad's car out for a ride around the block, but the engine died. We need your help pushing the car back into the garage."

Ollie took a deep breath while he debated with himself. Andy and Lane were his good friends, but he didn't want to become an accomplice to a crime. His strong urge was to say no, close the window, and climb back into bed. "Come on, Ollie!" Lane urged. "We need your help—*now!*" Suddenly, Ollie noticed a figure in the street. The man was carrying a flashlight and heading straight toward them.

1. Which aspect of the passage best shows an example of an external conflict?
   A. Ollie tries to decide whether to help Andy and Lane.
   B. Andy sneaks his father's car out of the garage.
   C. Lane and Andy pressure Ollie to help them.
   D. Ollie climbs out of bed and goes to the window.

2. What internal conflict does a character in the passage face?
   A. Andy wants to get the car back in the garage before his dad finds out what happened.
   B. Ollie wants to help his friends, but he does not want to get into trouble.
   C. Lane does not want Andy to get into trouble for sneaking the car out.
   D. Andy wants Ollie to help him avoid getting into trouble.

3. Which words from the passage indicate that a character is facing an internal conflict?
   A. "It's about time!"
   B. we're in big trouble
   C. We need your help
   D. while he debated with himself

4. Which of these details adds the most suspense to the passage?
   A. the reason Ollie gets out of bed
   B. the sudden appearance of the figure with the flashlight
   C. the exasperation with which Andy speaks
   D. the deep breath that Ollie takes

Literary Analysis: Author's Purpose

Read the expository passage about nougat. Then, answer the questions that follow.

You've seen the ads on television. A disembodied voice entices you with a barrage of delicious adjectives: "Rich milk chocolate, crunchy peanuts, and creamy nougat..." Wait! What exactly is nougat? Does anyone know? Where does it come from? What a funny word: *nougat*. It sounds French. In fact, it *is* French. The French word *nougat* comes from the Latin *nuca*, which is related to the word *nut*.

Traditional vanilla nougat is made from egg whites, sugar, honey, almonds, pistachio nuts, vanilla, and sometimes candied fruits. Today's candy makers depart from the traditional recipe by using lots of corn syrup and sucrose. Instead of egg whites, they often use hydrolyzed soy protein. And they add vegetable fats and milk powder. Sound good? On second thought, maybe we're better off not knowing what nougat is! Like so many highly processed foods, today's nougat seems to contain many ingredients that are not very healthful.

5. Which sentence in the passage most clearly reveals that one of the author's purposes is to persuade?
   A. the first sentence of the first paragraph
   B. the last sentence of the first paragraph
   C. the first sentence of the second paragraph
   D. the last sentence of the second paragraph

6. What are the author's two main purposes in the first paragraph of the passage?
   A. to describe and to persuade
   B. to persuade and to inform
   C. to inform and to entertain
   D. to tell a story

Literary Analysis: Irony and Paradox

7. What is the literary term for a seemingly contradictory statement that actually reveals a deeper truth?
   A. paradox
   B. dramatic irony
   C. verbal irony
   D. situational irony

8. In what way does the following sentence illustrate verbal irony?

   "Looks don't matter in this contest," Emily said, as she applied still more mascara and blush.

   A. The outcome of events is not what the reader expects to happen.
   B. Emily expresses a universal theme.
   C. Emily says the opposite of what she really means.
   D. Emily speaks with great emotional intensity.

9. Which of the following answer choices best defines situational irony?
   A. an expression of contradictory ideas that complement each other
   B. a situation in which the reader knows something that a character does not
   C. a statement that means the opposite of what it says
   D. an event that contradicts strong expectations

Reading Skill: Cause and Effect

Read the passage. Then, answer the questions that follow.

A natural wonder, Niagara Falls has attracted tourists for centuries. It has also attracted its share of daredevils. In 1901, Annie Taylor was the first person to survive a plunge over the falls. Stuffed inside a wooden barrel, the 63-year-old woman was towed into the middle of the Niagara River and then cut loose. The barrel bounced and bobbed its way toward the falls. Then, it took the long plunge and, after reaching the bottom, slammed into several rocks. Less than twenty minutes later, Taylor was pulled from the barrel, slightly dazed. "No one ought ever do that again!" she was heard to say.

Ignoring Taylor's advice, Englishman Bobby Leach rode the falls in a steel barrel. He sustained several fractures but recovered after a few months in a hospital—only to die later as a result of an accident. Walking on a street in New Zealand, he slipped and fell. Because of complications from the fall, one of Leach's legs had to be amputated. He suffered gangrene poisoning after surgery and died.

10. According to the selection, why are tourists attracted to Niagara Falls?
   A. People go to see the daredevils.
   B. The falls lie between two countries.
   C. The falls are a natural wonder.
   D. They go for recreation on the river.

11. Which detail best explains why Annie Taylor was dazed after going over the falls?
   A. The barrel that she was traveling in slammed into rocks.
   B. She was 63 years of age.
   C. She did not expect to survive.
   D. The barrel that she was traveling in bobbed in the water.

Read the information in the chart. Then, answer the questions that follow.

The Rise and Fall of Ancient Chinese Dynasties

1. New Dynasty Rises	2. New Dynasty Rules	3. Dynasty Fails
• Strong local rulers defeat others. • Rulers often acquire new land.	• It restores peace. • It chooses loyal officials. • It makes reforms.	• Rulers grow lazy and corrupt. • They lose control of provinces. • They cannot defend against rebellion, disaster, or invasion.

12. According to the chart, what is one effect of a new dynasty's taking control in ancient China?
   A. Local rulers fight for power.
   B. Rebellions take place.
   C. Reforms are put in place.
   D. Rulers lose control of provinces.

13. According to the chart, what is one cause of the failure of a dynasty?
  A. Rulers add captured land.
  B. Rulers become corrupt and lazy.
  C. Rulers make too many reforms.
  D. Rulers restore peace.

Reading Skill: Evaluate Sources

14. Which URL ending is likeliest to indicate a Web site with the most reliable information?
  A. .edu
  B. .biz
  C. .com
  D. .net

15. Which of these strategies would best help users analyze the credibility of a Web site?
  A. checking to see how many hits the site has gotten to date
  B. determining how easy the site is to navigate
  C. evaluating the quality of the graphics and design
  D. considering the credentials of the site's authors or sponsors

16. Which of the following answer choices is *not* an effective way to evaluate the credibility of a Web site?
  A. Check the information against another reliable source.
  B. Check to see when the information on the site was last updated.
  C. Ask a classmate if the site seems reliable.
  D. Consider whether the site's author or sponsor might be biased.

Grammar: Pronouns

17. Which of the following sentences contains three personal pronouns?
  A. I gave you my word.
  B. He went to the store to buy a card for his sister.
  C. He gave John his word.
  D. John went to the store to buy his mother and father a card.

18. Which personal pronoun should replace the italicized noun in this sentence?

"The triumph will be *Shirley's*," said Shirley.

  A. yours
  B. mine
  C. ours
  D. theirs

19. Which of the following sentences contains a personal pronoun?
    A. The entire team quickly ran around the field as the coach watched.
    B. Jennifer gave Trudy the funny book that was discussed in class.
    C. Americans are lucky to live in a strong democracy.
    D. Jake already gave that book back to you.

20. Which of the following sentences uses a relative pronoun correctly?
    A. The player whom was injured stood on the sidelines.
    B. The player which was injured stood on the sidelines.
    C. The player whose was injured stood on the sidelines.
    D. The player who was injured stood on the sidelines.

21. Which sentence contains a relative pronoun?
    A. He refused to go camping, and he would not go on a road trip.
    B. We ate lunch with our aunt and uncle and their son and daughter.
    C. The teacher who taught our workshop was an expert on the topic.
    D. Our instructor returns everyone's essays the day after we write them.

22. Which word is the relative pronoun in the following sentence?

    Who directed the movie that you and I saw last night?
    A. Who   C. you
    B. that   D. I

23. Which of the following sentences uses correct pronoun-antecedent agreement?
    A. Neither Julietta nor Maria had his annual sports physical yet.
    B. Neither Julietta nor Maria had her annual sports physical yet.
    C. Neither Julietta nor Maria had their annual sports physical yet.
    D. Neither Julietta nor Maria had my annual sports physical yet.

24. Which sentence uses correct pronoun-antecedent agreement?
    A. Neither George Washington nor Thomas Paine signed their name on the Declaration of Independence.
    B. Either Sally or LaToya will give her campaign speech this morning.
    C. When Mike and Ray presented the final project, he got a good grade.
    D. Both Alex and Bill will share his ideas for a school fundraiser.

25. What is the antecedent of the pronoun *their* in the following sentence?

    The trees lost several of their branches in last week's storms.
    A. trees   C. branches
    B. several   D. storms

Vocabulary: Roots and Prefixes

26. The root -ven- means "come" or "go." In the following sentence, what does the word *convention* mean?

    Representatives of student governments from every state attend the national convention each year.
    A. a problem that people solve
    B. a meeting that people attend
    C. a battle that people fight
    D. a formula that people prove

27. The words *international* and *interrupt* share the prefix *inter-*. Using this knowledge, what do you conclude the prefix *inter-* means?
    A. place
    B. before
    C. between
    D. after

28. One meaning of the prefix *ob-* is "against." Using this knowledge, what do you conclude a lawyer does when she objects to an opponent's line of questioning?
    A. She asks for more information.
    B. She asks that the questions be repeated.
    C. She expresses her approval of the questioning.
    D. She expresses her disapproval of the questioning.

29. The root -ver- means "true." Using this knowledge, choose the word that is formed from the root -ver-.
    A. overlook
    B. verify
    C. lever
    D. everything

WRITING

30. Write an anecdote, or brief story, that includes an ironic ending. The anecdote may be based on your own experience, may be a retelling of another story or film plot, or may be entirely invented by you. Set readers up for an expected outcome, but then surprise them with an unexpected outcome.

Name _____ Date _____

31. Write a proposal for a documentary in which you examine the greatest assets of the town or city in which you live. On a separate sheet of paper, list three people, places, or things that you will feature in your documentary. Briefly tell why each is an asset, and explain how you will present each one in the film.

32. On a separate sheet of paper, write a brief cause-and-effect essay about meeting a challenge. In your essay, explain the causes of the challenge and the effects of facing and overcoming that challenge. Include a diagram that shows the chain of causes and effects.

Vocabulary in Context

MULTIPLE CHOICE

Read the selection. Then, answer the questions that follow.

1. Each week, Mom gives us ten dollars each for our _____ .
   A. treasury
   B. luxury
   C. allowances
   D. cashed

2. I could buy the black shoes or the brown shoes, and I think I will choose the _____ .
   A. midst
   B. genuine
   C. latter
   D. extreme

3. Once the ingredients for the bread are in the bowl, I will show you how to _____ the dough.
   A. knead
   B. pursue
   C. waver
   D. barbecue

4. I was so thirsty that I was feeling _____ .
   A. awaiting
   B. parched
   C. subdued
   D. revealed

5. If you do not take care of your teeth, you will likely have _____ .
   A. brittle
   B. mottled
   C. agitated
   D. cavities

6. When the fire fighters arrived on the scene, the warehouse was already _____ .
   A. brazier
   B. astray
   C. sabotage
   D. ablaze

7. I decided to use a ladder to clean the leaves out of the_____ around the house.
   A. abode
   B. drainpipes
   C. casements
   D. parapets

8. These spices will give your dish a very special_____ taste.
   A. pungent
   B. bland
   C. dank
   D. extraordinarily

9. The school policy states that for every six students, there must be at least one_____ on field trips.
   A. governess
   B. reveler
   C. chaperone
   D. reinforcement

10. Thousands of years ago, monks lived, worked, and prayed in this old_____ .
    A. sloop
    B. elementary
    C. abbey
    D. stucco

11. After teaching for several years, he was hired to be the_____ of the boarding school.
    A. scribe
    B. associate
    C. headmaster
    D. colleague

12. When the shots rang out over their heads, the crowd_____ .
    A. separation
    B. unseated
    C. overrun
    D. dispersed

13. When the jury members did not reach a verdict by the end of the day, they were_____ overnight.
    A. coded
    B. sequestered
    C. termination
    D. clinched

14. I try to exercise and read some _____ quietly every day.
   A. sayings
   B. assumptions
   C. pacts
   D. meditations

15. Those movies about exploring outer space became his first _____ with spaceships.
   A. passionate
   B. characterization
   C. scenario
   D. preoccupation

16. He did not do his job, and he _____ his duties.
   A. ejected
   B. analyze
   C. persecuted
   D. shirked

17. I shouldn't take the vacation time now _____ I do need a break.
   A. logical
   B. consequence
   C. albeit
   D. doubtless

18. When we arrived in the city, we were amazed at the traffic and the _____ .
   A. monumental
   B. skyscrapers
   C. hillocks
   D. gothic

19. While serious areas of disagreement remain, our views are now more _____ .
   A. assailed
   B. recurred
   C. spectral
   D. convergent

20. When we graduated, we walked on stage and were handed our _____ .
   A. diplomas
   B. proverbs
   C. rubles
   D. postscripts

Diagnostic Tests and Vocabulary in Context
Use and Interpretation

The Diagnostic Tests and Vocabulary in Context were developed to assist teachers in making the most appropriate assignment of *Prentice Hall Literature* program selections to students. The purpose of these assessments is to indicate the degree of difficulty that students are likely to have in reading/comprehending the selections presented in the *following* unit of instruction. Tests are provided at six separate times in each grade level—a *Diagnostic Test* (to be used prior to beginning the year's instruction) and a *Vocabulary in Context*, the final segment of the Benchmark Test appearing at the end of each of the first five units of instruction. Note that the tests are intended for use not as summative assessments for the prior unit, but as guidance for assigning literature selections in the upcoming unit of instruction.

The structure of all Diagnostic Tests and Vocabulary in Context in this series is the same. All test items are four-option, multiple-choice items. The format is established to assess a student's ability to construct sufficient meaning from the context sentence to choose the only provided word that fits both the semantics (meaning) and syntax (structure) of the context sentence. All words in the context sentences are chosen to be "below-level" words that students reading at this grade level should know. All answer choices fit *either* the meaning or structure of the context sentence, but only the correct choice fits *both* semantics and syntax. All answer choices—both correct answers and incorrect options—are key words chosen from specifically taught words that will occur in the subsequent unit of program instruction. This careful restriction of the assessed words permits a sound diagnosis of students' current reading achievement and prediction of the most appropriate level of readings to assign in the upcoming unit of instruction.

The assessment of vocabulary in context skill has consistently been shown in reading research studies to correlate very highly with "reading comprehension." This is not surprising as the format essentially assesses comprehension, albeit in sentence-length "chunks." Decades of research demonstrate that vocabulary assessment provides a strong, reliable prediction of comprehension achievement—the purpose of these tests. Further, because this format demands very little testing time, these diagnoses can be made efficiently, permitting teachers to move forward with critical instructional tasks rather than devoting excessive time to assessment.

It is important to stress that while the Diagnostic and Vocabulary in Context were carefully developed and will yield sound assignment decisions, they were designed to *reinforce*, not supplant, teacher judgment as to the most appropriate instructional placement for individual students. Teacher judgment should always prevail in making placement—or indeed other important instructional—decisions concerning students.

Diagnostic Tests and Vocabulary in Context Branching Suggestions

These tests are designed to provide maximum flexibility for teachers. Your *Unit Resources* books contain the 40-question **Diagnostic Test** and 20-question **Vocabulary in Context** tests. At *PHLitOnline,* you can access the Diagnostic Test and complete 40-question Vocabulary in Context tests. Procedures for administering the tests are described below. Choose the procedure based on the time you wish to devote to the activity and your comfort with the assignment decisions relative to the individual students. Remember that your judgment of a student's reading level should always take precedence over the results of a single written test.

Feel free to use different procedures at different times of the year. For example, for early units, you may wish to be more confident in the assignments you make—thus, using the "two-stage" process below. Later, you may choose the quicker diagnosis, confirming the results with your observations of the students' performance built up throughout the year.

The **Diagnostic Test** is composed of a single 40-item assessment. Based on the results of this assessment, make the following assignment of students to the reading selections in Unit 1:

Diagnostic Test Score	Selection to Use
If the student's score is 0–25	more accessible
If the student's score is 26–40	more challenging

Outlined below are the three basic options for administering **Vocabulary in Context** and basing selection assignments on the results of these assessments.

1. For a one-stage, quicker diagnosis using the *20-item* test in the *Unit Resources:*

Vocabulary in Context Test Score	Selection to Use
If the student's score is 0–13	more accessible
If the student's score is 14–20	more challenging

2. If you wish to confirm your assignment decisions with a *two-stage* diagnosis:

Stage 1: Administer the 20-item test in the *Unit Resources*	
Vocabulary in Context Test Score	**Selection to Use**
If the student's score is 0–9	more accessible
If the student's score is 10–15	(Go to Stage 2.)
If the student's score is 16–20	more challenging

Stage 2: Administer items 21–40 from *PHLitOnline*	
Vocabulary in Context Test Score	**Selection to Use**
If the student's score is 0–12	more accessible
If the student's score is 13–20	more challenging

3. If you base your assignment decisions on the full 40-item **Vocabulary in Context** from *PHLitOnline:*

Vocabulary in Context Test Score	Selection to Use
If the student's score is 0–25	more accessible
If the student's score is 26–40	more challenging

Unit 1 Resources: Fiction and Nonfiction

Grade 10—Benchmark Test 1
Interpretation Guide

For remediation of specific skills, you may assign students the relevant Reading Kit Practice and Assess pages indicated in the far-right column of this chart. You will find rubrics for evaluating writing samples in the last section of your Professional Development Guidebook.

Skill Objective	Test Items	Number Correct	Reading Kit
Literary Analysis			
Plot and Foreshadowing	1, 2, 3, 4, 5		pp. 2, 3
Author's Perspective and Style	6, 7, 8, 9		pp. 4, 5, 6, 7
Reading Skill			
Make Predictions	10, 11, 12, 13, 14, 15, 16		pp. 8, 9
Analyze Structure and Format	17, 18		pp. 10, 11
Vocabulary			
Roots and Prefixes -cred-, -strict-, pro-, super-	19, 20, 21, 22		pp. 12, 13
Grammar			
Common and Proper Nouns	23, 24, 26		pp. 14, 15
Abstract and Concrete Nouns	25, 27, 29		pp. 16, 17
Possessive Nouns	28, 30, 31		pp. 18, 19
Writing			
Sequel	32	Use rubric	pp. 20, 21
Description	33	Use rubric	pp. 22, 23
Autobiographical Narrative	34	Use rubric	pp. 24, 25

Name _____   Date _____

Grade 10—Benchmark Test 2
Interpretation Guide

For remediation of specific skills, you may assign students the relevant Reading Kit Practice and Assess pages indicated in the far-right column of this chart. You will find rubrics for evaluating writing samples in the last section of your Professional Development Guidebook.

Skill Objective	Test Items	Number Correct	Reading Kit
Literary Analysis			
Plot; Conflict and Resolution	1, 2, 3, 4		pp. 30, 31
Author's Purpose	5, 6		pp. 26, 27
Irony and Paradox	7, 8, 9		pp. 28, 29
Reading Skill			
Cause and Effect	10, 11, 12, 13		pp. 32, 33
Evaluate Sources	14, 15, 16		pp. 34, 35
Vocabulary			
Roots and Prefixes -ver-, -ven-, inter-, ob-	26, 27, 28, 29		pp. 36, 37
Grammar			
Personal Pronouns	17, 18, 19		pp. 40, 41
Relative Pronouns	20, 21, 22		pp. 42, 43
Pronoun-Antecedent Agreement	23, 24, 25		pp. 38, 39
Writing			
Anecdote	30	Use rubric	pp. 46, 47
Documentary Proposal	31	Use rubric	pp. 48, 49
Cause-and-Effect Essay	32	Use rubric	pp. 50, 51

ANSWERS

Big Question Vocabulary—1, p. 1

Sample Answers

A. 1. comprehend: syn.—understand; ant.—misinterpret

   I do not speak Spanish, so I cannot comprehend it when I hear it spoken.

2. concrete: syn.—real; ant.—abstract

   I do not yet have concrete proof to show that my hypothesis is correct.

3. confirm: syn.—verify; ant.—disprove

   I can confirm that Shakespeare wrote that play by looking it up on the Internet.

4. context: syn.—background; ant.—isolation

   Considering the context of the story, which is set in the 1800s, I am sure that the author was not referring to space travel.

5. differentiate: syn.—distinguish; ant.—confuse

   I sometimes find it difficult to differentiate between the works of these two authors since their styles are so similar.

Big Question Vocabulary—2, p. 2

Sample Answers

1. F; One can discern the truth of a situation by eliminating anything that is not true or is an opinion.

2. T; *Evaluate* means to judge or weigh the importance of something. If you judge the facts upon which a person bases his or her opinion, you will be able to decide if the opinion is worthy of consideration.

3. T; Evidence tends to prove a theory or back up an opinion, so evidence would help a debate team win its argument.

4. F; The sun failing to rise tomorrow morning is completely improbable.

5. F; An objective opinion is one that is based on facts and logical conclusions.

Big Question Vocabulary—3, p. 3

Sample Answers

1. A truth is something that one can verify, or prove.

2. A person's perception of a situation can influence what he or she understands to be true. For example, if one person knows a fact that the other does not, he will have a different perception of the situation and might reach a different conclusion.

3. Emotions influence a person's perception of an issue, making her more subjective in her judgment.

4. You can match up elements of the novel with reality, and eliminate anything that gives you uncertainty. For example, a character talking to his mother who passed away years ago might indicate that a scene is actually meant to portray a dream.

5. Reality is simply what is real. Truth can also represent reality, but it is more subjective and is influenced by a person's perception.

Diagnostic Test, p. 5

MULTIPLE CHOICE

1. ANS: C
2. ANS: C
3. ANS: A
4. ANS: B
5. ANS: D
6. ANS: D
7. ANS: B
8. ANS: A
9. ANS: C
10. ANS: C
11. ANS: C
12. ANS: D
13. ANS: B
14. ANS: D
15. ANS: D
16. ANS: D
17. ANS: C
18. ANS: B
19. ANS: D
20. ANS: A
21. ANS: B
22. ANS: B
23. ANS: A
24. ANS: D
25. ANS: A
26. ANS: B
27. ANS: C
28. ANS: D
29. ANS: B
30. ANS: C
31. ANS: A
32. ANS: D
33. ANS: A
34. ANS: B
35. ANS: C
36. ANS: A
37. ANS: C
38. ANS: A
39. ANS: B
40. ANS: D

"Magdalena Looking" and "Artful Research"
by Susan Vreeland

Vocabulary Warm-up Exercises, p. 14

A.
1. chronology
2. whim
3. entailed
4. locales
5. eroded
6. defiance
7. auctioned
8. yield

B. Sample Answers

1. One good job for a very <u>meticulous</u> person is being an architect, because an architect needs to pay attention to many small details.
2. My friend Colleen would probably win a <u>trivia</u> contest because she knows a little bit about all sorts of subjects.
3. I do not think <u>muslin</u> would be warm enough for a winter scarf.
4. A <u>lute</u> sounds more like a guitar because both have strings that are plucked or strummed and similar shapes.
5. If someone is <u>ferociously</u> devoted to a hobby, he or she is extremely interested in it, almost to the point of obsession.
6. No; sometimes the best solution is more practical than <u>artful</u>.
7. Music that has a lot of high notes and strange sounds might be <u>evocative</u> of outer space.

Reading Warm-up A, p. 15

Sample Answers

1. (birth) (marriage) (death); A *chronology* is the order of events.
2. <u>the details of Vermeer's life</u>; When a rock is *eroded* by wind or water, parts of it are worn away.
3. (Paintings); Sculptures or antique furniture could also be *auctioned*.
4. <u>plenty of chances to observe and study paintings</u>; *Entailed* means "included or involved."
5. (interiors); In the movie I saw last weekend, two of the *locales* were a zoo and a diner.
6. <u>carefully selected and positioned</u>; I decided on a *whim* to make pancakes for breakfast last week.
7. <u>plenty of information about the way Vermeer used paint to create his rich illusions</u>; *Yield* means "to produce or result in."
8. <u>They boldly toss aside the normal ways of painting and follow their own goals.</u> *Defiance* is the refusal to obey or follow rules.

Reading Warm-up B, p. 16

Sample Answers

1. <u>important reflection</u>; One piece of *trivia* I know is the batting averages of every player for the Cleveland Indians.
2. <u>to get each detail just right</u>; My Aunt Sofia is very *meticulous* because she always takes at least an hour to get ready for any event.
3. <u>giving modern viewers insight into a world hundreds of years in the past</u>; *Evocative* means "bringing to mind images of another place."
4. (velvet) (satin); I might make an apron out of *muslin*.
5. <u>plucking the strings</u>; For example, violins, cellos, banjos, guitars, and fiddles are in the same family of instruments as the *lute*.
6. <u>First, apprentices learned to make exact copies of drawings and paintings</u>; I can make *artful* party invitations using my computer.
7. <u>forcing apprentices to redo work again and again until it was acceptable</u>; *Ferociously* means "intensely or fiercely."
8. (unreasonable); Five hours a day might be considered *excessive* by some people.

Susan Vreeland

Listening and Viewing, p. 17

Sample Answers

Segment 1. The glassware caused Susan Vreeland to think about the stories surrounding the creation of the piece, and her imagination enticed her to create stories and histories about artwork. Students may suggest that they would like to write about paintings, artists, sculpture, or film.

Segment 2. She wrote articles about local painters, did interviews, and wrote descriptions in her journal; students may suggest that these writings intensified her interest in art, sharpened her eye for detail, and improved her ability to write descriptively about paintings. According to Susan Vreeland, visual description can capture the reader's interest by offering exact details that make the reader feel like he or she is in a scene from the story.

Segment 3. Susan Vreeland "fills the holes" in a draft by reviewing the character motivations, issues of voice, and use of comparative language. Students may say that revising is important because a writer can improve what he or she has already written.

Segment 4. She would like her readers to see paintings as stories themselves, to explore art, and to identify with her characters. Students may suggest that they can learn about history, descriptive language, or different art forms.

Learning About Fiction and Nonfiction, p. 18

1. nonfiction
2. nonfiction
3. fiction

4. nonfiction
5. fiction
6. fiction
7. nonfiction
8. nonfiction
9. fiction
10. nonfiction

"Magdalena Looking" by Susan Vreeland

Model Selection: Fiction, p. 19

1. Amsterdam, 1696
2. Magdalena sees a notice for an art auction in the newspaper.
3. A. Magdalena, her father (J. Vermeer), Hendrick the baker;
   B. Magdalena is experiencing the events. Her father set them in motion by painting the portrait of Magdalena. Hendrick once owned the painting, and (as Magdalena expects) he has sold it.
4. A. It is told from the third-person limited point of view. The narrator knows only Magdalena's thoughts and feelings.
   B. *Sample answer:* She uses this point of view to show how a single individual relates to a painting and to art in general.

"Artful Research" by Susan Vreeland

Model Selection: Nonfiction, p. 20

1. the author, James Joyce, various authors and artists
2. the author's
3. *Sample answer:* Reading twenty printout pages on windmill engineering leads the author to the perfect metaphor for one of her characters, who learns to see that love is like the central shaft of a windmill.
4. *Sample answer:* In 1941 in the Netherlands, Jews were not allowed to keep pigeons. When researching *Girl in Hyacinth Blue*, the author consulted seventy-six books.
5. *Sample answer:* Research makes historical fiction richer and more interesting; good historical fiction "is about characters, not research."
6. *Sample answer:* The author's attitude toward the topic of writing historical fiction is positive and enthusiastic. This positive attitude is the result of the enjoyment she derives from writing historical fiction.

"Magdalena Looking" by Susan Vreeland

Open-Book Test, p. 21

Short Answer

1. The story contains imaginary events and characters, such as Magdalena herself.
   Difficulty: *Easy* **Objective:** *Literary Analysis*
2. "Magdalena Looking" is a short piece of fiction with one main plot. A novel is a longer work that usually has

chapters and subplots. A novella is longer than a short story but shorter than a novel.
   Difficulty: *Easy* **Objective:** *Literary Analysis*
3. General Setting: Time—seventeenth century; Place—the Netherlands (Holland) Opening Setting: Time—late afternoon, seventeenth century; Place—the Vermeer home, sentry post, Delft Closing Setting: Time—May 16, 1696; Place—auction gallery, Amsterdam, along a canal. Vreeland keeps the setting simple because short stories have to be focused in time and place.
   Difficulty: *Average* **Objective:** *Literary Analysis*
4. The story is told in the third-person point of view. The narrator is not a character in the story, but the thoughts and impressions are limited to the character of Magdalena.
   Difficulty: *Average* **Objective:** *Literary Analysis*
5. Magdalena likes to look at the world and to dream about painting it. Possible details include Magdalena "looking, looking"; Magdalena's observations from the sentry post involving color and form; her "pulsing wish" to paint; and her strong desire for her own colors and brushes.
   Difficulty: *Average* **Objective:** *Interpretation*
6. What most pains Magdalena is that he shows little interest in her and does not encourage her to paint. She most admires his artistic talent.
   Difficulty: *Average* **Objective:** *Interpretation*
7. Other examples of *defiance* would be refusing to do the mending or throwing the mending out the window.
   Difficulty: *Average* **Objective:** *Vocabulary*
8. Art can give people new understanding and can connect them to one another in a way that endures over time.
   Difficulty: *Challenging* **Objective:** *Literary Analysis*
9. She sees research as an adventure that helps give direction, depth, and authority to her fiction.
   Difficulty: *Average* **Objective:** *Literary Analysis*
10. Vreeland's main purpose is to inform. She seems to envision her main audience as people interested in writing.
    Difficulty: *Easy* **Objective:** *Literary Analysis*

Essay

11. Students should identify Magdalena's most powerful wish as her desire to become a painter. They should recognize that because of her gender and her father's attitude, the wish is unfulfilled. Some students may also say that even though Magdalena does not become a painter, she does have an artist's sensitivity to the world around her. Students should cite details from the story to illustrate Magdalena's wish and its outcome.
    Difficulty: *Easy* **Objective:** *Essay*
12. Students should recognize that Vreeland includes facts relating to the way she does research. These facts are valuable for other purposes, such as providing glimpses into Vreeland's writing process. They also illustrate her points about the research process, help persuade the

reader that the process works, and potentially inspire other writers. Students should include several facts from the essay to support their general statements.

Difficulty: *Average*   **Objective:** *Essay*

13. Students should note aspects of "Magdalena Looking" that suggest the author's research, such as geographical details about Delft and Amsterdam, information about Vermeer's paintings, and objects and accessories particular to the setting (such as iceboats, tapestries, and gold shoe buckles). Students who think the details enrich the story may suggest that they help capture Magdalena's artistic eye. Students who do not think researched facts add appeal may feel that there is too much detail, making the story less like a story than it should be. Students should support their opinions with evidence from the story.

Difficulty: *Challenging*   **Objective:** *Essay*

14. Students should recognize that not only Magdalena's society, but also her own father expect her to pursue a future only as a wife and mother. Both fail to notice her dreams of becoming an artist. They should cite details that illustrate Magdalena's keen eye for color and form—for example, observations from the sentry post. They could also discuss her artistic sensitivity—for example, her perceptions about art at the end of the story.

Difficulty: *Average*   **Objective:** *Essay*

Oral Response

15. Oral responses should be clear, well organized, and well supported by appropriate examples from the selection.

Difficulty: *Average*   **Objective:** *Oral Interpretation*

Selection Test A, p. 24

Critical Thinking

1. ANS: D	DIF: Easy	OBJ: Literary Analysis
2. ANS: B	DIF: Easy	OBJ: Literary Analysis
3. ANS: A	DIF: Easy	OBJ: Literary Analysis
4. ANS: C	DIF: Easy	OBJ: Literary Analysis
5. ANS: D	DIF: Easy	OBJ: Literary Analysis

Critical Reading

6. ANS: C	DIF: Easy	OBJ: Literary Analysis
7. ANS: A	DIF: Easy	OBJ: Comprehension
8. ANS: B	DIF: Easy	OBJ: Interpretation
9. ANS: B	DIF: Easy	OBJ: Comprehension
10. ANS: D	DIF: Easy	OBJ: Literary Analysis
11. ANS: A	DIF: Easy	OBJ: Interpretation
12. ANS: C	DIF: Easy	OBJ: Literary Analysis
13. ANS: A	DIF: Easy	OBJ: Interpretation
14. ANS: D	DIF: Easy	OBJ: Interpretation

Essay

15. Students should note that Magdalena's wish is to record life by painting what she sees. Some students may believe that if she had pursued her dream, she would have been successful. They may cite her love of "looking" and her deep sensitivity as evidence. Other students may believe that she would not have been successful, citing the social constraints on women at that time.

Difficulty: *Easy*   **Objective:** *Essay*

16. Students should define fiction as prose writing about characters and events from the author's imagination. They should point out that "Magdalena Looking" is a fictional story but that it contains some historically accurate information, such as details from the life of J. Vermeer, what the city of Delft looked like, and how paints were made in the 1600s. Finally, students should note that according to Vreeland, factual information makes a work of fiction more believable and more interesting.

Difficulty: *Easy*   **Objective:** *Essay*

17. Students should cite details that illustrate Magdalena's strong eye for color and form—for example, her observations from the sentry post. They could also discuss her artistic sensitivity—for example, her thoughts about art at the end of the story. Students should recognize that Magdalena's father, as well as the rest of society, expect her to be a wife and mother. They never notice her dreams of becoming an artist.

Difficulty: *Average*   **Objective:** *Essay*

Selection Test B, p. 27

Critical Thinking

1. ANS: D	DIF: Average	OBJ: Literary Analysis
2. ANS: B	DIF: Average	OBJ: Literary Analysis
3. ANS: C	DIF: Average	OBJ: Literary Analysis
4. ANS: B	DIF: Average	OBJ: Literary Analysis
5. ANS: A	DIF: Average	OBJ: Literary Analysis
6. ANS: D	DIF: Challenging	OBJ: Literary Analysis

Critical Reading

7. ANS: D	DIF: Challenging	OBJ: Literary Analysis
8. ANS: C	DIF: Average	OBJ: Comprehension
9. ANS: A	DIF: Average	OBJ: Interpretation
10. ANS: A	DIF: Average	OBJ: Comprehension
11. ANS: D	DIF: Challenging	OBJ: Literary Analysis
12. ANS: B	DIF: Challenging	OBJ: Interpretation
13. ANS: C	DIF: Challenging	OBJ: Literary Analysis
14. ANS: A	DIF: Challenging	OBJ: Interpretation
15. ANS: C	DIF: Average	OBJ: Literary Analysis
16. ANS: C	DIF: Average	OBJ: Interpretation

17. **ANS:** B   **DIF:** Average   **OBJ:** Interpretation

18. **ANS:** D   **DIF:** Challenging   **OBJ:** Comprehension

19. **ANS:** A   **DIF:** Challenging   **OBJ:** Comprehension

Essay

20. Students should note that Magdalena's most powerful wish is to paint, and that, because of her gender and her father's attitude toward her, her wish remains unfulfilled. Students may say that Vreeland seems to be urging her readers to value and pursue their own dreams—and thereby avoid the kind of regret Magdalena expresses at the auction when she sees the painting of herself.
    Difficulty: *Average*   **Objective:** *Essay*

21. Students should observe that Vreeland includes facts relating to her own research process and discoveries and that these facts are valuable not for their own sake but as glimpses into Vreeland's writing process. These facts help convince the reader that Vreeland's process works, and they may also inspire other writers to try the process on their own. Students should include at least two details from the essay.
    Difficulty: *Average*   **Objective:** *Essay*

22. Students should note aspects of "Magdalena Looking" that suggest the author's research, such as the geographical description of Delft from the perspective of the sentry post, the materials and processes her father used to make his paintings, and the objects and accessories particular to that time and place (such as iceboats, tapestries, and gold shoe buckles). Students may or may not agree that these details enrich the story, but they should support their opinions with evidence from the selection.
    Difficulty: *Challenging*   **Objective:** *Essay*

23. Students should recognize that not only Magdalena's society but also her own father expect her to pursue a future only as a wife and mother. Both fail to notice her dreams of becoming an artist. They should cite details that illustrate Magdalena's keen eye for color and form—for example, observations from the sentry post. They could also discuss her artistic sensitivity--for example, her perceptions about art at the end of the story.
    Difficulty: *Average*   **Objective:** *Essay*

"The Monkey's Paw" by W. W. Jacobs

Vocabulary Warm-up Exercises, p. 31

A. 1. torrent
2. persisted
3. preoccupied
4. pursued
5. haste
6. dubiously
7. unnecessary
8. virtues

B. **Sample Answers**

1. It was a <u>coincidence</u> that Jane and I wore *exactly the same* shirt today.
2. The ending of the story was so *surprising* that I felt <u>aghast</u>.
3. My sister hopes to get <u>apparel</u> like *a shirt or a belt* for her birthday.
4. Many people keep a horseshoe as *a lucky* <u>talisman</u>.
5. The politician seems <u>sinister</u>, so his promises *cannot* be trusted.
6. Your story was so <u>impressive</u> that I *read it aloud to my best friend.*
7. He accepted the <u>consequences</u> of his crime by *serving his prison term.*

Reading Warm-up A, p. 32

1. <u>as though she were being flooded</u>; A *torrent* is a quick flood or surge.
2. <u>very different paths</u>; I *pursued* the goal of singing with the school choir.
3. <u>forgot to call</u>; When I act in *haste*, I do things quickly and carelessly.
4. <u>(planning) (time management skills)</u>; A friend should have the *virtues* of honesty, reliability, and loyalty.
5. <u>(required)</u>; *Unnecessary* means "not required."
6. <u>questioning her own memory as well as the stranger</u>; *Dubiously* means "doubtfully."
7. <u>growing from vague suspicions to near certainty</u>; A synonym for *persisted* is *continued*.
8. <u>Amy never heard the favor</u>; People can become *preoccupied* when one topic becomes more important than anything else.

Reading Warm-up B, p. 33

Sample Answers

1. <u>attract good luck</u>; A *talisman* is something that people believe can attract good luck.
2. <u>(shirt) (socks)</u>; *Apparel* means "clothing."
3. <u>hardly aware of their actions</u>; *Absentmindedly* means "in a way that shows you are not aware of what you're doing."
4. <u>predict unfortunate or even tragic events</u>; A *sinister* plan could be a plan that has an evil or harmful goal.
5. <u>(serious) (unfortunate)</u>; *Consequences* are the results of an action, possibly serious or negative.
6. I would be *aghast* to see violence in the classroom.
7. <u>someone finds a four-leaf clover and then wins a huge prize in a contest</u>; Another *coincidence* would be a family winning a new car on the same day that the old car breaks down.
8. <u>convince others the clover really did bring good fortune</u>; I saw an *impressive* museum that helped people remember the struggle for civil rights.

Writing About the Big Question, p. 34

A. 1. improbable
2. differentiate
3. perception
4. comprehend

B. Sample Answers

1. The reality of what happens in a war might be different from the truth about the war.

2. In reality, one country is usually winning and one is losing in a way, but that **perception** can be hard to **verify**. The truth is that people on both sides are killed, so it is difficult to **evaluate** winners and losers.

C. Sample Answer

When people face personal hardship, they often have a hard time facing reality. Their perception of the future is bleak, even if concrete facts suggest a different truth. Although facing reality is tough, the truth behind any situation can often improve it.

Literary Analysis: Plot, p. 35

Sample Answers

1. exposition; foreshadows another fatal mistake—the first wish—that Mr. White will see after it is too late

2. rising action; foreshadows the Whites' interference with fate and their subsequent sorrow

3. rising action; foreshadows Mr. White's own third wish—for his dead son to return to the grave

4. rising action; foreshadows Herbert's death

Reading: Use Prior Knowledge to Make Predictions, p. 36

Sample Answers

1. The characters will try to wish and will come to sorrow.
   Clue: The man who put on the spell was "very holy" and wanted to teach people a lesson.
   Prior knowledge: I know that in horror stories, someone usually comes to sorrow.

2. The wish will come true.
   Clue: The paw moved.
   Prior knowledge: I know that in fiction, impossible wishes can come true.

3. The wife will wish her son alive again.
   Clue: When she asks for the paw, she does so "quietly"; she has made a decision.
   Prior knowledge: I know that most mothers will do anything to save their children.

Vocabulary Builder, p. 37

Sample Answers

A. 1. You should call the police.
2. I would probably not want to see it, as the reviewer said it was bad.

3. The candidate will probably lose the election.

4. The team lost, because the coach's *grave* expression showed serious thought or worry.

5. No, your *credulity* would make you ready to believe whatever the politician said.

6. The employer probably does not like the job, because the work load causes distress and discomfort.

B. 1. No, you would have no belief, or *credence*, in a report presented by someone who is untrustworthy.

2. Yes, this principle of belief, or *credo*, means you try to live in harmony with others.

3. The person is trying to cast doubt on the results and disgrace your reputation.

Enrichment: Problematic Wishes, p. 38

Answers will vary, but students should list six wishes, along with positive and possible negative consequences.

Sample Answers

Wish 1: A large sum of money

Positive consequences: wealth, freedom from want and debt

Possible negative consequences: The money could come to me at someone else's expense or as payment for something I don't want to do or to give up.

Wish 2: World peace

Positive consequences: no more suffering caused by war; increased life expectancy

Possible negative consequences: The world's population might explode, resulting in food shortages and starvation.

Wish 3: To become popular

Positive consequences: to have more friends; to no longer feel left out or inconsequential

Possible negative consequences: Popularity could result in a change in my personality that I wouldn't want.

Wish 4: To live forever

Positive consequences: no fear of death; to always be able to have another day

Possible negative consequences: I might get older and more infirm but never die.

Wish 5: To see the future

Positive consequences: no doubt or uncertainty about events; able to predict winnings at lotteries and contests

Possible negative consequences: I might see terrible things that I would rather not know.

Wish 6: To be happy

Positive consequences: no more unhappiness or suffering on my part

Possible negative consequences: I might not be able to register or understand others' suffering, which would make me less human.

Open-Book Test, p. 39

Short Answer

1. Life is cozy and affectionate. Supporting details include the warm fire, the chess game between Mr. White and

Unit 1 Resources: Fiction and Nonfiction

Herbert, and Mrs. White and Herbert's amused understanding of Mr. White's desire to win.
Difficulty: *Easy*   **Objective:** *Interpretation*

2. Remarks include Sergeant Major Morris's explanation
that anyone who interferes with the spell on the paw
will experience sorrow; his indication that the first
man's third wish was for death; his comment that the
paw has caused mischief already; and his remark that it
would be better to let the paw burn.
Difficulty: *Average*   **Objective:** *Literary Analysis*

3. Students should recognize that in many other plots that
involve granting wishes, things usually go wrong. For
example, students may cite the famous myth of King
Midas, who wishes that all he touches will turn to gold
and ends up turning someone he loves to gold.
Difficulty: *Average*   **Objective:** *Reading*

4. Possible events include the following: the sergeant
major arrives; the sergeant major gives the monkey's
paw to the Whites; Mr. White wishes for two hundred
pounds; Herbert's death results in the payment of two
hundred pounds. Students should then explain that
these events are part of the rising action because they
happen before the climax.
Difficulty: *Average*   **Objective:** *Literary Analysis*

5. Details include Mr. White's specific wish for two hundred pounds, the sergeant major's warnings about the
paw, and the sergeant major's explanation that people
who interfere with fate will feel sorrow.
Difficulty: *Average*   **Objective:** *Reading*

6. The Whites do not lack caring or emotion, which is what
apathy suggests. Instead, they care so much that they
have a hard time showing their strong emotions.
Difficulty: *Average*   **Objective:** *Vocabulary*

7. The climax happens when there is knocking at the door
after Mr. White wishes for Herbert's return. At that
moment the tension is very high, and the conflict is
about to be resolved.
Difficulty: *Challenging*   **Objective:** *Literary Analysis*

8. Mrs. White loves her son deeply. She is filled with grief
when he dies.
Difficulty: *Easy*   **Objective:** *Interpretation*

9. Mr. White wishes that his dead son will not return. After
Mrs. White makes her husband wish for Herbert's
return, something knocks at the door—probably Herbert's ghost. When Mr. White makes his last wish, the
knocking stops. This suggests that the ghost has gone
away.
Difficulty: *Average*   **Objective:** *Interpretation*

10. Mr. White has learned the fakir's lesson: sorrow will
come to him if he interferes with fate. He fears that Herbert will come back as a ghost, and that will make the
Whites even more unhappy.
Difficulty: *Challenging*   **Objective:** *Interpretation*

Essay

11. Students should identify two examples of foreshadowing, such as the sergeant major's discussion of fate, the
first man's wish for death, and the dire consequences of
using the monkey's paw. They might also bring up the
image of the monkey's paw in the fire or the twitching of
the monkey's paw in Mr. White's hand. Students should
then identify the future event foreshadowed by each
example.
Difficulty: *Easy*   **Objective:** *Essay*

12. Students should explain that Mr. White's wish for two
hundred pounds—his first attempt to change fate—
causes the death of his son. Mrs. White then tries to
change fate when she makes her husband wish for Herbert's return. She fails to recognize that the wish will
probably cause more sorrow. Mr. White has learned the
lesson, however. He uses the third wish to prevent Herbert's reappearance so that the Whites will not have a
ghost as a son.
Difficulty: *Average*   **Objective:** *Essay*

13. Students should identify two of the following decisions
that Mr. White makes: to keep the monkey's paw in
spite of being warned about it, to wish for two hundred
pounds, to wish that his dead son will reappear, and to
take back his second wish. Students might say that Mr.
White made his decisions too quickly and ignored the
consequences. Some students might say Mr. White was
smart and brave to make such a difficult final decision,
while others may feel he was only acting out of fear.
Difficulty: *Challenging*   **Objective:** *Essay*

14. Students should offer a different version of the plot. For
example, they might say that the monkey's paw never
twitches or appears in the fire; instead, Mr. White only
imagines these moments. Herbert's death and the payment of two hundred pounds could be mere coincidences. Finally, the knock on the door might simply be
another visitor—not Herbert's ghost—and the knock
ends because the visitor goes away.
Difficulty: *Average*   **Objective:** *Essay*

Oral Response

15. Oral responses should be clear, well organized, and well
supported by appropriate examples from the selection.
Difficulty: *Average*   **Objective:** *Oral Interpretation*

Selection Test A, p. 42

Critical Reading

1. **ANS:** C   **DIF:** Easy   **OBJ:** Interpretation
2. **ANS:** A   **DIF:** Easy   **OBJ:** Literary Analysis
3. **ANS:** A   **DIF:** Easy   **OBJ:** Comprehension
4. **ANS:** A   **DIF:** Easy   **OBJ:** Literary Analysis
5. **ANS:** D   **DIF:** Easy   **OBJ:** Interpretation

6. ANS: B	DIF: Easy	OBJ: Comprehension
7. ANS: A	DIF: Easy	OBJ: Reading
8. ANS: B	DIF: Easy	OBJ: Comprehension
9. ANS: D	DIF: Easy	OBJ: Literary Analysis
10. ANS: B	DIF: Easy	OBJ: Reading

Vocabulary and Grammar

11. ANS: A	DIF: Easy	OBJ: Vocabulary
12. ANS: D	DIF: Easy	OBJ: Vocabulary
13. ANS: A	DIF: Easy	OBJ: Grammar

Essay

14. Students must identify two examples of foreshadowing, such as the sergeant major's discussion of fate, the first man's wish for death, the sergeant major's warning of the consequences, and the image of the monkey face in the fire. Students must also fully explain what specific future event is foreshadowed by each of their examples.

Difficulty: *Easy* **Objective:** *Essay*

15. Students might predict that the Whites would have been overcome with horror at the corpse that waited outside the door. They might state that even Mrs. White would have tried to wish Herbert dead again. They should support their prediction with details such as Morris's statement that those who interfere with fate do it to their sorrow.

Difficulty: *Easy* **Objective:** *Essay*

16. Students should provide a different version of the plot. For example, they might say that the monkey's paw never twitches or appears in the fire; instead, Mr. White only imagines these moments. Herbert's death and the payment of two hundred pounds could just happen by chance. Finally, the knock on the door might just be another visitor—not Herbert's ghost—and the knock ends because the visitor goes away.

Difficulty: *Average* **Objective:** *Essay*

Selection Test B, p. 45

Critical Reading

1. ANS: D	DIF: Average	OBJ: Comprehension
2. ANS: C	DIF: Average	OBJ: Interpretation
3. ANS: B	DIF: Average	OBJ: Interpretation
4. ANS: C	DIF: Challenging	OBJ: Reading
5. ANS: A	DIF: Average	OBJ: Literary Analysis
6. ANS: B	DIF: Average	OBJ: Comprehension
7. ANS: A	DIF: Average	OBJ: Reading
8. ANS: C	DIF: Average	OBJ: Literary Analysis
9. ANS: D	DIF: Challenging	OBJ: Interpretation
10. ANS: A	DIF: Average	OBJ: Comprehension
11. ANS: C	DIF: Challenging	OBJ: Literary Analysis
12. ANS: B	DIF: Average	OBJ: Literary Analysis
13. ANS: B	DIF: Average	OBJ: Reading

Vocabulary and Grammar

14. ANS: B	DIF: Average	OBJ: Vocabulary
15. ANS: A	DIF: Average	OBJ: Vocabulary
16. ANS: B	DIF: Average	OBJ: Grammar
17. ANS: A	DIF: Average	OBJ: Grammar

Essay

18. Students must identify two examples of foreshadowing, such as the sergeant major's discussion of fate, the first man's wish for death, the sergeant major's warning of the consequences, and the image of the monkey face in the fire. Students must also fully explain what specific future event is foreshadowed by each of their examples.

Difficulty: *Easy* **Objective:** *Essay*

19. Students must explain why they would or would not make the second wish if they were in Mr. White's place. If they would make the wish, they must explain how they would word it and predict what would happen next. If they would not make the wish, they must explain why.

Difficulty: *Average* **Objective:** *Essay*

20. Students should offer a different version of the plot. For example, they might say that the monkey's paw never twitches or appears in the fire; instead, Mr. White only imagines these moments. Herbert's death and the payment of two hundred pounds could be mere coincidences. Finally, the knock on the door might simply be another visitor—not Herbert's ghost—and the knock ends because the visitor goes away.

Difficulty: *Average* **Objective:** *Essay*

"The Leap" by Louise Erdrich

Vocabulary Warm-up Exercises, p. 49

A.
1. anticipation
2. radiance
3. drama
4. collapsed
5. overcoming
6. culprit
7. carelessly
8. associate

B. Sample Answers

Answers with possible explanations.

1. F; A calculated risk is one that you have reasoned carefully.
2. T; Attaching each of the sequins by hand might be a slow process.
3. F; Boredom is likely if a plot has no surprises and is too predictable.
4. F; An extension ladder is a ladder whose length can be extended.
5. F; It is possible that a movie version is more effective than the written version.

Unit 1 Resources: Fiction and Nonfiction

6. T; You must be accurate to make miniature models.

7. T; The order of events in an experiment is important, and changing it can lead to very different results.

8. F; It is more likely that both basketballs will move if they crash together forcefully.

Reading Warm-up A, p. 50

Sample Answers

1. lit up the afternoon sky; *Radiance* means "brightness."

2. the next thrilling act; I would feel *anticipation* before the beginning of a concert.

3. the audience and the circus tent itself; A family disagreement about where to go for vacation could include a lot of *drama*.

4. falling to the ground; *Collapsed* means "fell down."

5. tossed match or cigarette; When something is done *carelessly*, people can get hurt or things can be damaged.

6. to have set the fire himself; A *culprit* is someone who is guilty of an action or crime.

7. (sadness), (loss); I *associate* the circus with fear because some children are afraid of clowns.

8. feelings of fear; *Overcoming* means "conquering" or "getting over."

Reading Warm-up B, p. 51

Sample Answers

1. (sparkle) (glisten); *Sequined* means "covered with sequins, which are small shiny metal discs."

2. so many fascinating sights; *Boredom* is possible in the waiting room at a doctor's office.

3. that the building was 620 meters long; *Calculated* means "figured using mathematics and reasoning."

4. I would like to have seen the last version because it seems to have been the most spectacular.

5. The efficient use of space; *Precision* means "accuracy" or "exactness."

6. (the limited schedule); An *extension* is something that extends or continues something else.

7. (First) (Then); The *sequence* of events in a tennis game includes the players coming to the court, playing a set, and then exchanging sides.

8. (bump); Two bumper cars might *collide* at a fair.

Writing About the Big Question, p. 52

A. 1. context

2. objective

3. subjective

B. Sample Answers

1. The reality and the truth about my best friend's talent for riding horses are different.

2. The reality is that my best friend is a talented horseback rider, which should **confirm** that she has always been fearless on horses. The **improbable**

truth is that she was afraid of horses when she was younger.

C. Sample Answer

The choices people make can have a variety of effects on their perception of reality. If you choose not to think about the views of others, you may create your own reality, but it is missing the truth found in other voices and points of view.

Literary Analysis: Plot, p. 53

Sample Answers

1. exposition; foreshadows the fire that the narrator will describe

2. rising action; foreshadows the fall that the narrator will endure with her mother

3. rising action; foreshadows the narrator's close brush with death

4. exposition; foreshadows the mother's later flawless escapes from death

Reading: Use Prior Knowledge to Make Predictions, p. 54

Sample Answers

1. A storm will cause the death of someone.

   Clue: The article calls the gale "deadly."

   Prior knowledge: I know that storms can cause terrible destruction.

2. The death will be due to an accident with the tent pole.

   Clue: The pole is cracked and splintered.

   Prior knowledge: I know that trapeze artists depend on the support of the tent poles.

3. The mother will try to save her child.

   Clue: The reader already knows the narrator lives.

   Prior knowledge: I know that most mothers will do anything to save their children.

Vocabulary Builder, p. 55

Sample Answers

A. 1. It will grow a little darker.

2. He or she is probably feeling fearful or nervous.

3. They are trying to remove people from the building.

4. The statue would be serious, because it honors fire fighters, including the memory of those who have died.

5. No, someone who trips constantly should probably not be carrying trays of breakable dishes.

B. 1. Your *district* is confined to your local area, so you would not compete against national students.

2. You are eating only apples when you *restrict*, or confine, your diet to that fruit.

3. The team should be worried, because the *stricture*, or unfavorable criticism, indicates that they did something wrong.

Enrichment: Decisive Moments, p. 56

Answers will vary, but students should list four events and explanations for the events' importance.

Sample Answers

Event: My mother gets an F on a biology test.

Why I Might Not Exist Without the Event: My mother hired my father to tutor her in biology—they would not have met otherwise, and I would not have been born.

Event: My grandfather comes to Canada from Norway to become a lumberjack.

Why I Might Not Exist Without the Event: My grandfather met my grandmother, a cook at the lumber camp; they married and gave birth to my mother, who gave birth to me.

"The Monkey's Paw" by W. W. Jacobs
"The Leap" by Louise Erdrich

Integrated Language Skills: Grammar, p. 57

A. 1. proper noun

Sample substitution: The woman

2. common noun

Sample substitution: Sergeant Major Morris

3. proper noun

Sample substitution: the company

4. common noun

Sample substitution: Herbert

B. 1. The narrator's mother was one-half of a blindfolded trapeze act.

2. Mr. and Mrs. White are horrified by the outcome of their wishes.

3. Louise Erdrich writes about a definitive moment in her own life.

4. The monkey's paw brings bad luck to anyone who uses it.

"The Leap" by Louise Erdrich

Open-Book Test, p. 60

Short Answer

1. They help the reader predict the accident that leads to the death of the mother's first husband.

Difficulty: *Easy* **Objective:** *Reading*

2. The flashback helps the reader predict that the narrator's mother will save her from a fire.

Difficulty: *Average* **Objective:** *Reading*

3. She no longer likes the limelight. Now she leads a quiet life and tries not to think too much about her dramatic past. Possible details include the mother showing little "drama or flair," her keeping no memorabilia from her youth, and the fact that the daughter learns about the accident not from her mother, but from old newspapers.

Difficulty: *Average* **Objective:** *Interpretation*

4. By saving her own life during the circus accident, the mother went on to give birth to the narrator.

Difficulty: *Average* **Objective:** *Interpretation*

5. It foreshadows the rescue of the narrator from the burning house. When she leaps to safety with her mother, she finds out for herself that there is time to think as you fall.

Difficulty: *Average* **Objective:** *Literary Analysis*

6. Among other things, she shows dexterity, daring, skillful training, and quick thinking.

Difficulty: *Easy* **Objective:** *Interpretation*

7. The mother can no longer physically fly as a trapeze performer. Now reading offers her escape and excitement, even though she is not going anywhere.

Difficulty: *Challenging* **Objective:** *Interpretation*

8. It applies to the mother when she hangs on to the heavy wire during the trapeze accident. It applies to the daughter when she hangs on to her mother as her mother saves her from the fire.

Difficulty: *Average* **Objective:** *Literary Analysis*

9. Most students are likely to identify the fire in the home, when the narrator's mother saves her life. They may note that all the details of the rising action build to this exciting moment. The narrator's resulting appreciation of her mother is central to the story's resolution.

Difficulty: *Challenging* **Objective:** *Literary Analysis*

10. She must *extricate* her daughter because the house is on fire.

Difficulty: *Average* **Objective:** *Vocabulary*

Essay

11. Students should identify two examples of foreshadowing, such as the opening remark about the mother's being "the surviving half" of a circus act; the narrator's memory of the fire in the second paragraph; the mother's statement that a person can do many things while falling; and the comment that the mother's burned palms had no lines, only "the blank scar tissue of a quieter future." Students should then identify the events that these details foreshadow.

Difficulty: *Easy* **Objective:** *Essay*

12. Students should describe the mother as talented, quick witted, and unselfish. They should recognize the big change when she goes from an illiterate circus performer who loves dazzling spectators to a quiet wife and mother who enjoys reading. They should also recognize the mother's courage as she faces blindness in her later years.

Difficulty: *Average* **Objective:** *Essay*

13. Students should compare and contrast the mother's leap during the circus act with her later leap into the burning house. They should recognize that the daughter actually makes two leaps, one emotional and one physical. She makes a leap of faith by trusting her mother while they literally leap together. Students may also

discuss the universal significance of the leaps of faith and love that parents and children make.

Difficulty: *Challenging* **Objective:** *Essay*

14. Students should cite precise details about the key events of the circus accident and the fire. They should then explain that the events reflect life's dangers in general. The characters' leaps could represent universal human truths about sacrifice, parental love, and the faith children put in their parents to guide them through life's dangers.

Difficulty: *Average* **Objective:** *Essay*

Oral Response

15. Oral responses should be clear, well organized, and well supported by appropriate examples from the selection.

Difficulty: *Average* **Objective:** *Oral Interpretation*

Selection Test A, p. 63

Critical Reading

1. ANS: B	DIF: Easy	OBJ: Literary Analysis
2. ANS: A	DIF: Easy	OBJ: Reading
3. ANS: C	DIF: Easy	OBJ: Comprehension
4. ANS: C	DIF: Easy	OBJ: Interpretation
5. ANS: B	DIF: Easy	OBJ: Comprehension
6. ANS: C	DIF: Easy	OBJ: Interpretation
7. ANS: D	DIF: Easy	OBJ: Literary Analysis
8. ANS: B	DIF: Easy	OBJ: Interpretation
9. ANS: C	DIF: Easy	OBJ: Reading
10. ANS: A	DIF: Easy	OBJ: Comprehension
11. ANS: A	DIF: Easy	OBJ: Literary Analysis

Vocabulary and Grammar

12. ANS: D	DIF: Easy	OBJ: Vocabulary
13. ANS: B	DIF: Easy	OBJ: Vocabulary
14. ANS: A	DIF: Easy	OBJ: Grammar

Essay

15. Students may note the narrator's memory of the smell of smoke and the sound of flames which suggest the later fire. They may also note the narrator's statement that a person can do many things within the act of falling, which suggests the leap the mother makes with the narrator during the fire.

Difficulty: *Easy* **Objective:** *Essay*

16. Students may note that the first event, in which the mother saves herself during her trapeze act, is entirely based on her background as a trapeze artist. The second event, in which the mother and father meet in the hospital, occurs as a result of the accident that is based on her background. In the final event, the fire, the mother's skill as a trapeze artist enables her to save her daughter.

Difficulty: *Easy* **Objective:** *Essay*

17. Students should choose a character and summarize the key events that the character experiences. They should then explain that the events lead to the truth about life's dangers in general. For example, the characters' leaps could suggest truths about how people make sacrifices for each other, how parents love their children, and how children put faith in their parents to guide them through life's dangers.

Difficulty: *Average* **Objective:** *Essay*

Selection Test B, p. 66

Critical Reading

1. ANS: B	DIF: Average	OBJ: Comprehension
2. ANS: B	DIF: Average	OBJ: Literary Analysis
3. ANS: B	DIF: Challenging	OBJ: Interpretation
4. ANS: C	DIF: Average	OBJ: Reading Strategy
5. ANS: A	DIF: Average	OBJ: Reading
6. ANS: C	DIF: Average	OBJ: Literary Analysis
7. ANS: C	DIF: Average	OBJ: Comprehension
8. ANS: C	DIF: Average	OBJ: Comprehension
9. ANS: C	DIF: Average	OBJ: Interpretation
10. ANS: A	DIF: Average	OBJ: Literary Analysis
11. ANS: C	DIF: Challenging	OBJ: Reading Strategy
12. ANS: A	DIF: Challenging	OBJ: Interpretation
13. ANS: A	DIF: Average	OBJ: Literary Analysis

Vocabulary and Grammar

14. ANS: C	DIF: Average	OBJ: Vocabulary
15. ANS: A	DIF: Challenging	OBJ: Vocabulary
16. ANS: C	DIF: Average	OBJ: Grammar
17. ANS: D	DIF: Average	OBJ: Grammar

Essay

18. Students may note the narrator's memory of the smell of smoke and the sound of flames, which suggest the later fire. They may also note the narrator's statement that a person can do many things within the act of falling, which suggests the leap the mother makes with the narrator during the fire.

Difficulty: *Easy* **Objective:** *Essay*

19. Students should note that the three events for which the narrator owes her mother her existence are the trapeze accident, the meeting of her mother and father, and her mother's rescue of her from the fire. Students may point out that the narrator is expressing gratitude toward her mother for her courage, her ability to weather change, and her love for her daughter.

Difficulty: *Average* **Objective:** *Essay*

20. Students should cite precise details about the key events of the circus accident and the fire. They should then explain that the events reflect life's dangers in general. The characters' leaps could represent universal

human truths about sacrifice, parental love, and the faith children put in their parents to guide them through life's dangers.

Difficulty: *Average*   **Objective:** *Essay*

from **Swimming to Antarctica** by Lynne Cox

Vocabulary Warm-up Exercises, p. 70

A. 1. fatigued
2. massive
3. focused
4. corset
5. torso
6. alternatives
7. mechanically
8. buffer

B. Sample Answers
1. The exterior of the house began to chip, so *the front of the house* looked awful.
2. When I swerved into oncoming traffic, I *made* a terrible driving mistake.
3. After Juan immersed the dumplings in water, they began to *get moist*.
4. The instructor explained how snorkels could be used for inhaling *air*.
5. After a prolonged soccer game, Bobby got home *later* than expected.
6. Only *boats* can travel on the strait that connects two waterways.
7. Tromping on thin ice is a bad idea.

Reading Warm-up A, p. 71

Sample Answers
1. (sleeping) (eating); Other alternatives include reading the newspaper or watching the morning news.
2. (on her training goals); *Focused* means "concentrated on."
3. (running); When I swim *mechanically*, I feel as if I'm a machine just going through the motions.
4. excruciating pain; *Buffer* means "to reduce shock or pain."
5. (stretching exercises); Muscles in the abdomen, or stomach, are also located in the *torso* of the body.
6. (imposing); It's a sharp, long uphill climb. When you go uphill at a sharp angle, it makes the climb that much harder.
7. difficult to take a deep breath; I felt greatly fatigued after exercising for an hour.
8. (laced too tightly around her chest); She compared it to the difficulty in breathing; A corset is an undergarment that shapes the waist.

Reading Warm-up B, p. 72

Sample Answers
1. down the banks of Cap Gris Nez, France. *Tromping* means "walking with a heavy step."

2. (sheep's grease); The *exterior* is the outer part of something.
3. She should have felt exhausted after swimming so long.
4. in the chilly waters of the English Channel; *Immersed* means "covered completely in a liquid."
5. (ice); I swerved my bicycle away from a dog running towards me.
6. (Dardanelles); A *strait* is a narrow body of water.
7. Compounding the physical difficulties, the choppy waters made her seasick.
8. (exhaling); He or she might breathe in water and drown.

Writing About the Big Question, p. 73

A. 1. concrete, objective
2. confirm, verify
3. uncertainty
4. discern

B. Sample Answers
1. I learned I could not run a mile. I learned that I could deliver an oral report without notes.
2. The **reality** is that I'm a good runner, but I could not run a mile. I did not **comprehend** how difficult it is to run that far, and I got tired and stopped running.

C. Sample Answer

People often learn deep truths about themselves when facing a dangerous or intimidating challenge. The reality might be that someone has never taken on such a big challenge, but that person's success will exist as a truth regardless of the reality.

Literary Analysis: Author's Perspective, p. 74

Sample Answers
1. Facts: Immersing the head could cause the heart to stop beating.

   Author's Reactions: She is hyperventilating and panicking.
2. Facts: Shore is within reach, and the author's arms and legs are as cold as the water.

   Author's Reactions: She is swimming strongly and feeling proud.

Reading: Use Prior Knowledge to Make Predictions, p. 75

Sample Answers
1. No; she is too strong to let the doctor psych her out.

   Details from the text that support my prediction: She has already swum in thirty-three-degree water; she is very determined.

   My own experiences that support my prediction: I know it is possible to shrug off something that scares me and focus on the problem at hand.
2. No; she will keep swimming.

   Details from the text that support my prediction: She knows a lot about the way her body reacts to the cold and can control it well; she desperately wants to complete the swim.

My own experiences that support my prediction: I know that I can get beyond panic by deliberately relaxing.

Vocabulary Builder, p. 76

Sample Answers
A. 1. He will probably get sunburned.
2. She could fall.
3. He probably doesn't like them or feels threatened by them.
4. She probably feels anger toward the person to whom she was speaking.
5. You should use a thermometer to measure, or *gauge*, the temperature of the water.

B. 1. When you *pronounce* your name, you announce it before others as you speak it aloud.
2. Yes, you avow before others and openly declare, or *profess*, your support.
3. No, they speak forcefully, because to *project* the voice is to throw it forward strongly.

Enrichment: Preparing for a Task, p. 77

Students should identify a specific task and list the physical and mental skills and preparations that are needed to accomplish it. In their answers, students should reflect an understanding of the task.

Open-Book Test, p. 78

Short Answer
1. Cox has mixed feelings. Part of her wants to be satisfied with the amount she has already swum, and she is scared to swim in colder waters. The other part of her is excited and determined to try the longer swim.
   Difficulty: *Average* **Objective:** *Literary Analysis*
2. Cox wants to fulfill her goal because she has been training hard. She also wants to experience the excitement of doing something no one has ever done before.
   Difficulty: *Challenging* **Objective:** *Interpretation*
3. Possible details include Cox's description of the test swim as the most dangerous swim she has ever done, the near-freezing water, Dr. Block's tracing of Cox's veins, and the potential for permanent nerve and muscle damage.
   Difficulty: *Easy* **Objective:** *Reading*
4. *Prolonged* exposure can cause permanent nerve and muscle damage.
   Difficulty: *Easy* **Objective:** *Vocabulary*
5. The first few moments are hectic and frightening. Cox mistakenly immerses her head in the water, which can be very dangerous.
   Difficulty: *Average* **Objective:** *Interpretation*
6. She gives herself a pep talk.
   Difficulty: *Average* **Objective:** *Vocabulary*
7. When the crew of the *Orlova* seems tense, it adds to Cox's feelings of danger. When the crew smiles, cheers, and laughs, it adds to her energy and makes her more certain that she can fulfill her goal.
   Difficulty: *Challenging* **Objective:** *Literary Analysis*
8. Unless Cox changes direction, she will not reach her goal of swimming the full mile.
   Difficulty: *Average* **Objective:** *Interpretation*
9. Perspective Before Shouting: uncertain and frightened Perspective After Shouting: certain about success, excited, motivated Cox's perspective becomes much more positive and inspired.
   Difficulty: *Average* **Objective:** *Literary Analysis*
10. Possible details include Cox's ability to find equilibrium, her smiling at the crew, Mrs. Stokie's remark about the captain, the appearance of the penguins, and the encouragement of the crew.
    Difficulty: *Average* **Objective:** *Reading*

Essay
11. Students who predicted a successful swim should identify details such as the selection's title, Cox's success in her test run, and Cox's determination. Those who predicted an unsuccessful swim should identify details such as Cox's bad start, the strong currents, the course's not being long enough, and the dangers of cold water.
    Difficulty: *Easy* **Objective:** *Essay*
12. Students should note Cox's determination, strength of purpose, and knowledge of her own limitations as qualities that help her succeed. They should illustrate their points with details such as Cox's continuing the swim even after it starts badly, her change of direction, and her speech to herself when she thinks about swimming farther than a mile.
    Difficulty: *Average* **Objective:** *Essay*
13. Students might mention talent, passion, and persistence as qualities of people who perform amazing feats. They also might mention a love of adventure and a desire for fame as possible motives. They should accurately cite examples from the selection, as well as examples of explorers, daredevils, sports figures, or other heroes.
    Difficulty: *Challenging* **Objective:** *Essay*
14. Students should recognize that in general, Cox prefers not to dwell on the full dangers of the swim because it might kill her motivation. She prefers to stay positive. Before she begins her swim, Cox has no idea that cold water can cause permanent nerve and muscle damage. She gets nervous and a bit angry when Dr. Block traces veins on her hand. She wishes Dr. Block had told her earlier because she wants to think positively. Cox tries to convince herself that she is doing well because it will help keep her going until the end.
    Difficulty: *Average* **Objective:** *Essay*

Oral Response

15. Oral responses should be clear, well organized, and well supported by appropriate examples from the selection.
Difficulty: *Average* **Objective:** *Oral Interpretation*

Selection Test A, p. 81

Critical Reading

1. ANS: B	DIF: Easy	OBJ: Interpretation
2. ANS: B	DIF: Easy	OBJ: Reading
3. ANS: D	DIF: Easy	OBJ: Literary Analysis
4. ANS: A	DIF: Easy	OBJ: Comprehension
5. ANS: D	DIF: Easy	OBJ: Comprehension
6. ANS: C	DIF: Easy	OBJ: Literary Analysis
7. ANS: B	DIF: Easy	OBJ: Comprehension
8. ANS: D	DIF: Easy	OBJ: Reading
9. ANS: B	DIF: Easy	OBJ: Literary Analysis
10. ANS: A	DIF: Easy	OBJ: Interpretation

Vocabulary and Grammar

11. ANS: C	DIF: Easy	OBJ: Vocabulary
12. ANS: A	DIF: Easy	OBJ: Vocabulary
13. ANS: B	DIF: Easy	OBJ: Grammar

Essay

14. Students might note that Lynne Cox shows her determination, her strength of purpose, and her knowledge of her own limitations. These all help her to succeed at her goal. Students might include details such as her change of direction against the current and her speech to herself when she thinks about swimming farther than a mile. These details illustrate her determination and self-knowledge.
Difficulty: *Easy* **Objective:** *Essay*

15. Students might note that the author's perspective is still one of pride in her achievement, which implies that she would have done the swim even if she had fully known the dangers. They might also point out that her desire and determination to do the swim were intense and probably would have overridden her fear of doing harm to herself.
Difficulty: *Easy* **Objective:** *Essay*

16. Students should recognize that the swim is dangerous because the cold water can cause permanent nerve and muscle damage. In general, Cox tries to avoid thinking about the dangers of the swim because she might decide not to do it. She wants to stay positive. Cox tries to convince herself that she is doing well because it will help keep her going until the end. Students should provide examples from the selection to support their points.
Difficulty: *Average* **Objective:** *Essay*

Selection Test B, p. 84

Critical Reading

1. ANS: B	DIF: Average	OBJ: Interpretation
2. ANS: B	DIF: Challenging	OBJ: Reading
3. ANS: A	DIF: Average	OBJ: Reading
4. ANS: A	DIF: Average	OBJ: Comprehension
5. ANS: D	DIF: Challenging	OBJ: Literary Analysis
6. ANS: C	DIF: Average	OBJ: Interpretation
7. ANS: D	DIF: Average	OBJ: Comprehension
8. ANS: D	DIF: Average	OBJ: Reading
9. ANS: A	DIF: Challenging	OBJ: Literary Analysis
10. ANS: B	DIF: Average	OBJ: Comprehension
11. ANS: B	DIF: Average	OBJ: Literary Analysis
12. ANS: A	DIF: Average	OBJ: Interpretation

Vocabulary and Grammar

13. ANS: B	DIF: Average	OBJ: Vocabulary
14. ANS: C	DIF: Average	OBJ: Vocabulary
15. ANS: D	DIF: Average	OBJ: Grammar
16. ANS: C	DIF: Average	OBJ: Grammar

Essay

17. Students may have predicted that she would complete her swim. They might note that her determination and her training would help her on the swim. They might note such quotations as "I am so ready." Students who predicted that she would not complete her swim might refer to the cold water temperature and the difficulties she encounters while swimming as support.
Difficulty: *Average* **Objective:** *Essay*

18. Students might note that Lynne Cox reveals her determination, her strength of purpose, and her knowledge of her own limitations. These all help her to succeed at her goal. Students might include details such as her change of direction against the current and her speech to herself when she thinks about swimming farther than a mile. These details illustrate her determination and self-knowledge.
Difficulty: *Average* **Objective:** *Essay*

19. Students should recognize that in general, Cox prefers not to dwell on the full dangers of the swim because it might kill her motivation. She prefers to stay positive. Before she begins her swim, Cox has no idea that cold water can cause permanent nerve and muscle damage. She gets nervous and a bit angry when Dr. Block traces veins on her hand. She wishes Dr. Block had told her earlier because she wants to think positively. Cox tries to convince herself that she is doing well because it will help keep her going until the end.
Difficulty: *Average* **Objective:** *Essay*

"Occupation: Conductorette" *from* **I Know Why the Caged Bird Sings** by Maya Angelou

Vocabulary Warm-up Exercises, p. 88

A.
1. tradition
2. intellectual
3. suspicions
4. proposal
5. immediate
6. reveal
7. indignation
8. dwellings

B. Sample Answers

1. If Mia had a good <u>academic</u> record, that means she made good grades. Therefore, I would encourage her to go on to higher education.
2. If my job has a <u>restricting</u> atmosphere, it means I do not have a lot of freedom.
3. If I <u>comprehended</u> the difficult reading, I would probably not need to ask for help.
4. If Maria showed <u>gumption</u>, that means she showed courage, so she wouldn't be ashamed.
5. If a popular band <u>resumed</u> playing, the audience might return to listen to the music.
6. His boss would probably be pleased to see Seth working <u>energetically</u>, or vigorously.
7. If I <u>encountered</u> troubles in the past, I would be sad that I hadn't been able to avoid them.

Reading Warm-up A, p. 89

Sample Answers

1. (She tried to become the first woman ever to study architecture at the Ecole des Beaux-Arts); *Tradition* means "a custom handed down through generations."
2. <u>she did very well in school</u>; *Intellectual* means "involving thought and reasoning."
3. <u>He suggested that she try to enter the famous school.</u> A *proposal* is "a suggestion of a plan."
4. (full of determination); *Reveal* means "to show or make known."
5. <u>she had to wait months to take the exam</u>; *Immediate* means "right away."
6. <u>Julia's exam got a lower mark than it deserved</u>; They had *suspicions* that something was wrong because Julia was so very qualified to enter the school.
7. (anger); Friends felt *indignation* at the school's prejudice toward Julia for being a woman and an American.
8. <u>Hearst Castle in California</u>; She designed everything from humble houses to castles; The *dwellings* on my street are small single-story ranch houses.

Reading Warm-up B, p. 90

Sample Answers

1. (setbacks); *Encountered* means "met with."

2. (African Americans); People treat others with *contempt* by speaking rudely to them or ordering them around.
3. <u>it was in his best interest to make the most of the opportunities he had</u>. *Comprehended* means "understood."
4. Marshall was rejected by the University of Maryland's law school because he was black. Then, he *resumed* his efforts to get into law school.
5. (at a good college); My own *academic* record is just okay, because I don't always take the time to study.
6. The policy was *restricting* because it did not admit people of color. Restricting means "limiting."
7. <u>led the fight against segregation</u>; *Energetically* means "with much strength."
8. One example of Marshall's *gumption*, or courage, was his fight to end restrictions at the University of Maryland.

Writing About the Big Question, p. 91

A.
1. reality
2. comprehend
3. concrete, objective

B. Sample Answers

1. I had the experience of finding out that I was not as good a soccer player as I thought I was, and of not getting to play much. I discovered that a person I thought was a good friend would ignore me because I made better grades than she did.
2. The **reality** of being ignored by my friend was hard to **comprehend**. It made me **evaluate** what I thought about friendship.

C. Sample Answer

People who see the truth behind problems in society must decide whether to help solve those problems or to ignore them. Choosing to accept reality that is based on false assessments means that "reality" and "truth" are disconnected.

Literary Analysis: Author's Perspective, p. 92

Sample Answers

1. Author's Reaction at the Time: Resistance to her efforts made her more and more stubborn.

   Author's Attitude Today: She admires her past self, but she wonders if she may have been a little crazy.
2. Author's Reaction at the Time: She was nervous.

   Author's Attitude Today: She admires the courage of her earlier self, but she realizes that she must have looked a little silly.

Reading: Use Prior Knowledge to Make Predictions, p. 93

Sample Answers

1. Yes, she will not give up.

   Details from the text that support my prediction: She is very determined and very angry.

My own experiences that support my prediction: I know that when I am angry, I can become much more determined to get my own way.

2. Yes, she will do as her mother recommends.

Details from the text that support my prediction: She respects and loves her mother.

My own experiences that support my prediction: Many aphorisms are based in truth, and I know that if I put my whole heart into something, I am more likely to succeed.

Vocabulary Builder, p. 94

Sample Answers

A. 1. She will probably say, "No, thank you, I'll do it myself."
2. The interviewer might write that the actor's attitude is full of contempt.
3. The room needs to be cleaned or renovated.
4. That person, intending to be hurtful, has uttered an insult or made a comment that was demeaning.
5. Eating a hamburger might reveal a vegetarian's *hypocrisy*.
6. She probably likes reading, writing, and playing with words.

B. 1. You do not need to save *superfluous* paper, because it is excessive and unnecessary.
2. You will remove the picture on the wall and replace it with your new artwork, which will replace, or *supercede*, the old one.
3. You have written the *superscript* above other writing at the outer edge of the page.

Enrichment: Create a Resume, p. 95

Whether for the student himself or herself or for an imaginary student, the information should be complete and clear.

from Swimming to Antarctica by Lynne Cox
"Occupation: Conductorette" by Maya Angelou

Integrated Language Skills: Grammar, p. 96

Sample Answers

A. 1. abstract: feelings
   concrete: swim
2. abstract: excitement
   concrete: water, beach
3. abstract: perversity, life, struggle, joy
4. abstract: panic
   concrete: wave
5. abstract: determination
   concrete: weeks, honeycomb, apertures, days

B. In their essays, students should summarize Lynne Cox's swim. Students should include at least four of the identified nouns and demonstrate an understanding of concrete and abstract nouns.

"Occupation: Conductorette" *from* I Know Why the Caged Bird Sings by Maya Angelou

Open-Book Test, p. 99

Short Answer

1. Angelou plans to leave school temporarily and get a job. If she fails, she will have to rely on other people. She will not be independent.
   Difficulty: *Average* **Objective:** *Vocabulary*
2. Because so many men are off fighting the war, there is a labor shortage at home. Women have replaced men in many jobs.
   Difficulty: *Average* **Objective:** *Interpretation*
3. Initial Motivations: needs money; thinks it's a good job; can get job without having age checked.
   New Motivations: unwilling to accept rejection; furious about racism toward African Americans Angelou's overall perspective on the job changes from hopeful to determined.
   Difficulty: *Average* **Objective:** *Literary Analysis*
4. The receptionist tells both of these lies because she does not want to say that the company does not hire African Americans. She is trying to make Angelou go away.
   Difficulty: *Average* **Objective:** *Interpretation*
5. Angelou will fight for the job even though she no longer finds it appealing.
   Difficulty: *Easy* **Objective:** *Reading*
6. At first Angelou forgives the receptionist's behavior because she sees the receptionist as a victim. Later she grows very angry at the woman because the receptionist supports unfair rules.
   Difficulty: *Average* **Objective:** *Literary Analysis*
7. Angelou feels that the whole city is rejecting her. She realizes that the city has helped create a society in which African Americans are treated unfairly.
   Difficulty: *Challenging* **Objective:** *Literary Analysis*
8. Details include the title of the selection, Angelou's persistence, her mother's assurance that Angelou will succeed, and the streetcar company's need to hire more workers.
   Difficulty: *Average* **Objective:** *Reading*
9. Angelou recognizes that she is being treated unfairly, but she ignores the difficulties and enjoys the job. Students should cite one example to support this analysis.
   Difficulty: *Easy* **Objective:** *Literary Analysis*
10. She is impressed by her daughter's determination to get (and to keep) the conductor job.
   Difficulty: *Easy* **Objective:** *Interpretation*

Essay

11. Students should write that Angelou is struggling against racism and the white power structure of her time. She is struggling against anyone who allows racism and unfairness to happen—including herself. Students should cite details from the selection to

support their interpretation of Angelou's feelings and situation.

Difficulty: *Easy*   **Objective:** *Essay*

12. Students should state and explain three of the mother's aphorisms. For example, "Can't Do is like Don't Care" means saying you can't do something is the same as saying you don't care about doing it. If you really care, you'll try harder. "Nothing beats a trial but a failure" means you can learn from trying, but you learn more from failing. Students should then explain how the aphorisms encourage Angelou to work hard and to persevere.

Difficulty: *Average*   **Objective:** *Essay*

13. As evidence that Angelou's lie is justified, students may point to Angelou's need for financial independence, her clear ability to do the job, and her right to bend the rules a little in a society that treats African Americans so unfairly. As evidence that Angelou's lie is wrong, students may note that Angelou plans to lie about her age even before she receives unfair treatment from the streetcar company.

Difficulty: *Challenging*   **Objective:** *Essay*

14. Students should recognize that the receptionist and Angelou both avoid the true reason Angelou will not be considered for the job—the color of her skin. Angelou never forces the receptionist to own up to the truth. Students should quote or paraphrase one of the following remarks showing the women's deception:
- "She gave me a face full of astonishment that my suspicious nature would not accept."
- "We were firmly joined in the hypocrisy to play out the scene."
- "We were like actors . . ."
- "I accepted her as a fellow victim of the same puppeteer."
- "The whole charade we had played out in that crummy waiting room had directly to do with me, Black, and her, white."

Difficulty: *Average*   **Objective:** *Essay*

Oral Response

15. Oral responses should be clear, well organized, and well supported by appropriate examples from the selection.

Difficulty: *Average*   **Objective:** *Oral Interpretation*

Selection Test A, p. 102

Critical Reading

1. ANS: C   DIF: Easy   OBJ: Interpretation
2. ANS: D   DIF: Easy   OBJ: Reading
3. ANS: A   DIF: Easy   OBJ: Comprehension
4. ANS: B   DIF: Easy   OBJ: Literary Analysis
5. ANS: B   DIF: Easy   OBJ: Reading
6. ANS: D   DIF: Easy   OBJ: Comprehension
7. ANS: C   DIF: Easy   OBJ: Literary Analysis

8. ANS: C   DIF: Easy   OBJ: Literary Analysis
9. ANS: C   DIF: Easy   OBJ: Interpretation
10. ANS: C   DIF: Easy   OBJ: Comprehension

Vocabulary and Grammar

11. ANS: B   DIF: Easy   OBJ: Vocabulary
12. ANS: A   DIF: Easy   OBJ: Grammar

Essay

13. Students may interpret the aphorisms as follows: "Give it everything you've got" means "Work as hard as you can"; "Can't do is like Don't Care" means "If you say you can't do something, it's the same as saying you don't care about doing it"; "Nothing beats a trial but a failure" means "You can learn from trying, but you learn more from failing"; and "God helps those who help themselves" means "God expects humans to work hard for what they want." Students may note that the author states that the sayings give her something to think about and act as encouragement to her. They may conclude that the aphorisms are very helpful.

Difficulty: *Easy*   **Objective:** *Essay*

14. Students might note that the author felt "disappointed" rather than angry when she learned that African Americans couldn't be conductors; now, she feels the appropriate response is anger. She refers to her haughtiness and her superciliousness in a way that shows some amused disapproval now; at the time, these were simply her responses to the situation. Students might also point out that at the end of the selection, the author states that she was "so much wiser and older, so much more independent" in a way that seems ironic, implying that this was how she felt at the time, but it was not actually true.

Difficulty: *Easy*   **Objective:** *Essay*

15. Students should provide a brief summary of the conversation. Then they should explain that the receptionist and Angelou are lying about the true reason Angelou will not be considered for the job—the color of her skin. Angelou never makes the receptionist own up to the truth. Students might quote or paraphrase one of the following remarks showing the women's deception:
- "She gave me a face full of astonishment that my suspicious nature would not accept."
- "We were firmly joined in the hypocrisy to play out the scene."
- "We were like actors . . ."
- "I accepted her as a fellow victim of the same puppeteer."
- "The whole charade we had played out in that crummy waiting room had directly to do with me, Black, and her, white."

Difficulty: *Average*   **Objective:** *Essay*

Selection Test B, p. 105

Critical Reading

1. ANS: B	DIF: Average	OBJ: Interpretation
2. ANS: B	DIF: Challenging	OBJ: Reading
3. ANS: C	DIF: Average	OBJ: Interpretation
4. ANS: B	DIF: Average	OBJ: Literary Analysis
5. ANS: B	DIF: Average	OBJ: Reading
6. ANS: C	DIF: Challenging	OBJ: Literary Analysis
7. ANS: A	DIF: Average	OBJ: Comprehension
8. ANS: C	DIF: Average	OBJ: Literary Analysis
9. ANS: B	DIF: Challenging	OBJ: Reading
10. ANS: C	DIF: Average	OBJ: Interpretation
11. ANS: C	DIF: Average	OBJ: Comprehension
12. ANS: D	DIF: Average	OBJ: Comprehension

Vocabulary and Grammar

13. ANS: A	DIF: Challenging	OBJ: Vocabulary
14. ANS: A	DIF: Average	OBJ: Vocabulary
15. ANS: C	DIF: Average	OBJ: Vocabulary
16. ANS: D	DIF: Average	OBJ: Grammar
17. ANS: A	DIF: Challenging	OBJ: Grammar

Essay

18. Students might note that the author felt "disappointed" rather than angry when she learned that African Americans couldn't be conductors; now, she feels the appropriate response is anger. She refers to her haughtiness and her superciliousness in a way that shows some amused disapproval now; at the time, these were simply her responses to the situation. Students might also point out that at the end of the selection, the author states that she was "so much wiser and older, so much more independent" in a way that seems ironic, implying that this was how she felt at the time, but it was not actually true. Students might also point out that though the author knows her reactions at the time were both innocent and uninformed, she respects the girl she once was and what that girl accomplished.
Difficulty: *Average* Objective: *Essay*

19. Students should note that the reference to the "marble lobby" is metaphoric. The author means that she was struggling against the mentality that rejected her. Her struggle has become epic and is now against everything that says that African Americans cannot hold the same jobs as whites can. The entire streetcar company is implicated in this struggle, as is the building that houses it and perhaps even those who run the building.
Difficulty: *Average* Objective: *Essay*

20. Students should recognize that the receptionist and Angelou both avoid the true reason Angelou will not be considered for the job—the color of her skin. Angelou never forces the receptionist to own up to the truth.

Students should quote or paraphrase one of the following remarks showing the women's deception:

- "She gave me a face full of astonishment that my suspicious nature would not accept."
- "We were firmly joined in the hypocrisy to play out the scene."
- "We were like actors . . ."
- "I accepted her as a fellow victim of the same puppeteer."
- "The whole charade we had played out in that crummy waiting room had directly to do with me, Black, and her, white."

Difficulty: *Average* Objective: *Essay*

"Marian Anderson, Famous Concert Singer"
by Langston Hughes
"Tepeyac" by Sandra Cisneros

Vocabulary Warm-up Exercises, p. 109

A. 1. critics
2. enthusiastically
3. recordings
4. outstanding
5. Publicity
6. debut
7. prejudice
8. racial

B. Sample Answers

1. Maria was <u>privileged</u> to have purchased the last ticket for the band's final concert.
2. I needed to get to the <u>pharmacy</u> before it closed to buy cough medicine.
3. When Cecee sang a <u>spiritual</u>, she felt a strong connection with her ancestors.
4. The truck's engine ran on <u>diesel fuel</u>, which the truck driver needed to buy.
5. The <u>canopied</u> bed was Nancy's favorite part of the early American bedroom set.
6. The family works with their accountant on all <u>financial</u> matters, including their taxes.
7. We keep a fan on to air out the <u>fumes</u> from the cleaning products.

Reading Warm-up A, p. 110

Sample Answers

1. (composer); (bandleader); *Publicity* is "special attention or notice."
2. (in 1912); *Debut* means "first appearance."
3. <u>expressed their admiration for the talented bandleader</u>; *Critics* are "people who review things like plays, movies, books, or concerts."
4. (black servicemen); I believe *racial* discrimination still exists today but less than it did years ago, thanks to the civil rights movement.

5. <u>White men didn't fight alongside black men.</u> *Prejudice* is "unfair, fixed opinions about a group of people."

6. (cheered); I applauded *enthusiastically* at the end of the Broadway musical.

7. Everyone thought the band was (amazing, talented, great).

8. <u>with his military band.</u> *Answers will vary.*

Reading Warm-up B, p. 111

Sample Answers

1. <u>to be his grandson.</u> *Privileged* means "having the advantage" of a special opportunity.

2. A *canopied* bed is a four-poster bed with a covering of material suspended across the top. An old-fashioned carriage can be canopied.

3. <u>on the screened-in porch, where he put a cozy sleeping bag on an army cot;</u> *Accommodations* are "places to stay or live."

4. A *spiritual* is a religious song from the African American tradition. A slow spiritual would make a good lullaby because it's so rhythmic and soothing.

5. <u>his old car with the diesel engine;</u> *Diesel* is a special kind of fuel.

6. I have been exposed to <u>fumes</u> from buses and trucks.

7. <u>his own medicine;</u> A *pharmacy* is a store where you can buy prescription drugs.

8. (money); It is probably expensive to travel 3,000 miles for a visit. His parents would need the financial means to send him that far away.

Writing About the Big Question, p. 112

A. 1. judge
2. to prove
3. to see something concealed
4. to understand
5. being in doubt

B. Sample Answers

1. When I was four years old, we had a huge stone fence in our front yard. It was so tall, I thought it was a castle wall and that we lived in a castle. For years, I told friends that I lived in a castle when I was small.

2. Years later, I went back to our old neighborhood and saw the reality was that the wall was only about three feet tall, and our house was just an ordinary house with a stone foundation.

C. Sample Answer

One person's idea of truth can be challenged when someone has a different idea about truth. I think that someone's idea of truth and reality may not alway be the same.

Literary Analysis: Style, p. 113

A. 1. A. Hughes's
B. Sample words: *church worker, croon, faith, school-teacher, farm boy*

2. A. Cisneros's

B. Sample words: *arabesque, scroll, whine, clang, lacework; uno, dos, tres; sopa de fideo, carne guisada*

3. Hughes uses simple, straightforward sentences that follow a subject-verb pattern. They are generally shorter than Cisneros's and contain only one or two ideas. Cisneros's long, rambling sentence is a string of images and memories that does not follow a traditional pattern. It contains a half-dozen or more ideas.

B. Paragraphs about "Marian Anderson . . ." may note that Hughes's purpose is to inform and that he uses a simple, factual style to achieve this purpose. Paragraphs about "Tepeyac" may note that Cisneros's purpose is to describe or express memories and that she uses a descriptive, impressionistic style to bring her memories to life. Paragraphs should include relevant examples from the text.

Vocabulary Builder, p. 114

A. Sample Answers

1. Isabel received two job offers. She decided to accept the more *lucrative* one because *she needed the money to pay off her debts.*

2. I am glad our patio is *canopied* because *it gives shelter on a rainy day.*

3. The toddler's *repertoire* consisted of *"Twinkle, Twinkle, Little Star" and the ABC song.*

4. The *irretrievable* balloon *floated up into the sky.*

5. A *staunch* fan of the football team, Jackson *attended every game.*

6. An hour before her *debut*, Ava felt *nervous* because *she had never performed for an audience.*

7. Her handwriting looked like a series of *arabesques*. It *looped and twirled across the page.*

8. My little brother's face becomes *dimpled* when he *sucks on a lemon wedge.*

B. 1. C; 2. A; 3. D; 4. B

Open-Book Test, p. 116

Short Answer

1. Anderson received strong support. Examples of support include the pawnshop owner's giving Anderson a deal on a violin, her church members' raising money for her singing lessons, her first singing teacher's refusing to charge for her lessons, and the Philadelphia Choral Society's sponsoring her further study.

Difficulty: *Easy* **Objective:** *Interpretation*

2. She had to overcome not having enough money to pay for singing lessons and prejudice against African Americans.

Difficulty: *Average* **Objective:** *Interpretation*

3. The incident shows that there was still a lot of prejudice against African Americans, but times were changing and many Americans thought prejudice was wrong.

Difficulty: *Challenging* **Objective:** *Interpretation*

4. Her memories are very strong, and they are important to her.

Difficulty: *Easy* **Objective:** *Interpretation*

5. It is more like a journal entry because she talks about her emotions and her personal life. A news report would focus more on facts.

Difficulty: *Challenging* **Objective:** *Literary Analysis*

6. Hughes's diction is simpler. He uses words that people use every day.

Difficulty: *Easy* **Objective:** *Literary Analysis*

7. Both selections are about an admirable person. Both authors admire and respect their subjects.

Difficulty: *Average* **Objective:** *Interpretation*

8. Type of Detail (Hughes): factual details about Anderson's life
Author's Purpose (Hughes): to express Anderson's musical and historical achievements
Type of Detail (Cisneros): personal and emotional memories of grandfather
Author's Purpose (Cisneros): to describe childhood memories, discuss grandfather's role in life Hughes wants to celebrate a person's entire life, while Cisneros wants to focus on one person's role in her own life.

Difficulty: *Average* **Objective:** *Literary Analysis*

9. The phrase describes Cisneros's long, complicated sentences that seem like poetry. The phrase does not apply well to Hughes's sentences because they are simple and easy to understand quickly.

Difficulty: *Challenging* **Objective:** *Literary Analysis*

10. No, she hadn't sung in Berlin before. A *debut* is a first public appearance.

Difficulty: *Average* **Objective:** *Vocabulary*

Essay

11. Students who especially enjoyed Hughes's style may mention his directness, simple syntax, and desire to celebrate the life of an important person. Students who especially enjoyed Cisneros's style may mention her poetic sentences, exciting word choice, and desire to share personal memories. Students should cite details from the selection to support their points.

Difficulty: *Easy* **Objective:** *Essay*

12. Students should identify Hughes's main purpose as a desire to inform his audience about a talented African American singer. They should identify Cisneros's main purpose as her desire to share a childhood memory or to show the significance of her grandfather in her life. Students may observe that Hughes's direct, informative style allows him to provide a large number of facts in an understandable way. Students may observe that Cisneros's winding, poetic style helps her capture the sights and sounds of the Tepeyac marketplace and shows her emotions. Her style helps bring the reader closer to her.

Difficulty: *Average* **Objective:** *Essay*

13. Students should recognize that Hughes's style would probably involve simpler words and shorter sentences. Extra details would probably change or be eliminated. Hughes would likely supply more facts and less emotion. Students should provide examples to demonstrate their understanding of the authors' styles.

Difficulty: *Challenging* **Objective:** *Essay*

14. Students who write about "Marian Anderson, Famous Concert Singer" should recognize that the truth of Anderson's remarkable talent overcame the prejudiced reality of a society that didn't want to recognize it. Students who write about "Tepeyac" should recognize that in the reality of a child, Cisneros fails to recognize the significance of the daily walks with her grandfather. However, she recognizes the truth and value of those walks now.

Difficulty: *Average* **Objective:** *Essay*

Oral Response

15. Oral responses should be clear, well organized, and well supported by appropriate examples from the selection.

Difficulty: *Average* **Objective:** *Oral Interpretation*

Selection Test A, p. 119

Critical Reading

1. ANS: C	DIF: Easy	OBJ: Comprehension
2. ANS: D	DIF: Easy	OBJ: Interpretation
3. ANS: A	DIF: Easy	OBJ: Comprehension
4. ANS: A	DIF: Easy	OBJ: Literary Analysis
5. ANS: D	DIF: Easy	OBJ: Interpretation
6. ANS: A	DIF: Easy	OBJ: Comprehension
7. ANS: C	DIF: Easy	OBJ: Comprehension
8. ANS: B	DIF: Easy	OBJ: Interpretation
9. ANS: A	DIF: Easy	OBJ: Literary Analysis
10. ANS: D	DIF: Easy	OBJ: Interpretation
11. ANS: B	DIF: Easy	OBJ: Comprehension
12. ANS: D	DIF: Easy	OBJ: Literary Analysis
13. ANS: B	DIF: Easy	OBJ: Literary Analysis

Vocabulary

14. ANS: A	DIF: Easy	OBJ: Vocabulary
15. ANS: C	DIF: Easy	OBJ: Vocabulary

Essay

16. Students should define style as the unique way in which an author writes. They may also identify diction and syntax as two important elements of style. Students may have most enjoyed the following aspects of each author's style: Cisneros's—its exotic words, its flowing sentences, its dreamy images; Hughes's—its directness, its traditional sentences, its "everyday" words.

Difficulty: *Easy* **Objective:** *Essay*

17. Students should identify Cisneros's subject as her grandfather and Hughes's as Marian Anderson. Cisneros's portrait is sympathetic and tender. She wants the reader to know that her grandfather was a hard worker and that he took good care of his grandchildren. Hughes's portrait is respectful and proud. He wants the reader to know that Anderson is a person who overcame social and racial barriers. Examples will vary but should adequately support students' claims.

Difficulty: *Easy* **Objective:** *Essay*

18. Students should recognize that the truth of Anderson's remarkable talent overcame the reality of people who didn't want to recognize it. Anderson also received help from the African-American community, which helped her rise above unfair treatment. Students should provide examples from the selection to support their responses.

Difficulty: *Average* **Objective:** *Essay*

Selection Test B, p. 122

Critical Reading

1. ANS: C	DIF: Average	OBJ: Comprehension
2. ANS: B	DIF: Challenging	OBJ: Interpretation
3. ANS: A	DIF: Average	OBJ: Comprehension
4. ANS: D	DIF: Average	OBJ: Literary Analysis
5. ANS: C	DIF: Challenging	OBJ: Literary Analysis
6. ANS: D	DIF: Challenging	OBJ: Interpretation
7. ANS: B	DIF: Average	OBJ: Comprehension
8. ANS: B	DIF: Challenging	OBJ: Comprehension
9. ANS: C	DIF: Average	OBJ: Interpretation
10. ANS: A	DIF: Average	OBJ: Literary Analysis
11. ANS: D	DIF: Average	OBJ: Literary Analysis
12. ANS: B	DIF: Average	OBJ: Comprehension
13. ANS: D	DIF: Challenging	OBJ: Comprehension
14. ANS: C	DIF: Challenging	OBJ: Interpretation
15. ANS: A	DIF: Average	OBJ: Literary Analysis
16. ANS: B	DIF: Challenging	OBJ: Literary Analysis

Vocabulary

17. ANS: D	DIF: Average	OBJ: Vocabulary
18. ANS: C	DIF: Challenging	OBJ: Vocabulary

Essay

19. Students should identify Cisneros's main purpose as describing a childhood memory, and Hughes's as informing his audience about a talented African American singer. Students may observe that Hughes's direct, informative style allows him to convey a large number of facts in a logical fashion; some students may also note that his style allows him to treat his subject objectively, without seeming biased. Students may observe that Cisneros's winding, poetic style allows her to bring the sights and sounds of the Tepeyac marketplace to life for her reader; some students may also note that her stream-of-consciousness style closely mirrors the act of remembering itself.

Difficulty: *Average* **Objective:** *Essay*

20. Responses will vary. Students may have most enjoyed the following aspects of each author's style: Cisneros's—its rhythm and cadences, its exotic words, its flowing sentences, its dreamy images, its tender expressions; Hughes's—its directness, its traditional sentences, its chronological sequence, its "everyday" words. Students are likely to say that Cisneros's style appealed more to their emotions and that Hughes's appealed more to their intellect. They may explain this difference in terms of each author's purpose—Cisneros's, to reminisce; and Hughes's, to inform.

Difficulty: *Average* **Objective:** *Essay*

21. Students who write about "Marian Anderson, Famous Concert Singer" should recognize that the truth of Anderson's remarkable talent overcame the prejudiced reality of a society that didn't want to recognize it. Students who write about "Tepeyac" should recognize that in the reality of a child, Cisneros fails to recognize the significance of the daily walks with her grandfather. However, she recognizes the truth and value of those walks now.

Difficulty: *Average* **Objective:** *Essay*

Writing Workshop

Autobiographical Narrative: Integrating Grammar Skills, p. 126

A. 1. James's; 2. women's; 3. coaches'

B. 1. My sister Bess works at a children's hospital near the city's oldest park.

2. Her nurse's training took several years to complete.

3. Bess's job as a night nurse begins at 9 P.M. and continues for eight hours.

Benchmark Test 1, p. 127

MULTIPLE CHOICE

1. ANS: A
2. ANS: B
3. ANS: A
4. ANS: D
5. ANS: C
6. ANS: D
7. ANS: A
8. ANS: A
9. ANS: A
10. ANS: D
11. ANS: C
12. ANS: B
13. ANS: A

14. ANS: A
15. ANS: C
16. ANS: C
17. ANS: A
18. ANS: B
19. ANS: C
20. ANS: D
21. ANS: B
22. ANS: A
23. ANS: B
24. ANS: B
25. ANS: D
26. ANS: C
27. ANS: A
28. ANS: B
29. ANS: B
30. ANS: C
31. ANS: A

WRITING

32. Students should provide a new plot that centers around a similar (or different) conflict. They should move from exposition to rising action to a climax, which should be followed by a resolution.

33. Students should identify the place and then describe it, incorporating information from their own prior knowledge and/or experience. They should provide vivid sensory details to capture a particular mood or atmosphere.

34. Students should write in the first person, providing a clear sequence of events. They should provide effective descriptions of the people and places involved. They should include an indication of why they find the incident funny or interesting and perhaps discuss an insight they gained from the experience.

"Contents of the Dead Man's Pocket"
by Jack Finney

Vocabulary Warm-up Exercises, p. 135

A. 1. astonishingly
   2. infinite
   3. intention
   4. fragments
   5. postponed
   6. protruding
   7. hopelessly
   8. comical

B. Sample Answers
   1. Most people feel a strong <u>yearning</u> for companionship.
   2. A tree branch is more <u>brittle</u> when it is dead and dry.
   3. My sister's handwriting is so sloppy it is <u>incomprehensible</u>.
   4. Running a marathon would be <u>impossibly</u> difficult for someone with no training.
   5. If visitors found out that artwork had been <u>duplicated</u>, they would be angry.
   6. I tried my <u>utmost</u> to play trumpet with the marching band and succeeded.
   7. My mother's singing voice was a <u>revelation</u> because I had never heard her sing.
   8. If Earth <u>accelerated</u> in its orbit, a year would last less than 365 days.

Reading Warm-up A, p. 136
Sample Answers
   1. <u>stop and stare</u>; *Astonishingly* means "amazingly."
   2. (limitless); I think that time is *infinite*.
   3. <u>my return</u>; The performance of a play could be *postponed*.
   4. (the corner of my journal); *Protruding* means "sticking out."
   5. <u>to jot down a brief description</u>; *Intention* means "aim."
   6. <u>incomplete ideas and words</u>; *Fragments* are incomplete pieces or parts of something.
   7. (the paper), (the poem); I would stare *hopelessly* if I spilled ink on a white shirt.
   8. <u>hugging the tree like it was a giant teddy bear</u>; Watching my grandmother trying to rap was *comical*.

Reading Warm-up B, p. 137
Sample Answers
   1. People in 1850 would find computers and the Internet *incomprehensible*.
   2. (reality); *Yearning* means "desire."
   3. (discovery); *Revelation* means "surprising information or discovery."
   4. (copied); Manufacturers *duplicated* the assembly line after Henry Ford invented it.
   5. The Internet *accelerated* change because people now share information very quickly.
   6. (support the stress and tension of a building); Glass can be a *brittle* substance.
   7. The *utmost* problem facing inventors today is finding ways to make computers faster.
   8. The goal of space tourism seems *impossibly* ambitious today, but it might be possible in 100 years.

Writing About the Big Question, p. 138
A. 1. context
   2. discern

3. differentiate
4. objective
5. subjective

B. Sample Answers

1. An event might be a serious illness, or losing a best friend or a parent, or failing at something really important, such as not making a team or failing an important test.

2. People who have lost someone they loved might change their **perception** about how they should treat people, and **evaluate** how they treat their friends and family, such as taking them for granted. They might see the **reality** about the **uncertainty** of life, and how they can never be sure what will happen tomorrow.

C. Sample Answer

The most important thing in life is family. When I was in fourth grade, our family went on a camping trip, and I got lost in the woods. I was lost for hours and really scared, and I began to think about how I had always taken my parents for granted. I was afraid then that I would never see them again, and I realized the truth about how much I loved and needed them.

Literary Analysis: Conflict and Resolution, p. 139

Sample Answers

A. 1. Internal conflict: "He kissed her then and, for an instant, holding her close, smelling the perfume she had used, he was tempted to go with her; it was not actually true that he had to work tonight."

External conflict: "He could not kneel here hesitating indefinitely till he lost all courage to act, waiting till he slipped off the ledge."

2. The story would have had no true meaning without Tom's internal conflict, which made him realize that his life and his relationship with his wife are more important than getting a promotion at work. If Finney had focused on external conflict only, the story would have been just a brief, suspenseful incident.

3. The title leads the reader to think that Tom will die, a suspicion that heightens the feeling of dread throughout the story.

B. Tom Benecke climbs into his apartment. He immediately gets up and places something large and heavy on the yellow paper to make sure it cannot fly away again. He spends the rest of the evening copying his notes three times, placing each copy in a different, secure place. When Clare gets home, Tom tells her that she is the most important thing in his life, which is why he is so determined to get a promotion. He wants to give her a life of luxury some day.

Reading: Reflect on Key Details to Analyze Cause and Effect, p. 140

Sample Answers

A. Effect 1: Tom convinces himself it will be easy and safe to retrieve the paper.

Effect 2: He goes out on the ledge and ends up nearly losing his life.

Effect 3: He realizes that the paper and his job are not as important as his relationship with his wife.

B. Tom and Clare spend more time together and have a much happier marriage. Tom's happiness at home allows him to relax about his work. He gets a promotion after all because he has such a positive attitude and has become a team player at work.

Vocabulary Builder, p. 141

A. Sample Answers

1. A seashell is more likely to be convoluted than a pebble because many seashells are twisted and have intricate designs.

2. The supervisor probably feels that she is a good, efficient worker.

3. paint drying, grass growing, rocks eroding, and so on

4. The doctor was not prompt because the wait seemed like it would never end.

5. *Verified* means proved true, so identity must be verified to make sure the person cashing a check is the one who should legally be cashing it.

6. Yes, because *reveling* means to be taking great pleasure in something.

B. 1. **verity:** the quality of being accurate; *-ver-* means "true" or "accurate."

2. **veracious:** honest or truthful; *-ver-* means "true."

3. **very:** truly or absolutely; *-ver-* means "true" or "real."

Enrichment: Making Decisions, p. 142

A. Sample Answers

1. The piece of paper contains notes that represent months of Tom's hard work. Tom needs the piece of paper to complete a report that he hopes will impress his boss enough to give him a promotion.

2. He can go out on the ledge to retrieve the paper.

3. He could fall off the ledge and die.

4. He could redo the work, which would take much more time, but would not endanger his life.

B. Responses will vary. Students should include sufficient details to indicate an understanding of the decision-making process.

Open-Book Test, p. 143

Short Answer

1. He seems to think his job is the most important thing in his life. Students may cite the detail of Tom's not going to a movie and instead staying home to work on a project for his job, even though he wants to see the movie and the project does not require immediate attention.
Difficulty: *Average* **Objective:** *Interpretation*

2. It causes trouble because Tom cannot open the window from the outside when he is on the window ledge.
Difficulty: *Easy* **Objective:** *Reading*

3. The detail shows that it will be quite a while before Clare comes home. Knowing that causes Tom to try to get

back into the apartment rather than risking a long time on the ledge waiting for Clare to return.

Difficulty: *Challenging* **Objective:** *Reading*

4. The paper flutters out the window. Tom is too focused on his work.

Difficulty: *Average* **Objective:** *Reading*

5. Tom spent months preparing the paper for work, and it contains information that would take him months to redo.

Difficulty: *Easy* **Objective:** *Interpretation*

6. Moving along the ledge or lighting a match with one hand requires *deftness.*

Difficulty: *Average* **Objective:** *Vocabulary*

7. Possible details include the slow pace of Tom's dangerous movements on the window ledge and the fear in his stomach. These details cause suspense because they draw out the action when the reader wants to know whether Tom will survive a dangerous situation.

Difficulty: *Average* **Objective:** *Literary Analysis*

8. The main external conflict is Tom's struggle to retrieve his paper and to survive. In the resolution, Tom survives.

Difficulty: *Average* **Objective:** *Literary Analysis*

9. He realizes that he has been placing too much importance on his job and should never have risked his life for it. He realizes that his relationship with his wife is far more important to him than his job and makes him much happier.

Difficulty: *Challenging* **Objective:** *Literary Analysis*

10. He sees how ridiculous it is that he's lost the paper that he almost died in the process of saving earlier. He has a sense of humor about it now because the paper is less important to him.

Difficulty: *Challenging* **Objective:** *Interpretation*

Essay

11. Students who discuss Tom's chief external conflict—his struggle to stay on the ledge and to get back into his apartment—should summarize Tom's actions in trying to stay alive, such as his careful steps, his lighting of the matches, and his breaking of the window. Students who focus on an internal conflict may discuss Tom's struggle to overcome his fears or to recognize what is really important in his life. Those focusing on the fears should trace Tom's changing attitude and eventual success in saving the paper. Those focusing on his struggle to change his values should discuss the importance he places on his job, his foolish risking of his life for his job, and his realizations as he risks his life and thinks about the contents of his pockets.

Difficulty: *Easy* **Objective:** *Essay*

12. Students should recognize that Tom is the dead man and that he calls himself dead because he imagines what others would think if he fell to his death and found the contents in his pocket. He is also somewhat emotionally dead when the story begins because he is not

enjoying his life and sharing it with the woman he loves. Students should explain that thinking about the contents of his pocket helps Tom reevaluate his life. This resolves the main internal conflict and points to a key theme of the story—that love and happiness are more important than financial success.

Difficulty: *Average* **Objective:** *Essay*

13. Students should begin by discussing the early questions that Finney prompts readers to ask. For example, in the first paragraph, readers may wonder about the nature of Tom's memo and the reason he has a guilty conscience. Students should then relate the suspense to the key conflicts in the story, especially the external conflict involving Tom's dangerous walk on the ledge and his efforts to reenter his apartment. They should cite specific details that show how Finney's slow building of detail upon detail and particular word choice add to the story's suspense.

Difficulty: *Challenging* **Objective:** *Essay*

14. Students should explain that Tom at first values his job above all things and wants a promotion more than anything. They should cite his foolishness in risking his life for his job, as well as his examination of his pocket's contents, as events that cause him to reevaluate his priorities. They should explain that his experiences on the ledge help him realize that it is his marriage, not his job, that makes him happy and means the most to him.

Difficulty: *Average* **Objective:** *Essay*

Oral Response

15. Oral responses should be clear, well organized, and well supported by appropriate examples from the selection.

Difficulty: *Average* **Objective:** *Oral Interpretation*

Selection Test A, p. 146

Critical Reading

1. ANS: D	DIF: Easy	OBJ: Comprehension
2. ANS: C	DIF: Easy	OBJ: Comprehension
3. ANS: C	DIF: Easy	OBJ: Reading
4. ANS: B	DIF: Easy	OBJ: Reading
5. ANS: B	DIF: Easy	OBJ: Literary Analysis
6. ANS: C	DIF: Easy	OBJ: Comprehension
7. ANS: B	DIF: Easy	OBJ: Interpretation
8. ANS: A	DIF: Easy	OBJ: Interpretation
9. ANS: D	DIF: Easy	OBJ: Literary Analysis
10. ANS: A	DIF: Easy	OBJ: Comprehension
11. ANS: C	DIF: Easy	OBJ: Interpretation
12. ANS: D	DIF: Easy	OBJ: Interpretation

Vocabulary and Grammar

13. ANS: C	DIF: Easy	OBJ: Vocabulary
14. ANS: D	DIF: Easy	OBJ: Vocabulary
15. ANS: B	DIF: Easy	OBJ: Grammar

Essay

16. At the beginning of the story, Tom values his job the most. He wants to get a promotion more than anything. He even risks his life for the paper he thinks will get him the promotion. While he is on the ledge, he really thinks about what he has done with his life so far. At the end of the story, he realizes that his relationship with his wife is the most important thing. When he gets back into his apartment safely, he goes out to find his wife and stops worrying so much about his job. He changes his mind about what is most important to him because he almost died.

Difficulty: *Easy* **Objective:** *Essay*

17. The external conflict of "Contents of the Dead Man's Pocket" is Tom's fight to retrieve his notes and get back inside. One internal conflict is Tom's struggle with his own fear. Another internal conflict is Tom's trying to decide what is most important in his life. He has to figure out whether his work or his wife is more important to him. Both kinds of conflicts are resolved when Tom breaks the glass of his window and gets safely back into his apartment. He is finally out of danger. That is the resolution to the external conflict. He also realizes at that point that his wife is more important than his work. That resolves the internal conflict.

Difficulty: *Easy* **Objective:** *Essay*

18. Students should explain that Tom risks his life for his job by going out on the ledge to retrieve the paper. While he is trapped outside, he realizes how foolish he is acting. He imagines someone finding the contents of his pockets after his death, and this also makes him feel foolish. These experiences help him realize that his marriage, not his job, makes him happy and means the most to him.

Difficulty: *Average* **Objective:** *Essay*

Selection Test B, p. 149

Critical Reading

1. ANS: D	DIF: Average	OBJ: Comprehension
2. ANS: C	DIF: Average	OBJ: Comprehension
3. ANS: B	DIF: Average	OBJ: Reading
4. ANS: C	DIF: Average	OBJ: Reading
5. ANS: B	DIF: Challenging	OBJ: Interpretation
6. ANS: C	DIF: Average	OBJ: Literary Analysis
7. ANS: A	DIF: Challenging	OBJ: Interpretation
8. ANS: D	DIF: Challenging	OBJ: Reading
9. ANS: D	DIF: Average	OBJ: Interpretation
10. ANS: B	DIF: Average	OBJ: Literary Analysis
11. ANS: D	DIF: Average	OBJ: Literary Analysis
12. ANS: D	DIF: Challenging	OBJ: Interpretation
13. ANS: B	DIF: Average	OBJ: Literary Analysis
14. ANS: A	DIF: Challenging	OBJ: Literary Analysis

Vocabulary and Grammar

15. ANS: C	DIF: Average	OBJ: Vocabulary

16. ANS: A	DIF: Average	OBJ: Vocabulary
17. ANS: B	DIF: Challenging	OBJ: Vocabulary

Essay

18. At the beginning of the story, Tom values his job the most. He wants to get a promotion more than anything. He even risks his life for the paper he thinks will get him the promotion. While he is on the ledge, he really thinks about what he has done with his life so far. He knows that what he had been doing wasn't making him happy. At the end of the story, he realizes that his relationship with his wife is what matters most to him. When he gets ready to hit the window, he thinks he will probably die. The last thing he says is his wife's name. That shows that he really values his wife the most. It makes him very happy when he realizes it. He even laughs when the paper flies out the window again, proving that he really has changed because of his experience on the ledge. He goes out to find his wife and stops worrying so much about his job.

Difficulty: *Average* **Objective:** *Essay*

19. The external conflict of "Contents of the Dead Man's Pocket" is Tom's struggle to stay on the ledge. The internal conflicts are Tom's struggle with his own fear and his thoughts about what is most important in his life. He has to decide whether his work or his wife is more important to him. Both conflicts are resolved when Tom breaks the glass of his window and falls into his apartment. He is finally out of danger, which is the resolution to the external conflict. He has also realized at that point that his wife is more important than his work, which resolves the internal conflict. I believe the resolution is a good one because it sends a positive message to readers—that they should really think about what's most important to them. It makes readers think about what they would be leaving behind if something terrible happened to them.

Difficulty: *Average* **Objective:** *Essay*

20. Students should explain that Tom at first values his job above all things and wants a promotion more than anything. They should cite his foolishness in risking his life for his job, as well as his examination of his pocket's contents, as events that cause him to reevaluate his priorities. They should explain that his experiences on the ledge help him realize that it is his marriage, not his job, that makes him happy and means the most to him.

Difficulty: *Average* **Objective:** *Essay*

"Games at Twilight" by Anita Desai

Vocabulary Warm-up Exercises, p. 153

A. 1. arid
2. misery
3. recognizable
4. passion
5. looting
6. skittering

7. stifled
8. successfully

B. Sample Answers

1. If a guest is *wholly* welcome, I would treat him kindly and hospitably.
2. You can *elude* cold weather by moving to a warmer region.
3. Yes, I think rhymes help you remember the words in a *refrain*.
4. A ball and a net are the *crucial* equipment for basketball.
5. If people in the crowd are smiling and dancing, their sound probably expresses *jubilation*.
6. No, I think that lying is always wrong, so there is no *legitimate* excuse for it.
7. I might give a sign of *congratulation* by hugging my friend.

Reading Warm-up A, p. 154

Sample Answers

1. After two weeks without rain; *Arid* means "very dry."
2. she was too far away; *Recognizable* means "identifiable."
3. decided right away he would trick Lona out of hers; I have a *passion* for comic books.
4. (toys); *Looting* means "stealing."
5. making dusty puffs as they bounced along; *Skittered* means "skipped across a surface."
6. (the young girl's trust); I have *successfully* completed two term papers.
7. (a laugh); I might have *stifled* a laugh during a wedding.
8. I saw you all alone; *Misery* means "a state of extreme sadness or pain."

Reading Warm-up B, p. 155

Sample Answers

1. (frivolous); *Legitimate* means "following recognized rules."
2. specific rules and details; The *crucial* elements of soccer are a ball and two nets.
3. I might try to *elude* a dog that was chasing me.
4. (delight); I might feel *jubilation* after passing a difficult test.
5. I find swimming in the ocean *wholly* enjoyable.
6. (from their hiding places); *Emerged* means "came out from."
7. repeated phrase; You can hear a *refrain* in many songs on the radio.
8. Someone might send a card of *congratulation* when I graduate from high school.

Writing About the Big Question, p. 156

A. 1. improbable
2. uncertainty
3. comprehend
4. discern
5. evidence

B. Sample Answers

1. A person may not realize that he or she is not as athletically talented as believed. A person may believe he or she is very well liked by others.
2. In some cases, a person may fail to qualify for a team. A person may have the perception that he or she will easily win an election, but the reality may be that others do not like him or her.

C. Sample Answer

You can tell how people really see you when you get in trouble and need someone to help you out. You may believe that you have a close friend who will always support you. When trouble happens, you learn the truth that the reality of your friendship was based on how you could be of benefit to him or her, not on mutual concern for each other.

Literary Analysis: Conflict and Resolution, p. 157

Sample Answers

A. 1. Internal conflict: "He wondered if it would not be better to be captured by Raghu and be returned to the milling crowd as long as he could be in the sun, the light, the free spaces of the garden and the familiarity of his brothers, sisters and cousins."

   External conflict: "He tore himself out of his mother's grasp and pounded across the lawn into their midst, charging at them with his head lowered so that they scattered in surprise."

2. The story would have been a very brief account of children playing a game of hide-and-seek without Ravi's internal conflict. Ravi's struggle against his fear, his determination to be a winner, and his bitter lesson about being forgotten give meaning to the story.

3. A moment of suspense occurs when Ravi realizes that he has not heard anyone looking for him in a very long time and that he must run to the "den" to win the game. This builds the reader's interest in both the internal conflict of Ravi's intense desire to be a winner and in the external conflict of having to physically expose himself to capture in order to make it to the veranda.

B. Ravi makes it to the veranda, sobbing in rage and misery. The other children stop their chanting and immediately gather around him in concern. They comfort him, realizing immediately that they forgot him in the game of hide-and-seek. They feel ashamed and acknowledge that he is the winner. Ravi calms down and feels happy that he won, but he realizes that he went too far with the game and ended up not having much fun because of his determination to win.

Reading: Reflect on Key Details to Analyze Cause and Effect, p. 158

Sample Answers

A. Effect 1: The others are surprised to see him, and they are puzzled about why he is so upset.

Effect 2: Ravi realizes that they had forgotten him.

Effect 3: He is crushed by the understanding of his insignificance.

B. Ravi may refuse to play with the other children on future evenings because he feels rejected and worthless. He may begin behaving badly in order to get more attention. His feeling of worthlessness may even affect him deeply enough to stay with him all his life, making it difficult for him to find happiness and success as an adult.

Vocabulary Builder, p. 159

A. Sample Answers

1. Her grades were probably poor.

2. You should get it fixed, throw it out, or donate it.

3. He is likely to finish the marathon because he is stubbornly continuing to run, no matter what.

4. I would probably try to cheer up him or her.

5. I would be happy, since they would settle the argument.

6. The person does not want to be seen by someone who is searching for him or her.

B. 1. **convent:** a place where nuns live together or "come together"

2. **ventilate:** to let fresh air in or to allow air to "go through"

3. **convene:** to assemble or "come together"

Enrichment: Science Connection, p. 160

Sample Answers

My Climate—Students should accurately describe their climate at the present time (typical temperatures, precipitation, humidity, etc.).

Different—Students might mention that air conditioning or central heating would make the children less anxious to get outside. They might also describe how their climate might change the progression of the game. For example, ice and snow in wintertime might keep Ravi from hiding so long.

Same—The children would probably still be excited about going outside to play, as children in all times and places tend to be. Ravi would still be anxious to win the game. Ravi might be forgotten by any group of children anywhere.

Rewritten Beginning—Students should incorporate their own climate and region into the descriptions of how the children felt and behaved both inside and outside.

"Contents of the Dead Man's Pocket"
by Jack Finney
"Games at Twilight" by Anita Desai

Integrated Language Skills: Grammar, p. 161

A. 1. First person: I; Second person: you, you; Third person: she, him, he, her, He, her, her

2. Third person: they, their, she, It

3. First person: I; Second person: You, you; Third person: she

4. Third person: they, he, He, his, it

5. Third person: It, him, they, him

B. 1. He did not want to lose it because he had worked on it for months.

2. He tried to get their attention, but none of them noticed him out on the ledge.

Open-Book Test, p. 164

Short Answer

1. They are eager to play because they have been inside the house all day and are feeling restless. Possible supporting detail: the children feel they will choke from being shut inside all day.
   Difficulty: *Easy* **Objective:** *Reading*

2. Because of the hot climate, the children are not supposed to go outside and play until it is evening. Once it is evening, they are allowed to go out.
   Difficulty: *Challenging* **Objective:** *Reading*

3. Ravi is frightened of Raghu and is jealous of the older boy's size and strength. Possible details include Raghu's long legs, Ravi's fear as Raghu approaches, Ravi's desperation to escape Raghu, and Ravi's wish to be tall and big.
   Difficulty: *Easy* **Objective:** *Interpretation*

4. First Cause: Ravi does not want Raghu to find him. Second Cause: Ravi wants to win at hide-and-seek. Ravi's behavior is playful, brave, and normal for a kid.
   Difficulty: *Average* **Objective:** *Reading*

5. Possible details include the shed's smelling of rats and dirt, its darkness, and Ravi's feeling something cold and slimy that he thinks is a snake. These details about scary things make the reader think that something scary or unpleasant is about to happen.
   Difficulty: *Average* **Objective:** *Literary Analysis*

6. He feels that defeating his much older, bigger, faster, and stronger brother would be a great victory. One detail is that he describes beating his brother as thrilling.
   Difficulty: *Average* **Objective:** *Interpretation*

7. He is determined and competitive. He does not give in easily.
   Difficulty: *Average* **Objective:** *Vocabulary*

8. Ravi struggles to decide if his desire to win the game is greater than his fear of the shed.
   Difficulty: *Challenging* **Objective:** *Literary Analysis*

9. Ravi struggles to beat the older children in the game of hide-and-seek.
   Difficulty: *Average* **Objective:** *Literary Analysis*

10. The other children have moved on to other games and have forgotten about Ravi. They are amazed at his tears and rage when he wins at hide-and-seek. Possible details: Ravi hears the children laughing and wonders what happened to them. They look at him as if they don't understand when he yells, "Den! Den! Den!"
    Difficulty: *Challenging* **Objective:** *Interpretation*

Essay

11. Students should accurately represent Ravi's experiences and feelings, explain whether or not they would have done and felt the same, and give reasons for their behavior and feelings. For example, some students may say that they would not have gone into a shed that seemed so dangerous because a hide-and-seek game should not be so important. Others may say that they would have felt just as angry if nobody had noticed their victory at hide-and-seek. Students should cite details from the story to support their points.

    Difficulty: *Easy* **Objective:** *Essay*

12. Students should recognize that Ravi resents and fears the older children, especially his brother Raghu. He thinks it would be thrilling to beat them in a game, and he thinks winning would earn their respect and admiration. Unfortunately, his plan backfires. Because he stays in the shed too long and the other kids generally pay little attention, he is forgotten and ultimately humiliated. Students should cite these details and others in their responses.

    Difficulty: *Average* **Objective:** *Essay*

13. Students should recognize that Ravi's conflict with the other children is his desire to beat them in hide-and-seek and to win their respect and admiration. At the story's end, he does win the game; however, he does not win the respect and admiration he thought would go along with victory. Instead, because he stayed in the shed so long, the other children have moved on to another game. They no longer care who won hide-and-seek, and they have forgotten about him. Ravi ends up being angry and hurt because, instead of doing something that gets him noticed, he proves that he is even less important than he thought. Most students are likely to find this resolution unsatisfying because Ravi is still experiencing the original conflict, even though the game is over.

    Difficulty: *Challenging* **Objective:** *Essay*

14. Students should recognize that while Ravi fears Raghu, many of the other children do not feel the same way. We know this because the older children force Raghu to be It in the hide-and-seek game. Students should recognize that the importance Ravi places on the hide-and-seek game is not shared by others. What he sees as a great ordeal in staying in the scary shed is meaningless to the other children, who have forgotten about him and moved on to other games. Ravi finds many small events and details more important than older people do.

    Difficulty: *Average* **Objective:** *Essay*

Oral Response

15. Oral responses should be clear, well organized, and well supported by appropriate examples from the selection.

    Difficulty: *Average* **Objective:** *Oral Interpretation*

Selection Test A, p. 167

Critical Reading

1. ANS: C	DIF: Easy	OBJ: Interpretation
2. ANS: D	DIF: Easy	OBJ: Interpretation
3. ANS: A	DIF: Easy	OBJ: Comprehension
4. ANS: D	DIF: Easy	OBJ: Literary Analysis
5. ANS: C	DIF: Easy	OBJ: Reading
6. ANS: C	DIF: Easy	OBJ: Literary Analysis
7. ANS: B	DIF: Easy	OBJ: Literary Analysis
8. ANS: C	DIF: Easy	OBJ: Reading
9. ANS: A	DIF: Easy	OBJ: Comprehension
10. ANS: A	DIF: Easy	OBJ: Interpretation

Vocabulary and Grammar

11. ANS: C	DIF: Easy	OBJ: Vocabulary
12. ANS: B	DIF: Easy	OBJ: Vocabulary
13. ANS: B	DIF: Easy	OBJ: Vocabulary
14. ANS: D	DIF: Easy	OBJ: Grammar
15. ANS: A	DIF: Easy	OBJ: Grammar

Essay

16. Ravi's conflict with the other children is his desire to beat them in hide-and-seek. At the end of the story, he wins the game. That resolves the conflict, but it is not very satisfying. The other children don't even care that he won. They totally forgot about him and the game. Ravi ends up being mad at the other children because they don't seem to care about him. He ends up with a whole new conflict. They want him to join their funeral game, but he refuses. He feels very hurt when he realizes how unimportant he is in his family.

    Difficulty: *Easy* **Objective:** *Essay*

17. If I had been Ravi, I would have been just as upset if my brothers and sisters forgot me and left me hiding all afternoon. I wouldn't have become hysterical like he did, though. I would have been too embarrassed to let them all see me so upset. I am not sure that I would have even made it to the end of the game. I would have become tired of waiting in the shed for so long. I might not have even gone in there in the first place if I thought that there were rats and spiders in there! I think that Ravi took the game much too seriously and that most kids would not have become that wrapped up in it.

    Difficulty: *Easy* **Objective:** *Essay*

18. Students should recognize that Ravi fears Raghu, but many of the other children do not feel the same way. We know this because the older children force Raghu to be It in the hide-and-seek game. Students should recognize that the older children do not think the game is as important as Ravi does. The other children forget about

the game quickly and move on to other games, while Ravi wants badly to win the game.

Difficulty: *Average* **Objective:** *Essay*

Selection Test B, p. 170

Critical Reading

1. ANS: B	DIF: Average	OBJ: Interpretation
2. ANS: D	DIF: Challenging	OBJ: Interpretation
3. ANS: D	DIF: Challenging	OBJ: Comprehension
4. ANS: B	DIF: Average	OBJ: Interpretation
5. ANS: A	DIF: Average	OBJ: Comprehension
6. ANS: B	DIF: Average	OBJ: Literary Analysis
7. ANS: C	DIF: Challenging	OBJ: Comprehension
8. ANS: A	DIF: Average	OBJ: Reading
9. ANS: B	DIF: Average	OBJ: Reading
10. ANS: C	DIF: Average	OBJ: Literary Analysis
11. ANS: C	DIF: Challenging	OBJ: Literary Analysis
12. ANS: B	DIF: Challenging	OBJ: Reading Skill
13. ANS: C	DIF: Average	OBJ: Comprehension
14. ANS: A	DIF: Average	OBJ: Comprehension

Vocabulary and Grammar

15. ANS: C	DIF: Average	OBJ: Vocabulary
16. ANS: B	DIF: Challenging	OBJ: Vocabulary
17. ANS: B	DIF: Average	OBJ: Vocabulary
18. ANS: A	DIF: Average	OBJ: Grammar

Essay

19. If I had been Ravi, I would have been just as upset if my brothers and sisters forgot me and left me hiding all afternoon. I wouldn't have become hysterical like him, though. I would have been too embarrassed to let them all see me so upset. If I were truly that bothered, I probably would have told them how I felt instead of laying on the ground crying like Ravi did. Truthfully, though, I don't think I would have even made it to the end of the game anyway. I would have become tired of waiting in the shed for so long. I might not have even gone in there in the first place if I thought there were rats and spiders in there! I think that Ravi took the game much too seriously and most kids wouldn't have become that wrapped up in it.

Difficulty: *Easy* **Objective:** *Essay*

20. The children decide to play hide-and-seek and Raghu becomes "It." Because he is bigger and older, the younger children fear him. Manu, who is small, is the first to be caught because his fear made him slow to hide. Ravi hears Manu get caught, which has the effect of making him panic about his own hiding place. Ravi realizes that Raghu will find him easily on the flower pot, so he goes into the shed. He stays there for three reasons. First, he fears being found by Raghu more

than he fears the shed. Second, he begins to get really excited about winning the game. Finally, he hears Raghu catch one of the girls nearby. The effect of these three things is that he stays in the shed for a very long time.

Difficulty: *Average* **Objective:** *Essay*

21. Students should recognize that while Ravi fears Raghu, many of the other children do not feel the same way. We know this because the older children force Raghu to be It in the hide-and-seek game. Students should recognize that the importance Ravi places on the hide-and-seek game is not shared by others. What he sees as a great ordeal in staying in the scary shed is meaningless to the other children, who have forgotten about him and moved on to other games. Ravi finds many small events and details more important than older people do.

Difficulty: *Average* **Objective:** *Essay*

"The Marginal World" by Rachel Carson

Vocabulary Warm-up Exercises, p. 174

A. 1. visibly
2. sensation
3. fragile
4. crevices
5. ominous
6. varied
7. dwellers
8. vital

B. Sample Answers

1. The watch was so intricate that even an expert could not fix it easily.
2. After the flood, the water receded, and the street was dry once again.
3. It is conceivable that a patient trainer could teach a cat to do tricks.
4. An art museum could show this exquisite frame because it is so beautifully carved.
5. The puddle got smaller and smaller due to evaporation.
6. My sister's announcement was a revelation to us all, so we were amazed.
7. The inorganic parts of this garden include rocks and lawn furniture.

Reading Warm-up A, p. 175

Sample Answers

1. (shoreline); Someone who is visibly angry might be red in the face, scowling, or stamping his or her feet.
2. to feel bare land under your feet where just a few hours ago there was water; At midnight, you might feel a sensation of cool mystery or cold fear.
3. (fish) (crabs) (clams); Rain forest dwellers include parrots, butterflies, and snakes.

4. Suddenly, birds and crabs come there to feed. Vital means "full of life."

5. depending on the water's location; People's reactions to a news report might be varied because they have different opinions about the events.

6. gaps in rock beds; Crevices are narrow places often caused by something cracking apart.

7. they could not survive these dramatic changes; The old lace on an antique tablecloth is very fragile.

8. the water may rapidly rush away from the beach; The slowing traffic was an ominous sign of the three-hour traffic jam that followed.

Reading Warm-up B, p. 176

Sample Answers

1. (Jamaica) (Peru); If I were a worldwide traveler, I would like to visit Puerto Rico, Madagascar, and Antarctica.

2. when I decided to visit Bolton Beach in early February. A revelation is a surprising discovery of something that is revealed.

3. like the delicate edge of a lace napkin; The tile floor at the community center has a very intricate pattern.

4. (beach ball) (swimsuit); Inorganic means "not coming from anything living."

5. that this was the same place that was so crowded and hectic during the summer; It did not seem conceivable that I had won the race, but I was the first person across the line.

6. leaving a long stretch of wet sand exposed to the sun; Receded means "moved back or away from."

7. (the sun); You might see evaporation if you spilled water in a very hot place.

8. (bright red); One of the most exquisite things I have ever seen was my grandmother's wedding dress, which was beaded and trimmed with beautiful lace.

Writing About the Big Question, p. 177

A. 1. subjective
   2. verify
   3. reality
   4. comprehend

B. Sample Answers

1. One time a friend of mine was accused of stealing. Even though all the **evidence** seemed to point to him, we learned the truth was that another person was guilty.

2. I sort of believed that my friend was guilty of stealing, even though I never thought he was a thief, but **evidence** seemed to point to him. Later, the truth was revealed when the guilty person confessed.

C. Sample Answer

Reality is sometimes best discovered by not trying too hard to be scientific, but by trying to see with your instincts or gut feelings. Once, in a biology class, I dissected a frog and saw all the inner organs and so forth. However, I did not really understand how a frog repro-duces and grows until I visited my grandparents' lake house in the spring and saw little clusters of eggs, and then a few weeks later saw tiny tadpoles that had hatched. By summer the tadpoles had lost their tails and were tiny frogs. It was an amazing experience to see.

Literary Analysis: Author's Purpose, p. 178

Sample Answers

A. 1. She is showing her admiration for the natural world and attempting to move her audience to feel the same way.

2. Her purpose is to make her readers feel awe for the timeless nature of the shore. She may also wish to convey to her readers a feeling of a human being's smallness compared to the shore.

3. Carson wishes to help her readers see how observing nature in different ways can bring new understanding of the world around us.

4. She again wants to convey her own sense of awe at the beauty of nature and living creatures' ability to survive and evolve.

B. Carson's thesis is that the beauty of the natural world makes people want to explore its mysteries and find answers about the meaning of life. Her description of what she felt when she saw the crab supports her thesis by showing that even a very experienced observer of nature can find new meaning by seeing something in a different way.

Reading: Reread Passages to Analyze Cause and Effect, p. 179

Sample Answers

1. Favorable winds and a lack of a sea swell are the causes that will allow the sea to drop below the entrance to the pool and make it visible (effects).

2. Carson sees horn shells on the beach, which causes her to wonder what the shore looked like in earlier times (the effect).

3. The tide rose, which caused the bird's tracks to disappear (the effect).

Vocabulary Builder, p. 180

A. In their answers, students should demonstrate their understanding of the meaning of each italicized word.

B. 1. interscholastic
   2. international
   3. interrupt
   4. intermission

Enrichment: Connecting to Science, p. 181

Sample Answers

1. Humans eat plants and animals from the sea and take oil and other resources from the oceans. Human activity affects the balance of marine life, sometimes for the better and sometimes for the worse.

2. If humans are not careful about what they harvest from the sea, they could destroy species or entire ecosystems. It is in humans' best interest to keep a natural balance in the marine world. This relates directly to Carson's observations of the intricate world of sea organisms.

3. Carson seemed most concerned with observing marine life. She wanted to preserve it and admire its beauty. Modern marine biologists figure out how sea creatures can be used as resources. They may see the oceans as a means of making money and serving humans' needs. A balance would be preferable so that marine resources can be preserved for future generations while helping to make life better for humans today.

Open-Book Test, p. 182

Short Answer

1. Carson means that on the flood tide, the shore takes on characteristics of the sea, but on the ebb tide, it takes on characteristics of the land. Students should paraphrase details from the first two pages of the selection to support their answers.
   Difficulty: *Average*   **Objective:** *Interpretation*

2. Six possible causes are glaciers melting or growing, underwater earthquakes, warping of coastlines, wind, rain, and the gravitational pull of the moon on the water. The sea level must be changing all the time.
   Difficulty: *Average*   **Objective:** *Reading*

3. Carson most admires that these life forms are tough and adaptable. Students should paraphrase parts of the essay to support their responses.
   Difficulty: *Average*   **Objective:** *Interpretation*

4. She suggests that the pool is a magical place.
   Difficulty: *Easy*   **Objective:** *Interpretation*

5. The outgoing tide has scattered the shells of sea creatures on the mud flats. Land creatures have left tracks in the sand.
   Difficulty: *Easy*   **Objective:** *Reading*

6. The world that Carson describes is literally marginal because it is found on the shore that separates land and sea. It is also marginal because life forms here are short-lived; they change quickly or die when the landscape changes from land to sea or vice versa.
   Difficulty: *Challenging*   **Objective:** *Interpretation*

7. They would live for a long time.
   Difficulty: *Average*   **Objective:** *Vocabulary*

8. The shore is a fragile, beautiful, and changing place that is perfect for examining the variety and adaptability of plant and animal life.
   Difficulty: *Challenging*   **Objective:** *Literary Analysis*

9. Carson wants readers to view nature as something that can teach human beings a great deal about the meaning of life. Details supporting this view include her romantic descriptions of the tidal pool and the ghost crab.
   Difficulty: *Average*   **Objective:** *Literary Analysis*

10. Carson uses the ghost crab as a symbol of how precious nature is. This helps convince her readers to see nature as worth preserving.
    Difficulty: *Average*   **Objective:** *Literary Analysis*

Essay

11. Students should provide details that show the edge of the sea to be strange and beautiful. For example, they might mention Carson's description of the "mysterious" tidal pool with its beautiful, fragile flowers; the "mysterious quality" of the Georgia coast and its ghost crab; and the "sense of creation" Carson gets from the southern coast, where she can imagine a flock of magnificent flamingoes.
    Difficulty: *Easy*   **Objective:** *Essay*

12. Most of Carson's descriptions of creatures support her idea that creatures along the shore are beautiful, strong, and adaptable. For example, she describes the hydroid Tubularia as a flower that is an animal, not a plant, and points out how fragile and beautiful it seems. She describes the mangrove periwinkle as a sea creature that has adapted to land over a long period of time. Students should paraphrase passages in the essay to support their points.
    Difficulty: *Average*   **Objective:** *Essay*

13. Students should recognize that Carson finds nature a valuable teacher that imparts important ideas to human beings and helps them understand the meaning of life. She believes nature gives people a sense of wonder and joy. Students should support their points with examples from the selection, such as the wonders Carson finds in the hidden pool, the beauty she sees in the starfish or hydroid Tubularia, and the philosophical ideas she perceives when she observes the ghost crab.
    Difficulty: *Challenging*   **Objective:** *Essay*

14. Students who describe the tidal pool should explain how the cave is usually hidden from view, and it reveals its secrets only during very low tide. Students may note that what appear to be plants are actually animals inside the cave. Students who describe the mud flats of the Georgia coast should discuss how nighttime is a world different from daytime's reality. Students who discuss the Florida coast should note how Carson can close her eyes and imagine an earlier time different from what the average observer experiences today.
    Difficulty: *Average*   **Objective:** *Essay*

Oral Response

15. Oral responses should be clear, well organized, and well supported by appropriate examples from the selection.
    Difficulty: *Average*   **Objective:** *Oral Interpretation*

Selection Test A, p. 185

Critical Reading

1. **ANS:** A   **DIF:** Easy   **OBJ:** Literary Analysis
2. **ANS:** C   **DIF:** Easy   **OBJ:** Reading

3. **ANS:** C	**DIF:** Easy	**OBJ:** Interpretation
4. **ANS:** B	**DIF:** Easy	**OBJ:** Comprehension
5. **ANS:** C	**DIF:** Easy	**OBJ:** Interpretation
6. **ANS:** D	**DIF:** Easy	**OBJ:** Comprehension
7. **ANS:** D	**DIF:** Easy	**OBJ:** Reading
8. **ANS:** B	**DIF:** Easy	**OBJ:** Comprehension
9. **ANS:** A	**DIF:** Easy	**OBJ:** Literary Analysis
10. **ANS:** A	**DIF:** Easy	**OBJ:** Literary Analysis
11. **ANS:** B	**DIF:** Easy	**OBJ:** Interpretation

Vocabulary and Grammar

12. **ANS:** A	**DIF:** Easy	**OBJ:** Vocabulary
13. **ANS:** D	**DIF:** Easy	**OBJ:** Vocabulary
14. **ANS:** C	**DIF:** Average	**OBJ:** Grammar

Essay

15. Carson described the hydroid Tubularia in detail. She did this to support the idea that shore creatures are strong and adaptable, even if they seem delicate. She describes the hydroid Tubularia as a flower that is an animal, not a plant. She points out how fragile and beautiful it seems. Then, she explains how such a delicate-looking creature does not seem as if it could survive in the crushing waves of the tidal zone. She goes on to explain how the hanging flower-like animals will come back to life when the tide returns. She seems impressed by how every delicate part of the creature is perfectly suited to its needs for survival. Carson uses the hydroid Tubularia as an example of how most shore creatures survive under harsh and changing conditions.

    Difficulty: *Easy* **Objective:** *Essay*

16. Students' responses will vary, but they should include a detailed description of a plant or an animal that was observed in nature. Students should then provide an explanation of the importance of the plant or animal.

    Difficulty: *Easy* **Objective:** *Essay*

17. Students who describe the tidal pool should explain how the cave is usually hidden from view, but you can see its secrets during low tide. What appear to be plants are actually animals inside the cave. Students who describe the mud flats of the Georgia coast should explain how nighttime is very different from daytime. Students who discuss the Florida coast should note how Carson can close her eyes and imagine an earlier time different from what most people experience today.

    Difficulty: *Average* **Objective:** *Essay*

Selection Test B, p. 188

Critical Reading

1. **ANS:** B	**DIF:** Average	**OBJ:** Interpretation
2. **ANS:** A	**DIF:** Average	**OBJ:** Literary Analysis
3. **ANS:** D	**DIF:** Average	**OBJ:** Interpretation
4. **ANS:** D	**DIF:** Challenging	**OBJ:** Interpretation
5. **ANS:** C	**DIF:** Average	**OBJ:** Reading
6. **ANS:** C	**DIF:** Average	**OBJ:** Interpretation
7. **ANS:** D	**DIF:** Challenging	**OBJ:** Interpretation
8. **ANS:** B	**DIF:** Average	**OBJ:** Comprehension
9. **ANS:** B	**DIF:** Average	**OBJ:** Comprehension
10. **ANS:** C	**DIF:** Average	**OBJ:** Reading
11. **ANS:** D	**DIF:** Average	**OBJ:** Reading
12. **ANS:** C	**DIF:** Challenging	**OBJ:** Literary Analysis
13. **ANS:** A	**DIF:** Challenging	**OBJ:** Literary Analysis

Vocabulary and Grammar

14. **ANS:** A	**DIF:** Average	**OBJ:** Vocabulary
15. **ANS:** D	**DIF:** Challenging	**OBJ:** Vocabulary
16. **ANS:** C	**DIF:** Average	**OBJ:** Grammar
17. **ANS:** C	**DIF:** Average	**OBJ:** Grammar

Essay

18. Sample response: Carson described several shore creatures in detail, including the hydroid Tubularia, the ghost crab, and mangrove periwinkles. She did this to support her statement that the life forms that live along the shore are particularly strong and adaptable. She describes the hydroid Tubularia as a flower that is an animal, not a plant. She points out how fragile and beautiful it seems. Then, she explains how such a delicate-looking creature does not seem as if it could survive in the crushing waves of the tidal zone. She goes on to describe a ghost crab that she sees alone on a beach at night. She is amazed at how this tiny creature is facing the giant, powerful ocean all by itself in complete darkness. Finally, she describes mangrove periwinkle snails. She uses these snails to show how she believes the process of evolution helps such creatures to survive. All three descriptions support Carson's points about shore creatures' adaptability, beauty, and strength under harsh and changing conditions.

    Difficulty: *Average* **Objective:** *Essay*

19. Students' responses will vary, but they should include a detailed description of a plant or an animal that was observed in nature. Students should then provide an explanation of the importance of the plant or animal.

    Difficulty: *Easy* **Objective:** *Essay*

20. Students who describe the tidal pool should explain how the cave is usually hidden from view, and it reveals its secrets only during very low tide. Students may note that what appear to be plants are actually animals inside the cave. Students who describe the mud flats of the Georgia coast should discuss how nighttime is a world different from daytime's reality. Students who discuss the Florida coast should note how Carson can close her eyes and imagine an earlier time different from what the average observer experiences today.

    Difficulty: *Average* **Objective:** *Essay*

"Making History With Vitamin C"
by Penny Le Couteur and Jay Burreson

Vocabulary Warm-up Exercises, p. 192

A. 1. development
2. effective
3. resulting
4. desirable
5. consuming
6. compelling
7. objectives
8. symptom

B. Sample Answers

1. <u>Initially</u>, the child might be curious and try to touch the flames.
2. An answer to a mystery can be <u>derived</u> by looking at the clues and finding the logical conclusion.
3. An <u>exotic</u> location would be unusual and interesting.
4. Two of my proudest <u>accomplishments</u> are learning to play the piano and writing an essay that won a school contest.
5. You might see a <u>demonstration</u> of how to paint a picture at a museum, an art center, or an art store.
6. You can protect yourself against <u>infectious</u> diseases by washing your hands carefully and not sharing utensils with other people.
7. There are twenty <u>decades</u> in two centuries.

Reading Warm-up A, p. 193

Sample Answers

1. (nutrients); *Consuming* means "eating."
2. <u>because liver is rich in vitamin A</u>; One *effective* cure for a bad mood is watching a movie that you enjoy a lot.
3. (night blindness); One *symptom* of the common cold is the "sniffles."
4. <u>lack of vitamin C</u>; *Resulting* means "happening as a consequence."
5. <u>a disease called beriberi</u>; One *development* in our city has been a new library expansion.
6. <u>polishing rice also removes an essential vitamin—B1—from the rice</u>; I saw a *compelling* bike safety ad that convinced me to always wear my helmet when biking.
7. (necessary); *Desirable* means "pleasant but not completely necessary."
8. <u>providing Recommended Daily Allowances (RDAs) of vitamins</u>; Two of my *objectives* for this school year are getting good grades and joining the soccer team.

Reading Warm-up B, p. 194

Sample Answers

1. <u>most people only read about in books</u>; I think that Antarctica would be an interesting and *exotic* place to visit.

2. <u>he was an apprentice on coal ships</u>; *Initially* means "at first."
3. <u>His careful maps of the coast of Newfoundland in Canada</u>; I could give a *demonstration* of my songwriting by playing one of my songs on my guitar.
4. (four); Two *decades* from now, I will probably be living with my husband and kids and working as a lawyer.
5. (from stories and legends); *Derived* means "concluded as a result of or established by."
6. <u>spread quickly from person to person</u>; Tuberculosis is an *infectious* disease that affects the lungs.
7. <u>proving that Terra Australis did not exist</u>; Two of my grandmother's *accomplishments* were learning English when she moved here and starting her own successful business.
8. <u>they would sail through the Bering Strait</u>; A *scenario* is an imagined series of events.

Writing About the Big Question, p. 195

A. 1. *Evaluate* is used correctly since it means to check or determine the truth or value of something.
2. *Uncertainty* is used correctly since doctors were unsure, or uncertain, about what caused scurvy.
3. *Improbable* is used correctly since people of the time did not think it was probable or reasonable that such a simple remedy could exist for such a terrible disease.
4. *Concrete* is used incorrectly since people would probably understand concrete ideas that could be put into practice.

B. Sample Answers

1. During the Middle Ages, people thought the Black Death was spread by bad air, or was a punishment from God.
2. Scientists later found the truth that the disease was spread by the fleas on rats.

C. Sample Answer

Ship's captains treated scurvy as a mysterious disease that was just part of the reality of life onboard ship, and nothing could be done about it. They later learned the truth that scurvy is caused by a lack of green vegetables or citrus fruits, and they learned to cure scurvy by giving sailors limes or fresh greens.

Literary Analysis: Author's Purpose, p. 196

Sample Answers

A. 1. The authors are showing that the lack of vitamin C affected people even in very ancient times. This gives readers an understanding of the historical importance of ascorbic acid.
2. The authors wish to show how important vitamin C was and how deadly its lack was. The comparison to other types of death at sea shows the huge impact of the ascorbic acid molecule on the course of history.

3. The authors wish to show how ignorance about things like vitamin C can cost people their lives.

4. The authors want to support the idea that many important discoveries could not have happened without vitamin C.

B. Le Couteur's and Burreson's thesis is that without vitamin C, many important historical discoveries could not have taken place. The sentence about Cook's discoveries provides specific examples of discoveries that would not have happened without Cook's understanding of the importance of sanitary living conditions and foods that contain vitamin C.

Reading: Reread Passages to Analyze Cause and Effect, p. 197

Sample Answers

1. The lemon juice was the cause of the lack of scurvy on the *Dragon*. The lack of lemon juice on the other three ships caused many to die of scurvy (the effect).

2. Cook's healthy crew allowed him to accomplish his goals. This caused the Royal Society to understand the importance of controlling scurvy. The effect was that the Royal Society gave Cook an award.

3. By offering sauerkraut only to the officers, Cook made the men think that it must be something special. This caused them to demand their share of sauerkraut. The effect was that Cook managed to trick the men into eating something that would prevent scurvy.

Vocabulary Builder, p. 198

A. In their answers, students should demonstrate their understanding of the meaning of each italicized word.

B. 1. object
2. obliterate
3. obsolete

Enrichment: Connecting to Social Studies, p. 199

Students should select a specific explorer and provide details and support in their explanation of how the course of history might have changed if the explorer had known about vitamin C.

"The Marginal World" by Rachel Carson

"Making History With Vitamin C"
by Penny Le Couteur and Jay Burreson

Integrated Language Skills: Grammar, p. 200

1. relative pronoun—which; subordinate clause—which is visible only at the lowest of the year's low tides; noun—cave

2. relative pronoun—that; subordinate clause—that Carson saw on the beach one night; noun—crab

3. relative pronoun—that; subordinate clause—that could prevent or cure scurvy; noun—remedies

4. relative pronoun—who; subordinate clause—who were used to hardtack and salted meat; noun—Sailors

5. relative pronoun—who; subordinate clause—who insisted on cleanliness and a good diet on his ships; noun—Captain Cook

Open-Book Test, p. 203

Short Answer

1. They mean that the disease is caused by a diet containing too little vitamin C. People can prevent scurvy by eating enough vitamin C.
   Difficulty: *Average* **Objective:** *Vocabulary*

2. Possible effects include exhaustion, weakness, swelling of the arms and legs, softening of the gums, excessive bruising, bleeding from the nose and mouth, foul breath, diarrhea, muscle pain, loss of teeth, lung problems, kidney problems, and death. A person with scurvy must feel horrible, tired, scared, and even panicked.
   Difficulty: *Average* **Objective:** *Reading*

3. During the Age of Discovery, sailors went on long voyages and ate food with very little vitamin C. Sailors in ancient Egypt, Greece, and Rome made shorter voyages near the coast. They had more access to fresh food, so their diets contained more vitamin C.
   Difficulty: *Average* **Objective:** *Interpretation*

4. Causes included the logistical problem of keeping citrus fruit or juice fresh for weeks at a time, the high cost and amount of time needed to create concentrated or preserved lemon juice, and the sailors' avoidance of eating fruits and vegetables while in port.
   Difficulty: *Average* **Objective:** *Reading*

5. Students should identify three of these achievements: Cook introduced better sanitation aboard ship. He established methods of preventing scurvy in the British navy. He made many impressive voyages to areas that were little explored by Europeans. He helped Britain create a worldwide empire.
   Difficulty: *Easy* **Objective:** *Interpretation*

6. Students should list two of the following reasons: Sauerkraut is a source of vitamin C that lasts much longer than fresh produce or juice. It does not lose its vitamin C to heat and light as much as fresh produce or juice does. It is less expensive to make than other long-term sources, such as concentrated or preserved lemon juice. It can be made from local plants.
   Difficulty: *Average* **Objective:** *Interpretation*

7. He wanted the rest of the crew to see sauerkraut as a special privilege. Then they would be more likely to eat sauerkraut—and therefore not get scurvy.
   Difficulty: *Challenging* **Objective:** *Interpretation*

8. The authors' main purpose is to inform readers about the historic role of vitamin C in European navigation, discovery, and colonization. The title stresses this important role.
   Difficulty: *Easy* **Objective:** *Literary Analysis*

9. The Age of Discovery would have had far fewer achievements if navigators had not come to realize the dietary importance of vitamin C.
   Difficulty: *Average* **Objective:** *Literary Analysis*

10. Cook's insistence on giving his crew vitamin C not only saved lives but also improved profits. Cook advanced the cause of exploration and helped Britain achieve worldwide political dominance. Cook's practices thus prove the authors' thesis—that history would have been different were it not for vitamin C.
    Difficulty: *Challenging* **Objective:** *Literary Analysis*

Essay

11. Students should explain that scurvy is caused by a lack of vitamin C in the diet. They should summarize the disease's effects on the body and explain that it often results in death. They should recognize that eating foods with vitamin C prevents or cures scurvy. They should cite details from the selection to support their statements.
    Difficulty: *Easy* **Objective:** *Essay*

12. Students should explain that vitamin C improved European navigation by making voyages of discovery and colonization more successful and profitable. They should cite details about Captain Cook's achievements and his crucial role in the widespread use of vitamin C.
    Difficulty: *Average* **Objective:** *Essay*

13. Students should recognize that sailors' lives were hard and often brief. They lived in dangerous conditions, had poor nutrition and sanitation, and often got deadly diseases. Many were forced into a life at sea by press gangs, and they were away from home for great lengths of time. Officers led better lives than the rest of the crew because they had privileges such as better nutrition.
    Difficulty: *Challenging* **Objective:** *Essay*

14. Students should mention that many people blamed salted meat or the lack of fresh meat for scurvy, while the disease is actually caused by a lack of vitamin C. They should recognize that sailors preferred meat and dairy products to fruits and vegetables. Many sailors were reluctant to try unusual foods. Ship owners thought they were saving money by not keeping citrus fruits and juices on board. In fact, the deaths of many sailors made voyages less successful and more expensive.
    Difficulty: *Average* **Objective:** *Essay*

Oral Response

15. Oral responses should be clear, well organized, and well supported by appropriate examples from the selection.
    Difficulty: *Average* **Objective:** *Oral Interpretation*

Selection Test A, p. 206

Critical Reading

1. ANS: A	DIF: Easy	OBJ: Comprehension
2. ANS: D	DIF: Easy	OBJ: Reading

3. ANS: D	DIF: Easy	OBJ: Comprehension
4. ANS: C	DIF: Easy	OBJ: Reading
5. ANS: C	DIF: Easy	OBJ: Interpretation
6. ANS: A	DIF: Easy	OBJ: Reading
7. ANS: B	DIF: Easy	OBJ: Literary Analysis
8. ANS: B	DIF: Easy	OBJ: Comprehension
9. ANS: A	DIF: Easy	OBJ: Reading
10. ANS: D	DIF: Easy	OBJ: Literary Analysis
11. ANS: C	DIF: Easy	OBJ: Literary Analysis

Vocabulary and Grammar

12. ANS: C	DIF: Easy	OBJ: Vocabulary
13. ANS: B	DIF: Easy	OBJ: Grammar

Essay

14. James Cook's crewmen were very healthy. Because they kept their ship clean and ate well, not very many of his men died. This was very unusual for the time. The crew did not like Cook's policies at first. They were used to living on dirty, moldy ships and eating nothing but dried meat and hard biscuits. But they eventually understood that he was thinking of their best interests. They realized that he was smart and that they were healthier because of it. As a result, Cook and his crew went on to make great discoveries. They went into the history books.
    Difficulty: *Easy* **Objective:** *Essay*

15. Many people did not believe the treatments for scurvy worked. They thought things like fresh meat, seawater, or vinegar would work instead. Also, it was hard to make things with vitamin C in them last for very long on a ship. Everything got moldy and covered with bugs. Ships did not come into port often enough to get fresh food. Plus, ship owners did not want to fill cargo space with healthy foods for the crews. Finally, even if they did have good food that would cure scurvy, sailors usually did not want to eat it. They did not like fresh fruits and vegetables. They wanted meat and bread. So, it was difficult to prevent scurvy on long sea voyages.
    Difficulty: *Easy* **Objective:** *Essay*

16. Students should mention that the way to prevent scurvy is to make sure people get enough vitamin C. Many people believed that salted or spoiled meat caused scurvy instead. They chose to believe the wrong information because they wanted to stick to meat and dairy products rather than eating fruits and vegetables. Many sailors did not want to try new or unusual foods. Finally, ship owners thought they were saving money by not keeping citrus fruits and juices on board.
    Difficulty: *Average* **Objective:** *Essay*

Selection Test B, p. 209

Critical Reading

1. ANS: A	DIF: Average	OBJ: Reading
2. ANS: B	DIF: Average	OBJ: Comprehension

3. ANS: C   DIF: Challenging   OBJ: Reading

4. ANS: A   DIF: Challenging   OBJ: Interpretation

5. ANS: B   DIF: Challenging   OBJ: Interpretation

6. ANS: C   DIF: Average   OBJ: Interpretation

7. ANS: D   DIF: Average   OBJ: Comprehension

8. ANS: A   DIF: Average   OBJ: Reading

9. ANS: B   DIF: Average   OBJ: Literary Analysis

10. ANS: D   DIF: Average   OBJ: Literary Analysis

11. ANS: D   DIF: Average   OBJ: Literary Analysis

Vocabulary and Grammar

12. ANS: A   DIF: Average   OBJ: Vocabulary

13. ANS: D   DIF: Average   OBJ: Vocabulary

14. ANS: B   DIF: Average   OBJ: Grammar

15. ANS: A   DIF: Average   OBJ: Grammar

Essay

16. Most seamen during the Age of Discovery ignored the known remedies for scurvy because they simply did not believe them. They often had their own theories about how to prevent and cure scurvy. For example, some thought sailors needed more fresh meat. Others thought things like seawater or sulfuric acid would cure it. Also, sailors had to eat mostly preserved foods like salted meat and hardtack. These foods did not have vitamin C, which prevents and cures scurvy. Even if they had foods with vitamin C in them, though, most sailors did not want to eat them. They liked meat, bread, and beer—not fresh fruits and vegetables. Finally, it was difficult and expensive to preserve foods with vitamin C in them.

Difficulty: *Average*   Objective: *Essay*

17. James Cook was the first ship's captain to keep his crews scurvy-free on long expeditions. He discovered scurvy-curing foods and insisted that his crews eat them. He also insisted on keeping a clean ship. As a result, very few of his men died. Because of his high standards, Cook was able to make many important discoveries. He also won an award for his good record. The authors wrote about Cook and his expeditions because he is the perfect example of how many discoveries would not have happened without vitamin C. Cook could not have accomplished what he did without a healthy crew. And he couldn't have had a healthy crew without vitamin C.

Difficulty: *Average*   Objective: *Essay*

18. Students should mention that many people blamed salted meat or the lack of fresh meat for scurvy, while the disease is actually caused by a lack of vitamin C. They should recognize that sailors preferred meat and dairy products to fruits and vegetables. Many sailors were reluctant to try unusual foods. Ship owners thought they were saving money by not keeping citrus fruits and juices on board. In fact, the deaths of many sailors made voyages less successful and more expensive.

Difficulty: *Average*   Objective: *Essay*

"Like the Sun" by R.K. Narayan
"The Open Window" by Saki

Vocabulary Warm-up Exercises, p. 213

A. 1. prospects
2. culinary
3. incessantly
4. assailed
5. sullen
6. imminent]
7. engulfed
8. medley

B. Sample Answers

1. **F**; If a soldier <u>shirked</u> her duty, it means she failed to do something she was supposed to do, so she would not be honored.

2. **F**; Jumping <u>headlong</u> into something means doing so without thinking ahead.

3. **T**; A caring letter might make someone feel better, and therefore would provide <u>consolation</u>.

4. **T**; A <u>scarcity</u> of gasoline means that it is in short supply, so that raises the price and causes crowds at gas stations.

5. **T**; Pageant winners often seem astonished that they have won, so their expressions looks <u>stupefied</u>.

0. **T**; Listening to someone who lectured, or <u>sermonized</u>, all the time would most likely be tiresome.

7. **F**; On the contrary, an arresting officer is required by law to <u>duly</u> inform people of their rights.

8. **T**; Artistic <u>inclinations</u> means a tendency to be artistic, so such a person would also be creative.

Reading Warm-up A, p. 214

Sample Answers

1. (kitchen), (cookbook), (recipes); The word *cooking* could replace *culinary* in the sentence.

2. <u>pinto beans, canned peaches, and sardines</u>; The deejay played a *medley* of disco tunes.

3. (dwell on); The opposite of *incessantly* might be *from time to time*.

4. The narrator's *prospects* for receiving more baked goods were improved; A synonym for *prospects* is *chances*.

5. <u>feelings of guilt</u>; The narrator will be *engulfed* by these feelings because he or she will have hurt the aunt's feelings.

6. We awaited the *imminent* arrival of the guests; *Imminent* means that something is definitely expected to happen, while *possible* means that it may or may not happen.

7. (mean-spirited); *Cheerful* is an antonym for *sullen.*

8. <u>feelings of uncertainty</u>; Another word for *assailed* is *attacked.*

Reading Warm-up B, p. 215

1. (financial resources); There is a *scarcity* of good book-stores in the downtown area.
2. writing.; The word *talent* would work well in this sentence.
3. Twain never *shirked* the task of writing about hypocrisy; *Avoided* means the same thing as *shirked*.
4. (preached); Twain got his views across by using humor and satire instead.
5. Aunt Polly *duly* reprimanded Tom Sawyer; She did so because she caught him lying.
6. (plunging); An antonym for *headlong* might be *careful* or *carefully*.
7. their irresponsible behavior; Twain used his being *stupefied* to poke fun at what politicians did.
8. (relief); A synonym for *consolation* is *comfort*.

Writing About the Big Question, p. 216

A. 1. perception
2. differentiate
3. confirm
4. objective
5. evidence

B. Sample Answers

1. My friends told me that the new boy in class was stuck up and unfriendly. When I first met him, he seemed as if he did not want to talk to me. I thought he was really unfriendly.
2. After I got to know him, I realized the truth was that he really was very nice. He was just shy and had trouble talking to people.

C. Sample Answer

When things do not turn out as you plan, sometimes it is because you did not understand the reality of a situation. I had planned on being elected captain of the basketball team even though I was not as good an athlete as another person. I was well liked by everyone. All the team members thought I was funny and fun to be with. When another person who was more serious and a better athlete was elected, I had to face the fact that just being a fun person did not mean you can always get what you want.

Literary Analysis: Irony and Paradox, p. 217

A. 1. It is ironic because the headmaster expects Sekhar to praise his performance; situational irony.
2. The irony is that Vera tells Framton he must put up with her; what is really happening is that she is finding a way to put up with him.
Type of irony: dramatic irony

B. 1. In "Like the Sun," Sekhar tells the headmaster the cruel truth about his singing. This keeps the headmaster from embarrassing himself in the future.

2. "The paradox is that it appears he has seen a ghost, but in reality he believes he has seen a ghost."

Vocabulary Builder, p. 218

A. 1. Tempering your tone might come in handy when disagreeing with a parent.
2. A person's signature might be scrutinized to determine its authenticity.
3. Many people find ingratiating behavior annoying because it is fake.
4. I would be upset if someone endeavored to harm me.
5. A person with stage fright might speak falteringly when giving a speech.

B. 1. D; 2. B; 3. B; 4. C

Open-Book Test, p. 220

Short Answer

1. Sekhar's wife does not expect him to be so honest.
   Difficulty: *Easy* **Objective:** *Literary Analysis*
2. The headmaster has unexpectedly accepted Sekhar's negative opinion of the headmaster's singing.
   Difficulty: *Average* **Objective:** *Literary Analysis*
3. Only people who do not need to succeed or to be liked by others can afford the "luxury" of practicing total honesty.
   Difficulty: *Challenging* **Objective:** *Literary Analysis*
4. With this question, Vera establishes that the way is clear for her to spin her dramatic story about the death of Mrs. Sappleton's husband and brothers.
   Difficulty: *Average* **Objective:** *Interpretation*
5. The derivation is ironic because Vera specializes in melodramatic fiction and not truth.
   Difficulty: *Average* **Objective:** *Literary Analysis*
6. Sekhar is completely honest, not very imaginative, does not succeed in what he sets out to do. Vera is not truthful, is imaginative, succeeds in what she sets out to do. Both have purposeful action and a goal. Students' choice of the more believable character should be reasonably supported.
   Difficulty: *Average* **Objective:** *Interpretation*
7. Sekhar believes people should tell the whole truth, no matter how inconvenient it may be. Vera believes it is entertaining and challenging to change the truth.
   Difficulty: *Average* **Objective:** *Interpretation*
8. In "Like the Sun," the headmaster changes his mind and tells Sekhar that he must correct one hundred exam papers and have them ready by the very next day. In "The Open Window," Vera starts off on another

fantastic story about Framton Nuttel's being hunted by a pack of dogs in India.

Difficulty: *Easy*   **Objective:** *Interpretation*

9. The authors' attitudes are different. Narayan's attitude is lighthearted and sympathetic while Saki's is more pointed and sharp.

Difficulty: *Challenging*   **Objective:** *Interpretation*

10. You would be carefully examining the document and paying close attention to its contents.

Difficulty: *Average*   **Objective:** *Vocabulary*

Essay

11. Ironic moments in "Like the Sun" include Sekhar's honest statement about his wife's cooking; his honest comments about the headmaster's singing; the headmaster's appreciation for Sekhar's honesty; and the headmaster's request for the one hundred graded papers the next day. These moments express the idea that truth may hurt, but it ultimately helps people. Ironic moments in "The Open Window" include Vera's account of the deaths of Mrs. Sappleton's husband and brothers; Mrs. Sappleton's rambling remarks about the shooting party; the reappearance of the three hunters; Framton's frenzied departure; and Vera's fiction about Framton's being hunted by a pack of dogs. These moments express the idea that certain individuals have a fanciful but creative imagination.

Difficulty: *Easy*   **Objective:** *Essay*

12. Ironic moments in "Like the Sun" include Sekhar's honesty about his wife's cooking; his comments about the headmaster's singing; the headmaster's appreciation of Sekhar's honesty; and the headmaster's request for the graded papers the next day. The irony helps Narayan say that the truth may be painful but is helpful, or truth can have unpredictable consequences. Ironic moments in "The Open Window" include Vera's account of the disappearance of her aunt's husband and brothers, which neither Frampton nor the reader expects; Mrs. Sappleton's rambling remarks about the shooting party, which Framton does not expect; the reappearance of the hunters, which neither Framton nor the reader expects; and Vera's explanation of Framton's hurried departure, which neither Mrs. Sappleton nor the reader expects. The irony helps Saki say that fanciful storytelling may have unpredictable consequences, but it is ultimately entertaining.

Difficulty: *Average*   **Objective:** *Essay*

13. Students may say that in "Like the Sun," the truth is shown to be blinding like the light of the sun, but unlike the sun, it casts a kind of paradoxical darkness over Sekhar's life during the course of his experiment. By hurting the feelings of others, the truth is shown to be chilling and hurtful rather than warm and healing. Ultimately, however, truth clarifies relationships and gives people a clearer perspective relating to others and to themselves.

Difficulty: *Challenging*   **Objective:** *Essay*

14. Students should point out that Sekhar perceives the whole truth as important. Unfortunately, however, this perception provokes conflict with others, including his wife, a faculty colleague, and the headmaster. The reality of the world around Sekhar is that truth has to be softened by tact and diplomacy. In contrast to Sekhar, Vera in "The Open Window" perceives truth as flexible. Her instinct for making up stories contrasts with the everyday, socially conventional world around her.

Difficulty: *Average*   **Objective:** *Essay*

Oral Response

15. Oral responses should be clear, well organized, and well supported by appropriate examples from the selections.

Difficulty: *Average*   **Objective:** *Oral Interpretation*

Selection Test A, p. 223

Critical Reading

1. ANS: D	DIF: Easy	OBJ: Comprehension
2. ANS: C	DIF: Easy	OBJ: Comprehension
3. ANS: B	DIF: Easy	OBJ: Interpretation
4. ANS: D	DIF: Easy	OBJ: Interpretation
5. ANS: D	DIF: Easy	OBJ: Literary Analysis
6. ANS: B	DIF: Easy	OBJ: Comprehension
7. ANS: D	DIF: Easy	OBJ: Interpretation
8. ANS: A	DIF: Easy	OBJ: Comprehension
9. ANS: D	DIF: Easy	OBJ: Literary Analysis
10. ANS: C	DIF: Easy	OBJ: Interpretation
11. ANS: A	DIF: Easy	OBJ: Interpretation
12. ANS: A	DIF: Easy	OBJ: Literary Analysis
13. ANS: C	DIF: Easy	OBJ: Interpretation

Vocabulary

14. ANS: C	DIF: Easy	OBJ: Vocabulary
15. ANS: B	DIF: Easy	OBJ: Vocabulary

Essay

16. Students should respond that in "Like the Sun," Sekhar's mission is to tell the absolute truth for one entire day. Most will say the mission is a success, based on the headmaster's acceptance of Sekhar's honesty. Students should respond that in "The Open Window," Vera's mission is to trick Framton into leaving. Students should state that Vera is successful, since Framton left hurriedly.

Difficulty: *Easy*   **Objective:** *Essay*

17. Ironic moments in "Like the Sun" include Sekhar's honest comment about his wife's cooking; Sekhar's honest assessment of the headmaster's singing; the headmaster's appreciation for Sekhar's honesty; and the headmaster's request for the one hundred graded papers the next day. These moments of irony help

Narayan express the idea that the truth may hurt, but that it ultimately helps people. Ironic moments in "The Open Window" include Mrs. Sappleton's rattling on about hunting, while Framton believes that is why her husband and brothers are dead, and Mrs. Sappleton's statement, "One would think he had seen a ghost." These moments express that our perceptions are shaped by our beliefs, whether those beliefs are true or are deceptive.

Difficulty: *Easy* **Objective:** *Essay*

18. Students should point out that Vera thinks the truth can be changed or seen in different ways. She uses her imagination to make up stories. The stories somehow seem just as real as the everyday, "true" world around her. Students should provide at least two examples from the story to back up their points.

Difficulty: *Average* **Objective:** *Essay*

Selection Test B, p. 226

Critical Reading

1. ANS: B	DIF: Average	OBJ: Comprehension
2. ANS: D	DIF: Average	OBJ: Literary Analysis
3. ANS: B	DIF: Average	OBJ: Comprehension
4. ANS: C	DIF: Average	OBJ: Literary Analysis
5. ANS: A	DIF: Average	OBJ: Interpretation
6. ANS: C	DIF: Challenging	OBJ: Interpretation
7. ANS: C	DIF: Challenging	OBJ: Comprehension
8. ANS: C	DIF: Average	OBJ: Interpretation
9. ANS: D	DIF: Average	OBJ: Interpretation
10. ANS: A	DIF: Average	OBJ: Literary Analysis
11. ANS: B	DIF: Average	OBJ: Comprehension
12. ANS: C	DIF: Challenging	OBJ: Literary Analysis
13. ANS: C	DIF: Average	OBJ: Interpretation
14. ANS: A	DIF: Challenging	OBJ: Interpretation
15. ANS: C	DIF: Average	OBJ: Literary Analysis
16. ANS: A	DIF: Challenging	OBJ: Interpretation
17. ANS: D	DIF: Challenging	OBJ: Interpretation

Vocabulary

18. ANS: A	DIF: Average	OBJ: Vocabulary
19. ANS: B	DIF: Average	OBJ: Vocabulary
20. ANS: C	DIF: Challenging	OBJ: Vocabulary

Essay

21. Ironic moments in "Like the Sun" include Sekhar's honest assessment of his wife's cooking, which she does not expect; Sekhar's honest assessment of the headmaster's singing, which the headmaster does not expect; the headmaster's appreciation for Sekhar's honesty, which neither the reader nor Sekhar expects; and the headmaster's request for the one hundred graded papers the next day, which neither the reader nor Sekhar expects. These moments of irony help Narayan express

the idea that the truth may be painful but is ultimately helpful; or that the truth can have unpredictable consequences. Students might note the following events in "The Open Window" as examples of situational irony: Framton Nuttel visits Mrs. Sappleton's country house to calm his nerves, only to end up fleeing in terror from the house shortly after he arrives; Vera, the confident young lady of fifteen whom he first meets at the house, at first seems like a serious, friendly person but turns out to be a mischievous sort who takes pleasure in spinning tall tales to manipulate people's feelings and actions. Students might also note the irony that Mrs. Sappleton remarks that Nuttel dashes off as if "he had seen a ghost," when that is exactly what Nuttel believes he has seen.

Difficulty: *Average* **Objective:** *Essay*

22. Students should respond that in "Like the Sun," Sekhar challenges the social system of "polite dishonesty" by vowing to tell the absolute truth for one entire day. He does this because he believes that if a person cannot be totally honest at least *sometimes*, life is meaningless. Students might suggest that in "The Open Window," Mrs. Sappleton's niece Vera defies the normal expectation of treating strangers with courtesy and respect; to the contrary, she seems to take delight in using fantasy and imagination to manipulate people's feelings and even scare them, as she does with Mr. Nuttel.

Difficulty: *Average* **Objective:** *Essay*

23. Students may say that in "Like the Sun," the truth is shown to be blinding like the light of the sun, but that unlike the sun, it casts a kind of paradoxical darkness over Sekhar's life during the course of his experiment. By hurting the feelings of others, the truth is shown to be chilling and hurtful rather than warm and healing. Students should note that in "The Open Window," Nuttel sees the open window as a symbol of the aunt's emotional distress after hearing Vera's made-up story about Mrs. Sappleton's delusional expectation that her dead husband and brothers will return through that window. Students might note that, at the end, Nuttel flees in terror at the sight of the approaching husband and brothers because he thinks they are ghosts. Students might suggest, then, that the paradox is that the open window turns out to be a symbol not of Mrs. Sappleton's emotional distress but of Nuttel's: instead of thinking the situation through logically and realizing that Vera has lied to him, he is easily unnerved and overcome by his fears. It is an open window into his state of mind.

Difficulty: *Challenging* **Objective:** *Essay*

24. Students should point out that Sekhar perceives truth as unvarnished and vital. Unfortunately, however, this perception provokes conflict with others, including his wife, a faculty colleague, and the headmaster. The reality of the world around Sekhar is that truth has to be softened by tact and diplomacy. In contrast to Sekhar, Vera in "The Open Window" perceives truth as flexible. Her imaginative instinct for making up stories contrasts with the everyday, socially conventional world around her.

Difficulty: *Average* **Objective:** *Interpretation*

Writing Workshop

Cause-and-Effect Essay: Integrating Grammar Skills, p. 230

A. 1. his or her; 2. they; 3. him

B. 1. Most of the tourists enjoyed their visit to the palace.

2. Everyone in the group had his or her chance to sit on the throne.

3. Either Eric or Todd had his picture taken with a palace guard.

Vocabulary Workshop—1, p. 231

A. 1. Students should circle **n.**; noun.

2. Students should underline the etymology, which is in brackets. Etymology is a word's origin or history.

3. *Perspective* comes from Middle English and Latin.

4. Students should write the number 3.

B. 1. **Sample answer:** insight—understanding something through intuition; wisdom.

2. ignorance (or any of the antonyms listed)

Vocabulary Workshop—2, p. 232

A. Students' dictionary entries will vary. They should include the word, pronunciation guide, part(s) of speech, etymology, definition(s), and perhaps word family words.

1. Students should circle the part(s) of speech in their copied dictionary entries.

2. Students should underline the etymology.

B. Students' thesaurus entries will vary. They should include the word, synonyms, and antonyms.

1. Students should write a sentence in which they correctly use the word they looked up.

2. In most cases, the synonym will be an easy substitute and will not significantly change the meaning of the sentence. Sometimes, however, one would have to revise the sentence to use a synonym correctly. And sometimes a synonym changes the meaning of the sentence because of differing connotations.

Benchmark Test 2, p. 234

MULTIPLE CHOICE

1. ANS: C
2. ANS: B
3. ANS: D
4. ANS: B
5. ANS: D
6. ANS: C
7. ANS: A
8. ANS: C
9. ANS: D
10. ANS: C
11. ANS: A
12. ANS: C
13. ANS: B
14. ANS: A
15. ANS: D
16. ANS: C
17. ANS: A
18. ANS: B
19. ANS: D
20. ANS: D
21. ANS: C
22. ANS: B
23. ANS: B
24. ANS: B
25. ANS: A
26. ANS: B
27. ANS: C
28. ANS: D
29. ANS: B

WRITING

30. Students' anecdotes should present a clearly stated contrast between a character's efforts and motives and what actually happens in the end.

31. Students should list three persons, places, or things, giving reasons for including each one and describing how each will be portrayed in the documentary.

32. Students should clearly describe the causes and effects of meeting a challenge. Their diagrams and essays should show the relationships between causes and effects.

Vocabulary in Context, p. 241

MULTIPLE CHOICE

1. ANS: C
2. ANS: C
3. ANS: A
4. ANS: B
5. ANS: D
6. ANS: D
7. ANS: B
8. ANS: A
9. ANS: C
10. ANS: C

11. ANS: C
12. ANS: D
13. ANS: B
14. ANS: D
15. ANS: D
16. ANS: D
17. ANS: C
18. ANS: B
19. ANS: D
20. ANS: A